Audio-Visual Media for
Education and Research
VOLUME I

POLITICS AND THE MEDIA:
FILM AND TELEVISION FOR THE
POLITICAL SCIENTIST AND HISTORIAN

POLITICS AND THE MEDIA:
FILM AND TELEVISION FOR THE POLITICAL SCIENTIST AND HISTORIAN

Edited by
M. J. Clark, B.A., Ph.D.
University of Southampton

Published for the
British Universities Film Council Ltd
by
PERGAMON PRESS
OXFORD · NEW YORK · TORONTO · SYDNEY · PARIS · FRANKFURT

U.K.	Pergamon Press Ltd., Headington Hill Hall, Oxford OX3 0BW, England
U.S.A.	Pergamon Press Inc., Maxwell House, Fairview Park, Elmsford, New York 10523, U.S.A.
CANADA	Pergamon of Canada, Suite 104, 150 Consumers Road, Willowdale, Ontario M2J 1P9, Canada
AUSTRALIA	Pergamon Press (Aust.) Pty. Ltd., P.O. Box 544, Potts Point, N.S.W. 2011, Australia
FRANCE	Pergamon Press SARL, 24 rue des Ecoles, 75240 Paris, Cedex 05, France
FEDERAL REPUBLIC OF GERMANY	Pergamon Press GmbH, 6242 Kronberg-Taunus, Pferdstrasse 1, Federal Republic of Germany

Copyright © 1979 British Universities Film Council Ltd.

All Rights Reserved. No part of this publication may be reproduced, stored in a retrieval system or transmitted in any form or by any means: electronic, electrostatic, magnetic tape, mechanical, photocopying, recording or otherwise, without permission in writing from the copyright holders

First edition 1979

British Library Cataloguing in Publication Data

Politics and the Media. (Audio-visual media for education and research).
1. Moving - pictures in historiography
2. Moving-pictures, Documentary
I. Clark, Michael Jeremy II. Series
909   D16   79-40426
ISBN 0-08-022483-0
ISBN 0-08-022484-9 Pbk

In order to make this volume available as economically and as rapidly as possible the author's typescript has been reproduced in its original form. This method unfortunately has its typographical limitations but it is hoped that they in no way distract the reader.

*Printed and bound at William Clowes & Sons Limited
Beccles and London*

Contents

Introduction to the series	vii
Acknowledgements	viii
Introduction *Michael J. Clark*	ix

I THE PRODUCTION CONTEXT — 1

The development of an approach to the presentation of political and current affairs on television: the experience of the BBC — 3
Peter Hardiman Scott

Television and current affairs — 9
Robert Hargreaves

Production and the political content of broadcasting — 17
Philip Elliott

America on screen? Hollywood feature films as social and political evidence — 25
Edward Buscombe

From October to *October*: the Soviet political system in the 1920s and its films — 31
Richard Taylor

II RELATIONSHIPS BETWEEN THE ACADEMIC USER AND PRODUCER — 43

Television-based history teaching in the context of the traditional university — 45
Nicholas Pronay

The political scientist as film-maker: some reflections concerning a German filmic documentation project on election campaigning — 59
Stig Hornshøj-Møller

III THE MESSAGE RECEIVED - A USER PERSPECTIVE — 70

An overview of recent research into the impact of broadcasting in democratic politics — 71
Jay G. Blumler

Political style on film: Neville Chamberlain — 87
Paul Smith

Film as a teaching resource: the possibilities of using film in American government and politics courses — 95
Philip J. Davies

Film analysis: the structural approach 105
Karsten Fledelius

IV SOURCES 127

Seizing the moving image: broadcast television archives 129
Alden Williams

Audio-visual sources and research into modern British politics 139
Kathryn Rowan

Some European film collections: an annotated list 151
James Ballantyne

Index 167

Introduction to the Series

For many years the British Universities Film Council has been concerned with a field of interest which extends far more widely than its name suggests. Every aspect of the use and production of audio-visual media at degree level comes within the Council's range, and its Associate Membership spreads to many countries other than Britain.

The intention of this series of texts on *Audio-Visual Media for Education and Research* is to provide hand-books in defined specialist subject areas in which aspects of the production and use of audio-visual media are discussed by teachers, researchers and producers. The emphasis is on producing a varied and informative introduction to the priorities of the subject area concerned, rather than on attempting either completely comprehensive coverage or exclusive presentation of advanced research results.

The Series is conceived as a means of consolidating the Council's longstanding interest in specialist publication. This first volume in the Pergamon format was inspired by a BUFC conference on Film and Television in the Study of Politics, although only some of the contributions originated as conference papers, and all have been re-written for publication. The views expressed are, of course, those of individual authors, not of the Editor or Council. Plans are in hand for future volumes - in particular, one on the use of computers for image-making and animation in education and research.

Further information about the Council may be obtained from The Director, British Universities Film Council Ltd, 81 Dean Street, London W1V 6AA.

Acknowledgements

The Editor and British Universities Film Council are most grateful to the many people who gave advice on the publication of this book. In particular Professor Martin Harrison of the University of Keele, Dr Jay Blumler of the University of Leeds and Dr Colin Seymour-Ure of the University of Kent guided the editor in the preliminary stages of the work.

Thanks are due to HMSO for permission to reprint part of Dr Blumler's submission to the Annan Committee on Broadcasting and to the Vanderbilt University Television Archive for permission to reproduce a page from the *Index and Abstracts*.

In particular, thanks are due to Yvonne Renouf who as Director of BUFC was instrumental in setting up the Conference on *Film and Television in the Study of Politics*, and played a leading role both in establishing the *Audio-Visual Media for Education and Research* series and in conceiving and structuring this first volume. Her successor as Director, Elizabeth Oliver, has continued this enthusiastic support for the series, and has taken a major part in text preparation and indexing.

BUFC is grateful to Sally Betts and Freelance Services for their assistance in preparing the typescript.

Introduction

Writing in *The Times Educational Supplement* for 1 October 1976, Carl Slevin commented that: 'The use of film in the study of politics is extremely new and so far almost completely undeveloped even in higher education where the best facilities are available. A considerable amount of material exists, but most teachers seem to be unaware of it or even to reject it because they suspect it may trivialize the subject and be at best an expensive frill.' He was, in fact, reviewing the BUFC conference on *Film and Television in the Study of Politics*, but the sentiment is equally appropriate as an introduction to the present volume - for both conference and book were born out of a feeling that the audio-visual media are under-utilized in education and research within the general field of political science and history. At the same time, however, the Council's international links suggested that work of this sort was in fact well advanced at a number of centres, so that the main problem was not so much the development of the field, but rather its formalization and wider acceptance as a valid focus for study.

Paradoxically, whilst many academics continue to approach audio-visual media with distinct reserve, there has been an upsurge in discussion on the relationship between politics, media and society amongst politicians, political commentators, the press, and 'media professionals' - the latter contributing to a period of detailed soul-searching on standards and priorities for the broadcasting of overt political material and current affairs in general. Against this background, it seems reasonable to assume that the public debate will increasingly find its counterpart in the academic world, and that when this interest is awakened the initial development of this field is most likely to take the form of a reinforcement and integration of the existing strands of study. It is within this context that the present volume has been designed, not as a compilation of pioneering research themes, but as an attempt to sample the recent achievements of the subject as a whole. Inevitably the sample is partial, but it does serve to indicate the range of attitudes and preconceptions through which the theme has been approached, and likewise reflects the very varied roles that have been found for media study by political scientists and historians.

The contributions have been arranged primarily with the media user rather than the producer in mind. Thus, the first two sections explore some of the ramifying problems of media production in the political field so as to introduce the user to the priorities and constraints within which the political message has been conceived, stored and transmitted. Against this essential background it is then possible to assess some aspects of the message as received and used, both by the general public in their experience of the broadcast media and by teachers, students or researchers interested either in the political media as such or in the political events that they depict. Having established the scope and potential of such studies, attention necessarily turns to problems associated with availability of material - a topic which encompasses consideration of the initial media coverage, the partial preservation of this coverage, and access to such material as has been preserved. It is hoped that this structure will provide a progressive and coherent introduction to politically-relevant audio-visual media, though preliminary discussion with contributors and with the BUFC's Editorial Advisers made it clear that this is only one of several possible approaches. The relationship between political event, media producer and media user is subtle, and a number of the contributions here published highlight points which have equal relevance to several of the volume's sections. Each section is, therefore, prefaced by a brief introductory note which sets out the context within which its constituent papers were assembled. The papers themselves have not been constrained to a standard format, since their differing style is regarded as being validly informative of the authors' varied backgrounds and interests.

SECTION I
The Production Context

The audio-visual media are vehicles for the creation, storage and transmission of messages, many of which have political content or implications. Whilst 'the medium is the message' is a valuable adage, focusing attention on aspects which might otherwise be overlooked or underestimated, it remains axiomatic that much of the message can be attributed to the producer - who in turn functions within the context of a complex framework of institutional, social, professional and commercial priorities and constraints. To understand the message we must appreciate something of this production context as well as its political setting and inspiration.

As several of the contributors intimate, there has in recent years been widespread questioning of the political coverage, depth and impartiality achieved by the broadcast media. A valid starting point for discussion is, therefore, a statement of the standards to which media professionals aspire, together with an indication of the pressures which mould both the aspiration and the actual level of achievement. This perspective is provided by Peter Hardiman Scott and Robert Hargreaves, reflecting the experience of the two main British television 'news' networks. An academic commentary on the same theme by Philip Elliott sets this discussion into a context directly applicable to the interests and problems of many media users.

To demonstrate that feature film production and distribution also operates within a definable framework of social, commercial and professional pressures, Edward Buscombe and Richard Taylor explore the background to Hollywood in the 1930s and Russia in the 1920s respectively. These two disparate examples develop principles which can be adapted to other areas and periods, and indeed very similar consideration of the relationship between a society and its films will be seen in Philip Davies' paper in Section III. It is also possible to discern in these introductory contributions something of the significant difference between film and television, extending to the nature of the medium, the very different distribution and viewing contexts, and contrasts in production constraints. This important distinction is implicit in many of the subsequent papers.

The Development of an Approach to the Presentation of Political and Current Affairs on Television: the Experience of the BBC

Peter Hardiman Scott

'It has been said that Parliamentary institutions are on their trial. If that be so, broadcasting is an instrument of great potential value in keeping Parliament before the minds of the people.'

That quotation came not, as you might think, from a contemporary politician. It was made just over 40 years ago by the committee, set up by Parliament under Lord Ullswater to look into the control of broadcasting content. Having recognized the political importance of broadcasting, it may seem a little illogical that the same committee concluded: 'Any direct broadcasting of Parliamentary proceedings we regard as impracticable.' However, the committee bravely thought that controversial topics should continue to be discussed. In fact, they had been discussed since 1928, and perhaps that was the genesis of political and current affairs broadcasting. Any consideration of current affairs in television, however, is really incomplete without at least some slight reference to the BBC's early struggles to broadcast politics and other controversial issues of the day.

It could be argued that one of the most effective forms of political broadcasting, and one which would give fresh impetus to current affairs programming generally, would be to televise the proceedings of Parliament in daily and weekly edited programmes, as well as being able to use the material in news and current affairs generally. In 1959 - that was a year after the BBC had been allowed to televise the pageantry of the State opening of Parliament - Aneurin Bevan suggested that there should be an investigation into the technical possibilities of televising Parliamentary proceedings because, he said, MPs should consider 're-establishing intelligent communication between the House of Commons and the electorate as a whole. That surely,' he said, 'is a democratic process'. The broadcasters are still waiting to be allowed to make that contribution to the democratic process.

The broadcasting of the proceedings in radio only started at Easter 1978, almost three years after the successful month's experiment in Parliamentary broadcasting. Yet in 1926, when Churchill was Chancellor of the Exchequer, Reith sought permission to broadcast the budget speech live from the Commons. He was unsuccessful. A few days later he had a letter from the Postmaster General saying: 'I see from the *Radio Times* that you propose to broadcast a talk about budgets. This could be controversial. May I have a script please?'

Peter Hardiman Scott is Chief Assistant to the Director General of the BBC.

In the BBC's early days it was forbidden to broadcast political, religious or industrial controversy. But in 1928, the BBC was told: 'After full consideration His Majesty's Government are of opinion that the time has come when an experiment ought to be made in the direction of greater latitude'. It would appear that the experiment is still going on! During the course of it, however, the BBC has had to suffer the inhibitions of first the fourteen-day rule and then the seven-day rule. These barred broadcast discussions of issues that were to be raised in Parliament within those periods. It meant that broadcasting producers had to acquire yet another skill, clairvoyance. These rules were not swept away until 1956. Very much earlier, in 1934 to be precise, the BBC had tried to get a radio debate about the budget. It produced this quaint reply from the government: 'The budget ought not to be the subject of a wireless debate before an unrestricted audience. The Chancellor' (it was Neville Chamberlain) 'should be treated not as a party leader, but as a national figure, speaking impartially'.

It was not until the early fifties that a Chancellor agreed to be interviewed about his budget. He was 'Rab' Butler and the interviewer was William Clark. The occasion was almost elaborately cosy, with the Chancellor introducing Mr Clark to a picture on the wall of a storm-tossed ship and using this as an analogy in explaining his budget strategy. There is a distinctly period atmosphere about it all. Yet looking through the BBC's film archives it is surprising to see how little things have changed. One format is tried, developed, exploited, changed, returned to. The manner of presentation differs over the years, but there is a remarkable similarity about content. Already in the same year (1953) the BBC used three interviewers to question Aneurin Bevan. The questions were pointed enough but the programme lacked the tighter form of more modern examples of the format. Ten years later the BBC was still using this form for another television interview with the then Chancellor, Reginald Maudling. The interviewers were William Clark, Robert Mackenzie and Andrew Schonfield. The questions were relevant and pointed, as could be expected from such experienced and knowledgeable men, but there was little hard follow-up.

The period of the 1950s could perhaps be seen as the point when television began to overtake other forms of political communication. Politicians began to suspect that if something needed to be said, or a subject of current concern, like housing or health, needed to be investigated, then television might be the medium to do it. Yet they were suspicious that the process might not necessarily lead to greater understanding, and consequently they were wary.

Many of them came into television studios diffidently. It was out of their wariness of this potentially powerful medium that politicians wanted to lay down conditions. They frequently expected to be told the questions they were to be asked, and sometimes even thought they had the right to decide the questions themselves. This attitude obviously had to be rejected, and doubtless this led to some of the early brushes between politicians and broadcasters.

To generalize and to simplify at one and the same time, politicians were aware of what they saw as the power of television, and although they were suspicious of it, they sought to use it to their advantage. Thus the most skilful of them developed the technique of never exactly answering the question put to them. Perhaps this is why it was the interviews with public figures who were not politicians which were often the most successful in eliciting information or deepening understanding. Nevertheless, it was probably the device of politicians only appearing to answer the questions put to them which led to the less polite, more aggressive type of interview. This has now become integrated into the many techniques which a practised and experienced interviewer regularly uses - not only to seek answers to questions of legitimate public concern but also to reveal something of the character of the person being interviewed.

The development of the more aggressive interview did not deter politicians. They had begun to see television as a powerful influence, and in this they were encouraged by the enthusiasm and commitment to the medium of the many new and young producers that the opening of a third channel demanded. So politicians tumbled over themselves to get into the studios. In spite of the admirable and varied research which is being undertaken it is unwise to be dogmatic about the real influence of television upon our daily lives. But in this context what was important was not any evidence of the powerful influence of television, but merely that MPs themselves believed it to be important.

This period of the sixties is often seen as the flowering of television. The mainstream current affairs programmes - both in the BBC and in independent television - were well-established. There was a lot of experiment in new techniques of inquiry. Producers developed a device which was convenient and which at the same time provided interesting television. This was the device whereby people were filmed setting out their arguments on a controversial issue and then they were intercut with other people advocating the opposing arguments. It seemed logical; it had pace; and at the end it looked cohesive. The technique in a modified way is still used. But it did lead directly to complaints of misrepresentation, of phrases and arguments being taken out of context and unnaturally juxtaposed. There is some truth in the complaint. At any rate it led, in the BBC, to the instruction that this technique should not be used without the participants being fully aware of the context in which their contributions were being broadcast.

There was a further and more important development. This was the studio confrontation between holders of opposing views - sometimes with a studio audience, sometimes without. This clash of opinion could, on occasion, produce riveting television. It could also result in a lot of noise and very little light, and a good deal of sterile argument. As a reaction to it came the technique, familiar to programmes such as *Panorama* and still followed, of a film report the aim of which is to set out the facts of a subject as fairly as they can be ascertained, followed by interviews, a studio discussion, or an examination of the facts unearthed in the film report. There are other formats for the broadcasting of politics and current affairs, but the above have been specifically mentioned because they seem to grow out of each other and out of the requirements of the time. They do not, of course, take account of other areas of broadcasting where politics are frequently examined in depth and detail. Such an area is Further Education, where programmes such as an examination of the whole background to Northern Ireland, and an investigation into political ignorance, to take only two recent examples, are part of the staple diet for viewers.

But to return to the 1960s. These were also the years of the political satire programmes. Political leaders found themselves lampooned in a way that had not been seen since the political cartoons of the previous century. The more experienced and philosophical men - like Harold Macmillan, who had a sense of history - could take it: but most of them could not. The satire shows altered the climate; they helped to loosen up political programmes generally and to sharpen interviews. That was a benefit, but there is little doubt that these programmes embittered MPs against the BBC in particular and against the media in general.

The criticism came almost as much from Iain Macleod as from Harold Wilson, but since much of this programming was during the period of Labour government, the criticism naturally developed more on the left because of the traditional belief of the Labour Party that the media are ranged against it. It is a belief which is understandable because, unlike the other two parties, which grew out of the Parliamentary system, the Labour Party had its birth outside Parliament in the struggle of the working people and the early trade union movement. It was obvious at that time to see the whole machinery of the established order, including the press, as against these new political forces. It is an attitude which dies hard. The satire programmes and the brighter current affairs programming, stimulated it. This led to the repeated charge of trivialization, which culminated, at the end of the decade, in Richard Crossman's Granada lecture.

Crossman had a serious point. He specifically excluded news. His charge was directed against current affairs, and there was some justification for it. But without seeming to realize it, Crossman was complaining as much about the nature of the medium as the treatment of the subject, because he contended that five minutes on radio's *World At One* was far more useful in expressing a complicated political idea than the same period of peak television time. The reason he gave was one which anyone who has appeared at all frequently on television has experienced - the tendency of the viewer to take more notice of the picture than the content of what is being said. This is not always because of the treatment of the subject; it is more often the nature of pictures themselves - the broadcaster's hunched shoulders, the colour of his suit, his tie slightly askew, the kind of spectacles he is wearing - these are all distractions to the assimilation of information or the understanding of argument and opinion. So television producers have a natural preference for film which can illustrate a subject; film which, married to words, can hold the attention and, it is hoped, deepen understanding.

Robin Day has recently pointed to the inherent weakness. '...Television's dependence on pictures', he has said, 'makes it not only a powerful means of communication, but a crude one, which tends to strike at the emotions rather than the intellect'. (Ref. 1). That is true. But television producers are much more aware of the problem today than they were when the medium itself seemed almost to be its own justification.

In tackling any contemporary subject in a television current affairs programme the search is always for the format which can best explore the subject, convey information and lead to greater understanding. This means striking not only the right balance between words and pictures, studio talking and film; it means trying to find the kind of pictures and the kind of talk which strike less at the emotions and more at the intellect, and in a way that increases, and not obscures, understanding.

John Birt and Peter Jay, in their critique of television journalism, (Ref. 2) maintained that the system had an inbuilt bias against understanding. Their paper caused a lot of discussion; it usefully made broadcasters think about their craft. On the other hand it seemed to ignore a great deal of evidence that was contrary to its main thesis. Thus the kind of programmes which Birt and Jay said are not being done - because there is not enough examination and exposition of complicated issues - are being done, and have been done over many years both in independent television and in the BBC. There have been scores of them, ranging from quite alarming medical investigations to examinations of the structure and efficiency of the steel industry. This is not to say that greater exposition and deeper analysis of current issues are not sometimes desirable.

But what often stands in the way of greater exposition and more detailed examination, is not the way programmes, or the staff to do the programmes, are organized, but sometimes the sheer impossibility of collecting the information. For example, there are whole areas of the world where reporters and television crews cannot operate at all or, if they can, can only do so under restrictions which prevent them getting at all the facts. Even in this country we have the Official Secrets Act. It would be more helpful to have something nearer the American Freedom of Information Act, which gives any citizen the right of access to government papers, providing they don't deal with defence and foreign policy secrets or commercial secrets.

It is not the role of broadcasters, as Birt and Jay conceive, to tell 'the citizenry at large what is happening to the world and the society in which they live'. The broadcasters are not gods in their industry - although angry politicians sometimes say they behave like them. Broadcasters cannot look down from their lighting gantries and say what is happening to the scurrying viewers beneath them. They can only try to provide all the ascertainable facts, and a variety of opinion about those facts, and leave the people themselves to decide what is happening to their society. Anything else would require of the programme staff - the editor, the producer, the reporter - a commitment to a point of view. As a result of their collection of information, their presentation of argument and opinion, they would come to a view of their own and present that to the viewer. That is not the broadcasters' job. It would not even be their job if there were a dozen television channels.

An interesting suggestion was recently made to the BBC by two executives in one of Britain's 'controversial' industries. They suggested that two BBC current affairs producers should each produce a committed programme. One producer would be told: 'Now it is your job to take a totally committed view and produce a programme as convincingly as you can in favour of this industry, the way it is run, the processes it uses, their total safety and so on. You have got to justify it up to the hilt.' The second producer would be told: 'Now you have got to be just as committed to a programme against this industry, the way it is organized, its processes and so on.' Then both programmes would be shown, one immediately after the other, and perhaps they would be followed by a studio discussion.

Even overlooking the possibility that the producer making a programme deliberately hostile to the company might find it difficult to get the necessary co-operation, it remains an interesting idea. It might even be worth trying. But those two company executives were told that it might prove extraordinarily difficult to find two producers who could make the programmes. Commitment is so foreign to their upbringing - to the whole ethos which they acquire in their work throughout their broadcasting career - that each of them would automatically be seeking other evidence, other opinions, so as to present a less partial view. It is doubtful whether their commitment would turn out to be all that convincing.

In future there will inevitably be experiments in new ways of examining issues and analysing problems, but one of these ways will not be with reporters and producers with a committed point of view. Neither is there likely to be any alteration in the distinction which the BBC has always drawn between the reporting of news and the presentation of current affairs. In news the BBC rightly restricts itself to reporting the ascertainable facts and deductions which can properly be made from those facts. Current affairs programmes present a range of opinion, argument and discussion about them, and examines many of the public issues of our times. The BBC has always maintained that it is important to draw this line between news and current affairs so that there should be no confusion in the mind of the listener or viewer between the reporting of news and the presentation of opinion about it. This does not mean that the staffs of news and current affairs cannot work closely together. Co-operation between the two has developed in recent years and will doubtless increase. Whether or not a total merging of staffs is necessarily the most efficient way of doing the job is a matter of controversy, but both can surely be used within the single context of a news and current affairs programme, one staff complementing the other, as one programme develops naturally from its predecessor - the news.

There is clearly room for experiment in this way, because the search for better ways of presenting current issues is a continuing process. But in that search producers cannot help recognizing that, over the years, audiences for programmes like *Panorama* and *World in Action* have slowly declined, whereas the audience for *Nationwide* has steadily gone up. That does not mean that broadcasters should always aim at brevity. There are many complicated issues that cannot be dealt with briefly. But equally broadcasters should understand that brevity need not necessarily mean triviality.

A lot of research has been done, and is being done, into the effect of television upon people who watch it. It is valuable that this research should continue, but nevertheless there is a great deal we still do not know. It is much too simple, for example, to say that television defeated Nixon and won the presidential election for Kennedy because, after the first television debate, Nixon 'never got up off the floor'. There were other factors that helped Kennedy - his appearance before Protestant ministers in Houston; his telephone call to Mrs Martin Luther King Jr. when her husband was in jail in Atlanta, to mention but two. Nevertheless it was probably the Nixon-Kennedy experience which, up to now, has persuaded leaders of the two major political parties in Britain not to confront each other in a television studio. It would, however, be very difficult to establish a direct causal relationship between certain television programmes and subsequent public behaviour.

But if not enough is yet known about the effect of television, it is known that most people get most of their news information from the television screen. It might, therefore, seem astonishing that the very heart of our democratic process itself should voluntarily cut itself off from the largest of the mass media. In spite of its many imperfections it is important that the system of politics enjoyed in this country, and the Parliamentary democracy it produces, should be upheld. The alternative is dictatorship. For all sorts of reasons, which are not the subject of this paper, Parliamentary democracy is in great and urgent need of reform. One of the most potent aids to achieve it could be the televising of Parliament. This would not only enable people to see the process of discussion, and bring politics dramatically and authentically to the screen, it could also make MPs desperately aware of their own inadequacies and the inadequacy of present Parliamentary procedure to control the power of the executive with a mighty civil service behind it. That awareness might gradually lead to Parliament itself demanding more influence, more control, more power in the decision-making processes. And an obvious way that MPs might see of achieving that would be through a more highly developed and more efficient select-committee system, which could not only call Ministers and their civil servants to account, but which could constructively contribute to the decision-making of government.

That would not merely be good television. It would be important television. It would be bringing to people in their homes an insight into the very purpose of politics and the way Parliament and government work. It would be the best way of screening politics. It would also be good for democracy itself.

REFERENCES

1. R. Day, Troubled Reflections of a TV Journalist, *Encounter* May (1970). Reprinted in *Day by Day*, (1975) Kimber, London.

2. J. Birt and P. Jay, *The Times*, 28 February, 30 September, 1 October 1975.

Television and Current Affairs

Robert Hargreaves

The days have passed when journalists working for television thought of themselves as pioneers, constantly pushing forward against technical, editorial and even legal barriers as they created an exciting new medium of communication. Today, we are on the defensive, under attack for our so-called bias against understanding according to the thesis recently presented by Peter Jay and John Birt (Ref. 1); and under attack for bias of a more political sort in a book entitled *Bad News*, published last year by a study team from the University of Glasgow (Ref. 2).

I want to add that I am in no way entitled to speak on behalf of my employers, Independent Television News. The views I put forward are my own - those of an individual television reporter, responsible not for high policy, but for dealing day by day with the news as it arises in my particular field. As Home Affairs correspondent of ITN, that field covers four of the great domestic departments of the state: the Home Office (which of course includes news in the delicate areas of race relations and immigration); the Department of the Environment (which takes in, for example, local government and public housing policy); Education & Science; and the Department of Health and Social Security - all of them subjects particularly liable to the dangers of bias.

For the broadcaster these are potential minefields of controversy - controversy not only in deciding how such subjects should be covered in the context of a television news programme, but even on many occasions controversy in deciding what should be covered in the first place. Is it right, for example, to give an interview to Mr Enoch Powell after he has claimed to have revealed mistakes in the immigration statistics? Or again, should we look into allegations made by prominent politicians that the Social Security system in Britain is being widely abused?

These, and questions like them, present problems of balance and judgement with which working journalists have to grapple almost every day. I should like later to introduce some examples of the problems that have arisen in the field of Home Affairs, and to discuss how we have tackled them in practice, with particular reference to the problems of impartiality. But first, I will look briefly at the broader picture: and here, I suppose, the most frequently heard criticism of television news is that it is too shallow, too superficial, and too short. Every night on *News at Ten*, we condense into a bare half-hour some fifteen or twenty news items: everything from

---

Robert Hargreaves is Home Affairs Correspondent, Independent Television News

foreign and political news to sport and crime. On an average night, the most important items might rate four minutes of air time. Secondary film or studio spots might get two or two and a half minutes. The so-called newscaster stories - those not backed up with film or specialist studio reports - are usually dismissed in just three or four paragraphs. And how, ask the critics, can such an atomised formula possibly avoid trivialisation? How can it offer the viewer the interpretation and analysis of events that are, we all admit, essential to a proper understanding of complex problems?

Such critical analyses of news presentation often begin by quoting an experiment conducted many years ago now by an American television producer, Mr Fred Friendly of CBS, who had set into type the entire verbal content of one evening's news programme. He found that it filled less than a column and a half of the front page of the *New York Times* - proof, indeed, one might think, of how much television has to leave out; of how relatively shallow its coverage must perforce be.

But I am not sure that this is a proposition that stands up to closer scrutiny. Another, and perhaps wiser journalist who also worked for CBS - the late Ed Murrow - once observed that the really important journey undertaken by the television signal was not its voyage by satellite across the Atlantic, nor its transmission from the TV tower into the individual home. The really important journey was from the tube in the drawing room into the mind of the individual viewer. On that criterion of received information, the average member of the public might actually absorb more information from television than he does from his daily newspaper.

The viewer of *News at Ten*, for example, receives almost a full half-hour of news every weeknight. Even the well-informed readers of this volume probably absorb no more than that in terms of hard news from their daily newspaper - and most will almost certainly spend far less than half an hour reading the news columns of that newspaper before they move on to the leader page, the features, the letter columns or the crossword puzzle. This applies even to the minority of viewers who read the serious press: those who subscribe to one of the popular papers clearly receive an even smaller proportion of real information from their newspaper than they do from the television news programmes.

The real difference between television and newspapers is that the reader of a newspaper can choose for himself the items he wishes to read in depth, those he wishes merely to skim, and those he ignores altogether. On television, by contrast, the news director makes that choice for him. It can be argued that, as a result, the viewer actually receives a broader perspective from television than he does from the newspapers. None of us, of course, would claim that on individual stories the coverage will always be as deep - and it is this lack of depth, rather than the lack of breadth, that gives most concern to the broadcasters whose job it is to provide an adequate forum for the tens of millions of people who nightly view the main news programmes on both ITV and the BBC.

But let us avoid looking at television news in isolation. No viewer does; and the news programme is after all only one of the sources from which he draws his understanding of the world. Let us recognise, too, that the various arms of the media are in fact complementary one to the other. Perhaps it takes newspapers to dig out the concealed background to the Watergate affair - but it takes television to bring home to the public the full impact of the Erwin enquiry. People who really want to understand what is going on in the world rarely rely on one medium only. We are all newspaper readers and viewers of television, and we all occasionally listen to the radio. Taking these sources in combination, we are probably getting a fuller and more rounded picture of the world we live in than our parents or our grandparents ever did.

Television news, therefore, does not exist in a vacuum, but within its own confines we must acknowledge that it has serious limitations in providing an adequate flow of explanation, analysis and background. What the news programmes lack today is depth. There are many reasons for this, some of them inherent in the nature of the medium, some due to historical factors, others to the limited structure of the programmes.

One important limitation stems from the technical revolution that transformed television news roughly in the decade of the 1960s. At the beginning of that decade, the inflow of pictures in the form of film or videotape was only a fraction of what it is today. Viewers first took in their information on foreign affairs, for instance, from the morning newspaper - and then later saw pictures of the same event on television, which merely reinforced what the newspapers had already told them. Today, those roles have been reversed. Thanks to satellite and Eurovision sources, it is now possible to watch the fall of Saigon on the day it happened, to bring in coverage within the hour of Mrs Thatcher's press conference in Australia, or to watch the nomination of Jimmy Carter live, as it is actually happening. Today, we see these events first on television, and read about them afterwards in the newspapers.

But television's very success in organising its inflow of coverage has also greatly increased the pressures on already scarce air time, and so actually made more acute its problems of analysis and explanation. It is in part this sheer pressure of available material that leads to the charge that television news displays a bias against understanding. We try to cram too much in. With so much dramatic material to choose from, there is a temptation, not always resisted, to over-illustrate and under-explain; to choose the arresting picture and not the dull; the spectacular and not the representative.

Even if we avoid all these temptations, there is another pitfall in store: that some pictures are of such emotional force they drown out the perhaps more significant news. One recent example is the film of a riot at the Notting Hill Carnival - dramatic, forceful, in its way unforgettable, as are all images of violence. And yet, how representative is such coverage of the state of race relations in Britain today? And will it also drown out the more muted, more thoughtful expositions of racial deprivation carried in the same programme on quieter nights?

I do not profess to know the answer; but the same question is reinforced by a comparison of three film items carried on *News at Ten* that have touched on the specific problems of the West Indian community in London. First, a report based on the initiative taken by the former Conservative minister, Mr Peter Walker: second, the drama of the hot news event of the riot at Notting Hill, filmed at very short notice: and finally, the coverage transmitted the following day in an attempt to explain why the violence had occurred. From this small selection of newsfilm the image that lingers is the image of violence - however hard we have tried as reporters to give a fair and balanced assessment of the wider problems which perhaps led to the violence. But even in these brief sequences, an impression remains not only of violence, but also of problems - of the overall nature of the deprivation and discrimination suffered by the black community in Britain, of the attitude of the police towards the blacks, and of the blacks towards the police. It is not a complete picture, of course; it could not hope to be in the time available. But it is not a partial picture, either, and we would claim that it is as fair and balanced as honest journalists working under pressure could make it.

Sometimes, of course, the dilemma we face is the opposite one: the knowledge that television can be 'used' by groups or individuals to promote their own ends, and that this in itself can lead to a further polarisation of our society. In the late 1960s, this phenomenon became a cause of real worry as many student demonstrations turned to violence partly at least in response to the presence of television cameras. One can observe the same phenomenon at work today in groups who burn buses in Belfast specifically for the purpose of getting the event on television, or at National Front marches and attempts by minority groups of all sorts to command national attention through street drama, protest and violence. They have learned that television pays attention to action rather than argument; to shock rather than explanation; and to emotions rather than ideas. They have also learned that success comes not through the old politics of negotiation and compromise, but through the new politics of theatricality. And the chief characteristic of this world, as seen by television, is that life is apocalyptic.

This is the real bias of television, whether it arises from the nature of the medium, or from the shortcomings of its practitioners. We often persuade ourselves that our first priority is to present the viewer with a plain and unvarnished account of events in words and pictures. But let us also not lose sight of the fact that the events we are recording may themselves have been influenced in fundamental ways by the presence - or hoped-for presence - of television.

An example from my own experience came recently at Winchester, during the enquiry into the proposal to extend the M3 Motorway: an enquiry which was systematically disrupted by protestors, representing both local and national interests. You may see this as evidence that people will not put up with arbitrary government - and you would be right. At one level, this was a heartening week, watching people fighting passionately against what they saw as an oppressive bureaucracy for a cause they believed to be just. But where does that leave the supposedly impartial broadcaster who covered the hearing? For there is no doubt that the course of the enquiry was affected in fundamental ways by the presence of television. Should we have been more impartial than we were? Should we have meekly stood back when ordered not to film? Were we right to cover the event in the first place, knowing - as we did - that our presence would be 'used' by the protestors? All of these are questions which show, once again, that for the reporter in the field matters of selection and impartiality are not abstract or academic issues, but practical problems that have to be faced every working day.

The basic rule for the conduct of controversy on the air can be summed up in just three words: 'Give both sides.' In spite of the taunts of some that impartiality is a false and unattainable goal, it remains the central creed of most broadcast journalists - avoid editorialising; hold the ring, but keep out of it yourself. Many of us still believe that it is through this code that news on television continues to be believed, trusted and respected. But as the former editor of ITN, Sir Geoffrey Cox, has recently pointed out, impartiality alone is not enough. It is the essential guide to the treatment of events; but it cannot provide an adequate guide to the selection of events - and clearly, the mere decision to cover, or not to cover, any given event involves the exercise of as much judgement and discretion as the coverage itself.

'Give both sides' is an indispensable rule for the reporter sent out to cover a specific assignment but, for his editor, it begs one important question: both sides of what? The power of selection of the issues to be probed and debated has been called the broadcaster's most important responsibility. He exercises it through the deployment of what is usually known as 'news sense.' Contrary to popular belief, however, there is no special mystique about news judgement, nor is there always a common consensus even among journalists about what news is. Indeed, the fiercest arguments about news values have taken place in my experience, not with the Sociology Department of the University of Glasgow in its authorship of *Bad News*, but in the newsroom of ITN. We frequently disagree about what to cover and what to omit. What is important, I think, is the fact that these are arguments based not on political grounds, nor on sociological grounds, nor most emphatically of all, on commercial grounds - but on an honest attempt to be impartial in deciding what to report in the public interest.

If you ask me who decides what the public interest is, I can only reply - the working journalist. If he allows someone else to decide for him - the government, some pressure group, or an ideology - then he forfeits his freedom. If you deny the journalist that freedom of choice, you deny the freedom of the press. Journalists do not live in a vacuum, and the determination of what is in the public interest and how it is reported of course reflect values and ideals that are current in our society. None of us would deny that, many of us would applaud it. We would, however, deny that we represent only one section of that society, with a common class and a common background. The journalists at ITN come from all walks of life: old Etonians and the sons of miners; women who went to Oxford and men who covered crime in Gateshead; Tribunites and High Tories; Scotsmen and Yorkshiremen; black people and white; women as well as men. In terms of background and social assumptions, what is remarkable is how little they have in common - and this, too, is a variety that helps to ensure that the judgements that are applied to news events are in fact the judgements of professional journalists in general, and not the mere political or social prejudices of a particular class.

I know of no mechanical formula to substitute for that professional judgement, of the sort that says that because textile workers make up 20% of the workforce they should get 20% of the coverage. You cannot edit news with a tape measure, although just such a formula has been used by some of our critics to suggest that we should carry, for instance, more interviews with women, since their research has shown (with remarkable precision) that only 7.7% of the people interviewed on ITN in 1975 were women. From this they conclude that ITN has a bias against women, although in fact it is more likely to be - dare I say it? - an impartial reflection of the world we live in. In the present British Cabinet of twenty four members, there is only one woman: in the whole House of Commons only twenty eight. If we granted equal time to each member, that would give women only 4.4% of the air time. Then again, I know of no leading Trades Unionist, no important industrialist who is a woman. If there was one, we would interview her on equal terms with the men.

These arguments, supposedly based on scientific analysis, are in fact based on a false premise, and may themselves be biased, because they grow from partial assumptions. The broadcast reporter is an educator, not a reformer. It is not his job to lead or guide society in any direction. He is not elected by the public and has no mandate to do anything of the sort. Today, more than ever, the broadcaster's role is to maintain his impartiality and his freedom from bias in seeking out and examining the truth about our world - but the world as he thinks it is, not as he thinks it ought to be.

It is sometimes argued that there are subjects which should remain taboo on television, or on which the broadcaster need not be impartial. We are often told, for instance, that broadcasting should not remain neutral over clear cases of right and wrong. Sir Hugh Greene, then director-general of the BBC, once declared: 'I should not for a moment admit that a man who wanted to speak in favour of racial intolerance had the same rights as the man who wanted to condemn it. There are some questions on which one should not be impartial.' Today, the taboo subject is race; yesterday it was the Royal Family; before that perhaps the Christian religion - subjects on which it was permissible to give only one side in order to preserve what were once known as 'standards.'

Personally, I find such strictures misguided. The cause of good race relations in Britain is not well served by well-meaning attempts at self-censorship, nor by concealing a problem we all know exists.

If the ultra right-wing National Party is active in Blackburn and likely to gain a significant proportion of the votes in the local elections, that is news - and should be reported, and the views of its spokesmen, however outrageous, subjected to scrutiny. When a speaker for the same party delivers his inflammatory and now notorious attack on immigrants - saying, after an Asian boy had been killed: 'One down, and a million to go,' - that is news, too. News because of the appalling insight it gives into the mentality of the racist parties in Britain today, and news because it helps to explain the feelings of outrage and discrimination felt by the immigrant community when they are subjected to such provocative taunts.

Not long ago, I interviewed a rather right-wing Conservative MP on a contentious social issue. He was characteristically forthright and outspoken in his views. After the broadcast, someone phoned through to ITN to protest that we had carried the item, saying: 'That was rather like interviewing Hitler about the Jews.' My answer to that is: yes - if this were 1938, one should indeed try to interview Hitler about the Jews. And to go further: it was the failure of many western newspapers fully to report Hitler's threats against the Jews before the war that led in part to the complacency and the refusal to believe what was happening in Europe until the shocking discoveries at Belsen and Buchenwald finally brought it to our understanding. Some lives might have been saved, a greater urgency might have driven the leaders of the West, greater efforts made to evacuate and rescue the inhabitants of the ghettoes, if the racist views of Adolf Hitler had been more widely reported and more widely understood in the 1930s.

What is important, of course, is the balance with which one reports delicate subjects like race. Here again, the picture is not perfect. None of us in the media can look back with much pride on our role in reporting on the Asian family from Malawi who were put up in a hotel near Gatwick Airport by the local Social Services department. The manner in which this item was reported is widely held to have inflamed racial passions in Britain, and there may well be some truth in that claim. Headlines proclaiming 'the scandal of the £600-a-week Asians' are themselves racist and unfair, but that is a complaint about treatment of the story not about selection. This was a legitimate news story, raising several issues of public concern that it was right to discuss openly and fairly. As far as I am concerned, the subject was most certainly not taboo. But let us make it clear that the scandal, if there was one, was not of the Asians' making.

Another contentious subject that has been in the British news recently is that of alleged abuses of the social security system. There are many people whose opinions I respect who claim, with passion, that to report cases of abuse only serves to bolster the views of those who are against all forms of Social Security payment, and whose real target is the basic concept of the Welfare State. There may be some truth in that claim but, after long discussion, ITN recently went on the air with a series about abuse, taking the view that no area should be regarded as off-limits to television. We tried to take care, though, that the series was balanced. First, we presented the case against; then we gave a number of specific examples of abuse; and finally, the case in favour - we would say these were all legitimate items of news, fairly covered.

That brings me to my next question: are there any issues which should rightly be regarded as off-limits to the television journalist. The answer is, yes: and here I am referring to subjects which are none of the public's business, - people's private lives, for example, or intrusions into personal grief. Here again, though, the dividing line is not an absolute one, but one for judgement and discretion. Sometimes private lives do force themselves on our attention, as in the case of Mr John Stonehouse, or in the events which preceded the breakup of Princess Margaret's marriage.

Another, more disturbing example, led up to the resignation of Mr Jeremy Thorpe as leader of the Liberal Party. Normally, news broadcasters would regard the alleged sexual affairs of public figures to be off-limits. In themselves, they are not news and they are none of our business. In the Thorpe case, the allegations which were made should - arguably - not have been reported. But special factors were at work which made it impossible not to report the affair.

In the first place, it had already been widely discussed, first in *Private Eye*, and then, with more serious consequences, in the *Daily Mail*. Because of this, a sort of Gresham's Law began to operate, as the bad news drove out the good, and newsroom after newsroom began its pursuit of the unsavoury tale, so that by the time Mr Scott did make his allegations in the tiny Devon courtroom - which, incidentally, gave both him and the press the cover of privilege - it was packed with reporters, all knowing in advance what was likely to occur. 'For who will stop his ears when loud rumour flies abroad?'

But this was not simply a question of climbing on the bandwagon, of not wanting to be 'scooped' and left behind by one's competitors. Although that was an important factor, it was not the over-riding one. For once this case was in the open, and once the Liberal Party had decided to take the allegations seriously and interrogate their own leader, even the most high-minded members of the press and broadcasting were obliged to report the distasteful story and to investigate the roles of the various participants. It was an episode which did, after all, drive Mr Thorpe from his office. For any news organisation, however self-righteous, to report simply his departure without giving the reasons for it was obviously unrealistic. At the same time, the pace was clearly being set by the more prurient and sensational newspapers, with the others being forced with varying degrees of reluctance to follow.

It was an episode which also raises some serious questions about the practice of journalism in Britain, in the area where it relates to an individual's rights to privacy and to the laws of defamation and privilege. The legal remedies have been well rehearsed elsewhere, but the news coverage of the Thorpe affair illustrates very clearly the way in which we are all sometimes obliged to follow the herd - and by so doing may actually influence, rather than simply report, the course of events. Is there any remedy for that? If we believe in a genuinely free press, no there is not. To impose restrictions on the freedom to report is no remedy at all.

If impartiality is our code, it can admit of no exceptions. And here, finally, is where I part company with ITN's former editor Sir Geoffrey Cox, who has argued in recent articles that it is the primary duty of broadcasters to sustain and support to the utmost the democratic system and, in particular, the rule of the law which is the necessary partner to that system. He makes his stand upon the principles of the British Constitution; upon the principles of civil and religious liberty; upon the rule of the law and the freedom of the press; upon the institutions of Parliamentary government and an independent judiciary.

This is our code as Englishmen: it is a noble code, and as citizens we have a duty to defend it. Yet, as impartial journalists, even adherence to the principles of our constitution is not enough, for as John Stuart Mill wrote 150 years ago: 'The law of England is as unfavourable to the liberty of the press as that of the most despotic government which ever existed; and consequently, whatever degree of that liberty is enjoyed in this country, exists, not in consequence of the law, but in spite of it.' Fifty years ago, during the General Strike, John Reith called upon precisely this code (the rule of the law) to deny air time to the TUC, on the grounds that the strike had been declared illegal: the rule of the law must be preserved, therefore those who break the law are not entitled to be heard.

Broadcasters today would regard such a ruling as offensive and ludicrous. And yet, by an exactly parallel ruling, we would bind ourselves when it comes to interviewing terrorists, or racists, or members of the IRA who act outside the law. Such barriers - whether erected in the name of the constitution, or the rule of the law, or the public interest - are in fact barriers against an impartial search for the truth, and they are a hindrance to the justified scrutiny of an important aspect of our society.

A journalist's first concern must not be for the law, nor the preservation of the existing establishment. It must be to report and probe, without fear and at the journalist's own discretion, any of the issues that affect the society in which we all live.

That is our code and we find our motto in the words of Marcel Proust:
'Cherish those who seek after truth. But beware of those who say they've found it.'

REFERENCES

1. J. Birt and P. Jay, *The Times*, 28 February, 30 September, 1 October (1975).

2. Glasgow University Media Group (1976) *Bad News*, Routledge and Kegan Paul, London.

Production and the Political Content of Broadcasting

Philip Elliott

There was a time when documents tyrannised history. As E. H. Carr put it, 'documents were the Ark of the Covenant in the temple of fact' (Ref. 1). At present the public is convinced by television news. It could be argued that this amounts to a tyranny of the visual. The reason most often given for believing television news is the illusion it gives of seeing for oneself.

There is more to it than that however. One of the main aims in the production of broadcast news for both radio and television has been to make it authoritative and credible (Ref. 2). Changes in presentation, for example, have been assessed by weighing advantages in terms of interest and comprehension against possible losses in terms of broadcasters' authority and credibility. These efforts to achieve credibility have been greatly assisted by the transparency of both broadcast media. Visuals in television are an added bonus to the illusion which is possible through both radio and television of allowing the audience to know the truth about the world with a minimum of intervention. Where the press journalist with the help of newspaper technology has to translate his experiences into a written account, broadcast journalism appears to offer simpler channels through which knowledge or, in the case of television, experience can be made available to the audience.

Broadcasters have capitalised on this illusion to justify their activities. Like the historians before them, they argue that they have the techniques to render objectively and impartially a true account of important events in the world. Pressed to explain how a selected account can ever amount to the truth, they fall back on the position that this is the only possible way of working if the medium is to retain its credibility. More than that, it is the only way of working to avoid broadcasting propaganda. The only choice is between witting and unwitting bias and if the broadcaster is to retain his independence, the latter is the only alternative. For one thing it is easier to deny unwitting bias. Reuven Frank, President of NBC News, concluded from his experience as a television newsman in the United States that 'this country is best served if the power over television news is in the hands of people who have no idea of what to do with it' (Ref. 3). It is too great a mystery to understand, and the attempt to do so may be positively dangerous by opening the way for manipulation or intervention. There is a good chance however that there will be no need to deny it. What is hidden may not be noticed. Most important of all, it is less likely to upset the public and the authorities who have set up the system within which broadcasting operates.

Philip Elliott is Research Fellow at the Centre for Mass Communication Research, University of Leicester, U.K.

The positive claim that broadcasters render truth objectively and impartially can therefore be expressed more negatively. Broadcasters have developed routines and techniques for hiding bias. The most important, to which I shall return below, is the technique of sticking closely to the basic assumptions, what might be termed the general bias, of the culture.

Historians and political scientists are more likely to find broadcasters' claims to deal in truth convincing as ordinary viewers rather than in their professional capabilities. This is not because such academics have universally accepted some form of the relativist argument. Far from it. To quote E. H. Carr again 'The belief in a hard core of historical facts existing objectively and independently of the interpretation of the historian is a preposterous fallacy, but one which it is very hard to eradicate' (Ref. 4). Rather it is because broadcasting is clearly dealing in a different order of truth from that which has been the traditional concern of historians and political scientists.

This difference may be subdivided into three types; permanence, importance and public consumption. The first difference is again illustrated by the contrast between documents and broadcasting or film. Documents had the particular attraction for the historian that they were a lasting record. Once captured and archived for historical purposes, they could serve those purposes for all time. By contrast, broadcasting and film were ephemeral media. The fact that relatively cheap and convenient means of storage and retrieval are beginning to be developed may go some way to account for historians' interest in their value to their subject. The problems associated with archiving are discussed elsewhere in this volume, but it seems that the time has almost arrived when film and broadcasting will cease to be ephemera and become a recoverable resource. In so far as film and broadcasting organisations have kept their old material themselves, this is already the case. But their archives have been founded on the policy of keeping what might be useful to the future activities of the organisation and there have been considerable problems of access for those outside. Those archives also illustrate the further problem of selection criteria.

This brings us to the second difference between historical accounts and broadcasting accounts, differing definitions of importance. In a sense historical documents were selected by history. They were the records of any period which happened to survive. There are some grounds for arguing that this fortuitous selection was made, however unconsciously, on grounds of historical importance. Documents of state and the papers of prominent public figures were more likely to find a safe home in some permanent public building or family house. What is more, the relationship may be argued the other way round. Rather than the subject defining which records survived, it was the survival of that type of record which decided the main thrust of the subject. The political history of public figures was founded on the type of material readily available. It is only with difficulty that other records have been discovered to support other types of history - popular, social and economic.

The traditional concerns of politics and history are shared by some broadcasters and film makers. Those working in news and current affairs tend to be pre-occupied with the activities of political office holders and others in constitutional positions of power. But they are a small minority of those working in these media. There have even been others, for example those involved in the British documentary movement, mass observation and more recently producers of drama-documentaries, who have shared the same interests as social historians. But they are an even smaller minority. To pick out this type of output, which is itself directly concerned with political and historical subjects as traditionally understood, would therefore be to take a small and unrepresentative sample of film and broadcasting output. To justify this on the grounds that it is the only part of the output concerned with history and politics would be to perpetuate a narrow view of those subjects.

Setting these problems aside for the time being, there is a third difference between historical accounts and the account of historical and political subjects produced by the media. The latter is produced for immediate public consumption. This is more than a point about simplification for a mass audience or the restrictions which limited time and resources inevitably place on topical coverage. In the case of news and current affairs there is the more significant problem that such output is limited to what it is possible and permissible to say in public about the issues of the day. In so far therefore as film and broadcasting report the activities of the powerful and important, they are dealing with the way such people present themselves in public. They are also dealing with accessible presentations. Some producers have tried with striking success to minimise the extent to which film crews and reporters interfere with the subject they are recording and reporting. But the general run of coverage uses such familiar techniques as the statement, the interview and the filmed report to build a story or a programme with the material to hand. The results are easily caricatured by reference to common news stories like VIP arrivals at airports, pre-negotiation pleasantries in the negotiating room or outside broadcasts from outside the place where negotiations are taking place. The technology allows an account which is physically close to the scene of the action but which can only reach the substance of the action in so far as the participants are prepared to make that available.

Newspapers have always been treated as a special kind of documentary record in history precisely because it was clear that their content had to be interpreted with the purposes of their producers very much in mind. It is unlikely that historians and political scientists would be less suspicious of film and television. Even more than some newspapers, they are mass media produced for general consumption whose value for interpreting the policies and activities of élites are clearly limited. Nevertheless, the social responsibility theory of the press is sufficiently credible in the case of some papers to suggest that their record is worth considering as evidence (Ref. 5). According to this theory, because of monopolist or oligopolist conditions of press competition the role of newspapers has changed or should change (there is some ambiguity as to whether the theory is descriptive or normative) from political partisanship, attempting to influence events, to neutral recording of the activities of the times. This theory is echoed and amplified in the ideology of broadcast journalism. Controls have been imposed on the few transmission channels available in radio and television to prevent partisan or propagandist use. The result is a more powerful creed of how to report accurately and impartially. In the press the problem of identifying and packaging a commodity called news to reach the most profitable audience was founded on commercial considerations. So too was it in the cinema when the mass cinema audience was provided with newsreel services. But in broadcasting such considerations have been backed up by government control over the broad form of organisation and principles of practice.

The strength of the broadcast journalists' creed, which is well represented by the first two papers in this volume, does allow the claim to be made that broadcast news and current affairs has value as an accurate record of events. In their accounts of broadcasting, both Peter Hardiman Scott and Robert Hargreaves start from the broadcasters' responsibility to inform the public, developing a series of contrasts to show how this should be done. Broadcasting should deal in information rather than opinion, impartiality rather than bias and intellect rather than emotion. Both admit to some misgivings on the last count partly because a visual medium seems inherently more emotional in its handling of some subjects than a verbal one and partly because of the charge that the presentation of information as short reports of events in news bulletins deprives the audience of the context which is necessary for them to understand what is going on. Both are complex arguments which can hardly be resolved in the context of this short paper. Nevertheless both illustrate a fundamental point about the treatment of news and current affairs in broadcasting.

The central feature of the mediating process which produces broadcasting accounts is the framework of controls within which the broadcast media operate. In the case of other media which have been used by historians and political scientists the important problem has been to compensate for the mediating effects of intentionality, or even to study those as the way policies and reputations were built among different sectors of society. This latter type of analysis is very relevant to broadcasting. The subject of study in such cases is the way the intentions of people outside the media are realised through it, for example in the different techniques political leaders have used in this century to reach the public through radio and television (Ref. 6). But so far as broadcasters themselves are concerned, their work in the media is organised in such a way as to screen out or at least conceal the mediating effect of their intentions.

Desmond Taylor, then Editor of News and Current Affairs at the BBC gave a personal account of what this meant to the individuals concerned when he wrote of the 'considerable self-discipline' necessary 'for ordinary sinners to adopt this slightly saint-like role. As an example of what it means, let me tell you that I cannot recall having made, in the 21 years I have worked for the BBC, a single overtly political statement in public......Most BBC journalists are equally careful. Their attitude sometimes leads the layman to think that we are intellectual eunuchs who act without thinking. The reality is that we suppress our views and it is an effort' (Ref. 7).

In studying the implications of production for the content of film and broadcasting therefore we are mainly concerned with systemic rather than individual effects. The two cases referred to above which worried Peter Hardiman Scott and Robert Hargreaves both illustrate this point. The problem of the emotionalism of visual coverage is a problem of how to introduce the same kind of control over what might be called the overlay of communication, the range of connotative meanings and associated symbolism carried by any message, in the visual as in the verbal case. Considerable attention is given to controlling the niceties of verbal meaning in news bulletins. The cliché that one man's freedom fighter is another man's terrorist has been adopted as one key illustration of the phenomenon. But its intricacies, as described for example by Richard Francis (Ref. 8) when Controller of BBC Northern Ireland, take one into realms which are more usually associated with such abstruse semantic analysis as 'kremlinology'. The differences between 'the army says', 'the army alleges' and 'according to the army' are fine ones which may not be apparent to those outside broadcasting and the army who do not know the code, particularly if they are ordinary news consumers simply scanning the output in an inattentive way. Nevertheless, as Francis makes clear, they were matters of great moment to those who were in the know. The verbals are an aspect of the communication which appears potentially controllable and so debate rages over the exact way this should be done. By contrast, the meaning of visuals is less certain and how to control it is less clear. There is less agreement on the basic vocabulary which might pin down visual meaning to a single denotation, and it is not at all clear how there could be such agreement. The intellectual tradition is a literary and verbal one. Faced with the problems of predicting and controlling visual communication, the tendency is to write it off as emotional, as Robin Day does in the passage quoted above by Hardiman Scott (Ref. 9).

The second problem, the Birt and Jay (Ref. 10) 'bias against understanding', illustrates the same phenomenon. It is the importance of control in broadcasting rather than something inherent in the medium which produces this bias. By control I do not mean censorship or day to day interference in journalistic affairs. Both Hardiman Scott and Hargreaves rightly emphasise the independence of the broadcast journalist in Britain. Nor do I mean the specific processes of editorial control used by the two broadcasting organisations, though they illustrate how the overall system works out particular cases. My concern is with the general political and economic conditions under which broadcasting operates. This gives rise to general styles of coverage, and one of these is the style of factual news. The factual style can largely be equated with event-oriented reporting. The heavier the weight of general control becomes over any area of politically sensitive news, the closer is the equation between fact and event.

The process can be illustrated by reference to the reporting of Northern Ireland. The main broadcast style has become a record of the 'who, what, where, when' of events. There have been occasional changes in the way even those bare details have been recorded in further attempts to avoid sensitive issues. Thus for example the religious identification of victims, itself an oversimplification if not a distortion of the issues involved, has been dropped from most reports. Without it however the implications of any new incident are even less clear. In a comparative study of the reporting of Northern Ireland in the press and broadcast media in London, Dublin and Belfast, Elliott (Ref. 11) found that the most controlled medium Radio Telefís Eireann (RTE) also produced the most bald reports. It was the most controlled in the sense that the continual friction between politicians and broadcasting over the reporting of the North, characteristic of relationships in both Britain and the Republic, had been translated there into action under Section 31 of RTE's Charter. Some types of broadcasting had been prohibited and to enforce the ban members of the authority had been sacked.

Other findings from the same study underline the general importance of control in setting the style of broadcast news. Of all the media studied, British radio and television bulletins carried the highest proportion of violence and law enforcement stories. There was a clear difference between all the media produced in London and those produced in Dublin on this dimension. The Dublin morning papers carried a higher proportion of political and other types of story which were not about law enforcement and violence, than did their British counterparts. This general difference is to be explained by the different definition of the problem of the North which is to be found in the political culture of the two countries. These definitions may be crudely summarised as violence in Britain and politics in the Republic. There are special factors relevant to both radio and television which go someway towards accounting for their interest in violence. These include both immediacy and visual impact. A more general explanation however is to be found in the concern to report those events which appear to be facts within the dominant definition of the problem. There is a certain irony in the way this lays broadcasting open to the charge from politicians among others that it encourages violence by giving it attention (Ref. 12). Broadcasting attended to violence because it was following the political definition of what was important and within that, picking those items which lent themselves to factual reporting, pre-eminently violent incidents.

Extrapolating, it can be argued that this 'bias against understanding' produced by control will be greatest on those topics which are most sensitive and difficult to handle. These are precisely the issues which are of most interest to the present generation, and will be to historians and political scientists representing future generations.

Another consequence of the general structure of control within which broadcasting operates is that it operates within, one is tempted to say under the cover of, the general media culture. Broadcasting is particularly subject to the law of occluded communication. It is a medium in which it is very difficult to say anything which has not already achieved widespread public currency. In *The making of a television series*, Elliott (Ref. 13) identified three contact mechanisms through which material became available for inclusion in the series. All three provided different routes into the general media culture through other contemporary productions in the whole range of media, through pressure groups and other organisations with a public relations function and through the personal contacts of the production staff built up from working in the industry on other productions. The result tends to be a reworking of a somewhat haphazard sample of the current conventional wisdom.

Baldly stated, this underestimates the novelty which producers strive to introduce into their programmes but even the novelty takes predictable forms. One is that it is much more in evidence at the beginning of the production process than at the end. Another is that it is a novelty of form rather than content. A premium is placed on finding novel illustrations of familiar themes. Screening hitherto unused archive film for example is a type of novelty particularly appreciated in another vehicle of the media culture, the producer's colleague group. A third aspect of novelty is the translation of subjects believed by such groups to be 'boring' or 'bad television' into interesting, televisual treatments. Politics for example tends to be translated into politicians, an aspect of the subject which can be dealt with almost completely in personal terms, as in the case of *Yesterday's Men* (Ref. 14).

Television's dependence on the general media culture introduces another type of bias into its output. This has been spotted by Robert Hargreaves above in his references to specific cases like the Asian family from Malawi, the abuse of the social security system and the Jeremy Thorpe affair. Discussing the latter he moves towards a generalisation suggesting there is a Gresham's law of news by which the bad will drive out the good. Hargreaves' implication is that bad news is salacious news which comes to the fore ultimately because the public have a taste for it. His discussion of these issues however also includes several references to the competition, to the fact that broadcast journalists could not ignore stories which had already achieved widespread currency for fear of appearing ill-informed. At this point the argument that public taste is responsible for the selection of topics begins to break down.

The mechanisms through which that taste is realised, are pre-eminently the selection decisions of the national press and the press is a predominantly conservative institution, conservative with a small 'c', and for most newspapers with a large 'C' as well. Too much cannot be made of the independence of the press itself in defining the cultural agenda. It, too, works within a general culture which includes a limited range of meanings and assumptions, stereotypes and predictable positions which effectively limit what it is possible and practical to say on any topic. A useful example of the general bias of the culture was the reaction to the recent May Day bank holiday, newly introduced in 1978. Instead of celebrating or commercialising the new holiday, general media reaction was to condemn it as a foreign, political innovation, out of place compared to Britain's usual regal and religious ceremonial. The three cases Hargreaves cites also illustrate the way in which the limits on action through the media culture are broadly political, exploitable for the right and not the left and exploited in that way by the press and those whom the press reports.

Hargreaves' discussion of the way he and his colleagues decided to handle the issue of social security abuse is particularly illuminating on the strengths and weaknesses of broadcast journalism. The story was presented as a balanced account for and against the incidence of abuse. The balance was introduced over a series of bulletins. Ignoring the question of whether such balance can be effective in balancing the story for a viewer, when he may miss installments and when he is exposed to treatment of the same subject by other, unbalanced, media, the important point is that the balanced presentation accepts the general definition of which aspect of social security is 'legitimate news'. Abuse is news. Hardship on benefit, difficulties claiming benefit, cases not covered by benefit are not news or at least much less important news. (During the period when this was the main topic on the national media agenda a few stories of the latter type did appear in papers like *The Observer* and *The Guardian*). The reason why abuse was news is recognised by Hargreaves in his account of the planning of the way to deal with the story. It was a convenient political campaign for those 'who are against all forms of Social Security payment and whose real target is the basic concept of the Welfare State' (Ref. 15). For broadcasting or any other form of journalism to move in following such a campaign and attempt simply and impartially to investigate the facts of the matter is to miss the point that however it does it, it has accepted someone else's definition of the way the subject should be approached. Broadcast news can only avoid intentional bias by allowing others in other parts of the media system to express their intentions. Then it can follow along and work impartially within the framework they have set up. An alternative strategy would be to report not the facts within the campaign but the fact of the campaign, to abandon the pose that intentionality has been eradicated, that it is possible to reach the truth by dealing simply with facts about the world and instead to report clearly why a topic is news in terms of where the story comes from and who has an interest in seeing it widely disseminated.

This paper has concentrated on the value of television to history and politics echoing both the balance of the papers which precede it in this book and the balance of attention in media research which has mainly focussed on factual television, news, documentaries and current affairs. I have tried to sketch some of the factors which give this type of broadcasting limited value for an understanding of the political history of our time. Nevertheless it should be clear from what I have said that broadcasting has its own value as a subject rather than a tool of history. The complex processes of mediation involved in broadcasting production which make the account it renders of the world inadequate in absolute terms, are themselves an important subject of study alongside the output they produce. This is the point which Edward Buscombe takes up in his discussion of the relationship between Hollywood films and American society (Ref. 16). In this case we are concerned with more than factual production but with the whole range of output which goes to make up what Walter Lippman called the 'pseudo environment' of the modern world. The processes of mediation involved in creating this environment direct our attention to a much wider conception of politics than competition for an exercise of political office. If politics is the exercise of power over the distribution of scarce resources, then in looking at the media we have both a forum in which power is exercised over the distribution of ideas and images through scarce technology and the evidence of the output on the results of that distribution. The illusion that film and television mirror society is particularly dangerous if our purpose is simply to ransack them for images. The challenge however is to develop a new science of the optics involved, a science which has both historical and political dimensions.

REFERENCES

1. E.H. Carr (1964) *What is History*, Penguin Books, Harmondworth, 16.

2. There is a growing sociological literature on the production of television news. See, for example: J.D. Halloran, P. Elliott and G. Murdoch (1970) *Demonstrations and Communication*, Penguin Books, Harmondsworth; E.J. Epstein (1973) *News from Nowhere: television and the news*, Random House, New York; P. Schlesinger (1978) *Putting 'reality' together: BBC News*, Constable, London; P. Golding and P. Elliott (forthcoming) *Making the News*, Longman.

3. Reuven Frank, An anatomy of television news, *Television Quarterly 9*, no 1, 11-23 (1970).

4. *Ibid.*, 14.

5. The theory is one of those discussed in Fred S. Siebert, T. Peterson and W. Schramm (1956) *Four Theories of the Press*, University of Illinois Press, London.

6. For a recent discussion of the techniques of political broadcasting in Britain see J. Blumler, M. Gurevitch and J. Ives (1978) *The Challenge of Election Broadcasting*, Leeds University Press, Leeds.

7. Desmond Taylor (13 November 1975) *Editorial Responsibilities*, BBC Lunchtime Lecture, 4.

8. Richard Francis (22 February 1977) *Broadcasting to a community in conflict - the experience in Northern Ireland*, Lecture to the Royal Institute for International Affairs.

9. See this volume, page 6.

10. J. Birt and P. Jay, *The Times*, 28 February, 30 September, 1 October (1975).

11. Philip Elliott, Reporting Northern Ireland: a Study of News in Great Britain, Northern Ireland and the Republic of Ireland, in *Race, Ethnicity and the Media*, UNESCO, Paris, 263-376 (1977).

12. As for example, the Secretary of State for Northern Ireland, Roy Mason's attack at 'the second battle of Culloden' in November 1976. The lecture by R. Francis *Loc. cit.* was a response to Mason's attack *inter alia*. See the discussion in P. Schlesinger *op. cit.*, Chapter 8.

13. Philip Elliott (1972) *The Making of a Television Series*, Constable, London.

14. One of the cases discussed in Michael Tracey (1978) *The Production of Political Television*, Routledge and Kegan Paul, London.

15. See this volume, page 14.

16. See this volume, pages 25-29.

America on Screen? Hollywood Feature Films as Social and Political Evidence

Edward Buscombe

In *Footlight Parade*, produced by Warner Brothers in 1933, there is a concluding musical number, entitled 'Shanghai Lil', in the middle of which the chorus girls hold up a huge picture of Franklin D. Roosevelt. In *Twilight's Last Gleaming*, directed by Robert Aldrich in 1977, a crazed American general tries to blackmail the President into broadcasting 'the truth' about the war in Vietnam. What, if anything, can these films tell us about American history and politics? Quite a lot, possibly; certainly there is no question that increasingly feature films, particularly American ones, are being used as sources of evidence in history and politics courses.

But evidence of what, exactly? There is no novelty in using feature films to illustrate certain features of the society which produced them. Just over thirty years ago Siegfried Kracauer wrote *From Caligari to Hitler*, a scholarly study which set out to show that the German films of the 1920s revealed a mentality in the German people which predisposed them towards Hitler. Films, according to Kracauer, 'reflect not so much explicit credos as psychological dispositions - those deep layers of collective mentality which extend more or less below the dimension of consciousness'. (Ref. 1)

Since Kracauer made the practice academically respectable it has become almost commonplace to 'read' films in terms of the special insights they can give into what a country feels or thinks. Thus Arthur Schlesinger Jr. wrote that film in the 1930s had 'a vital connection with American emotions - more, I think, than it ever had before...The movies were near the operative center of the nation's consciousness'. (Ref. 2) Whether films are held to reveal the conscious or, as Kracauer prefers to think, the unconscious mind of the nation, it is probably fair to say that the most important claim made for the use of feature films in the teaching of politics or history is that they can capture the feel or the mood of the times in a way that few other kinds of documents can. Films present not just facts, though they may provide us with information; nor do they simply present ideas. Rather, they can show us how the facts were experienced, and what people felt about ideas.

Of course, literature and other art forms can do the same. But film, especially American film, has one big advantage as a source of evidence about how people felt. The cinema has always been a popular art; in 1945, for example, weekly attendances in America reached 90 million, in a population of around 140 million. Thus films, it is assumed, tell us not just what was being felt, but what nearly everybody felt.

Edward Buscombe is Editor of Publications, Educational Advisory Service, British Film Institute

People went to see films in such numbers because they gave them what they wanted to see. Movies, so the argument goes, are the collective mind of the populace, particularly as caught in its off-duty moments. Movies embody the hopes, dreams and fears of the people. If you want to know what Americans really felt about things, especially in the second quarter of the century, then the movies will tell you.

Such a view has much to recommend it. After all, movies do have something in common with dreams. They happen in the dark, to each of us privately; anything can occur and for their duration our conscious everyday self is suspended. But in fact the analogy does not end there. For just as, according to Freud, dreams are not the direct expression of our unconscious desires, but a distorted representation of them after the work of repression has been performed, so with movies, whatever in them does correspond to the audience's own thoughts and feelings has been worked upon by other factors. To look at movies as the unmediated, pure expression of popular consciousness can lead to misleading, even dangerous assumptions.

To begin with, the movies were not actually made by the American people, but by a tiny proportion of them, of dubious representativeness. For instance, towards the end of the 1930s, when Hollywood was at its peak, around 30,000 people were employed in production in the Los Angeles area. Of these, however, perhaps only a tenth were in a position to influence the content of the films they worked on. One estimate reckoned that at this time there were 159 producers, 1753 actors (not counting extras), 232 directors and between 600 and 700 writers (let us say 650). According to Rosten (Ref. 3) this makes for a total of 2794 people expressing the consciousness of a population calculated as 131,409,000 in 1940.

Such figures surely urge caution in any statements as to what the movies tell us about America. But, it may be argued, these people did not produce just what suited them. Production was regulated by the box office, which operated as a powerful mechanism of feedback, encouraging Hollywood to make only what the audience wanted. The fact that a small number of people had charge of production does not in itself prove that the content is not representative of the majority. Certainly, it would be foolish to deny that there is some truth in this. Hollywood was not in business to give people what it thought they ought to have. It made money by, if not exactly giving people what they wanted, at least making them like what they got. But while the effects of the box office on production cannot be denied, those effects always operated in association with other factors.

Even on its own, the box office cannot be a perfect indicator of what the audience likes. Firstly, because it cannot tell you whether the audience might like not only what it is getting but also other things which it is not getting. Secondly, people pay for a film before they have seen it. Box office receipts therefore strictly only record how many people have seen a film, not how many people liked it, or thought it expressed what they felt. But in any case to assume that box office figures can in any simple way dictate what is produced is seriously to misunderstand the nature of the production system. People cannot make films strictly to order like fish fingers. Of course there are similarities; but the production of successful films must involve some kind of commitment beyond merely clocking on and off. While one should never underestimate the extent to which Hollywood film production was based on formula patterns, or forget that any kind of film-making requires a certain amount of industrialisation in the form of technology and organisation, nevertheless every film in order to have a value in the market place has to be different. Something new has to be created; one cannot simply produce another order of the same. And the invention of something new does seem to require the investment on the part of the makers of something more than mere mechanical skills. In order that this 'something extra' is given, it seems necessary to ensure that film makers can, at least to some extent, make what pleases them rather than follow slavishly what the public wants. In one sense the history of production in Hollywood is a struggle between those who hold the purse strings and do, precisely, demand that the public be given what it wants (or what they say it wants), and those who sell their labour and in exchange demand (besides considerable financial rewards) the freedom to 'express' themselves.

So, in treating American movies as evidence concerning the nature of American society, one cannot ignore the element of personal expression in them. Of course, in film studios the emphasis has, at least until very recently, been all the other way. The rise of the auteur theory led towards a view of Hollywood films which treated them as the products exclusively of creative individuals, seen as existing largely outside history, expressing a vision which owed little to social formations, to geographical or political boundaries. Possibly the attack on the auteur theory has reached a point where it is in danger of obscuring the part that the individual does play in the production of commercial cinema, for certainly the personal cannot be ignored. Accidents of individual biography and psychology undoubtedly contribute to the totality of any Hollywood film.

At the same time, though, one has to recognise that the individuals who are doing the creating have themselves been formed in a social process. To take one example, Frank Capra (a director perhaps more used than any other in American Studies courses) did not invent himself. The ideas and feelings to be found in films such as *Mr Deeds Goes to Town* or *Mr Smith Goes to Washington* can be found in other films and indeed in books of the time. They can thus be said in some sense to reflect what concerned people in the 1930s. True, these ideas and feelings do occur in a specific form in Capra's films, differently from elsewhere, and we may say that this is because Capra's individual personality formed his films. But, this personality did not spring up out of nowhere. Capra was born in Sicily; his father was a peasant farmer; he remained a Catholic all his life; he trained as an engineer. Such biographical details, among others, made him what he was. And so, in reading one of Capra's films in terms of its relation to the American society of its time, one has to recognise both that Capra put something of himself into it, and also that this self was also a product of the society he commented on. What we may say, therefore, is that American films are neither simply the unmediated expression of a collective consciousness, nor individual acts of self-expression, but the products of some possibly rather complicated relationships between the two.

Thus the fact that Hollywood films are made by small numbers of people, and are in some sense personal expressions may be no bar to seeing them as evidence of what the nation as a whole felt. But at this point one has to ask, which nation? To speak at all of *a* national consciousness assumes that the nation is a unity, that there are certain ideas and feelings which are common to all Americans. But it scarcely needs a moment's thought to recognise that at no time in its history has America been united. Divisions between North and South, East and West, between black and white, rich and poor, between city and country, Protestant and Catholic and many others must surely make any notion of one national consciousness highly suspect. About the safest thing one could say about Hollywood in relation to these divisions is that it has usually existed within them rather than above them. For example, Hollywood has traditionally spoken for whites rather than blacks; indeed the existence of a separate black cinema, with its own production and exhibition centres, confirms this, though all too little is known as yet of its history. As regards some of the other divisions, the picture is perhaps a little more complicated, for although Hollywood can be seen as tending towards the northern and protestant tradition, one could also point to the considerable number of Westerns and costume dramas glorifying the South, and the marked influence of Jews and Catholics.

The most important division in American society, however, is that between the classes, and this presents perhaps the most difficult problem. If the movies do not in fact speak for everybody, as I have suggested they do not, then are they the voice of the working class or of the middle class? There seems to be a tendency to assume that since they are 'mass' entertainment they must make their appeal primarily to 'ordinary' people, to the majority. This is indeed their value to historians in the first place, that the movies are representative of the 'people'. Now there is no doubt that large numbers of the working class did indeed go to the movies in their heyday. But the available evidence strongly suggests that large numbers of the middle class went too. What is hard to ascertain is whether they went to the same films, whether Hollywood was catering for a unified audience or a divided one. What we know about the audiences does not at present allow us to make any confident assertions.

However, if we turn from exhibition to production things become a little clearer. For example, Leo Rosten (Ref. 4) showed that at the end of the 1930s those involved in making films in Hollywood were overwhelmingly middle class. The number of actors, directors, film editors or cameramen whose fathers were semi-skilled or unskilled labourers was statistically insignificant, and only 7% had fathers who were skilled labourers. On the other hand, two-thirds of writers had been to college, and nearly half of actors, producers and directors. The 'masses' may have consumed the movies, but it certainly does not appear that they produced them. Nor could they be said to be in control of those institutions which regulated production and consumption; it seems a fair assumption, for example, that the critics who reviewed movies in the press were equally as middle class as those who made them. One institution in particular which had a significant influence on production from the early 1920s to the 1950s was the Hays Office and its notorious Production Code. Set up in order to head off mounting criticism of Hollywood from various pressure groups, the Code took its moral and social attitudes from the middle class WASP section of American society, the section which, however much it may have failed to transform the actual behaviour of the rest of the country was certainly successful during this period in controlling its visible manifestations. The fact that in the 1930s and 1940s nobody committed adultery in the movies with impunity can in no sense be taken to indicate a universal intolerance of adultery. What it does indicate is that one section of society had the power to impose itself on others, through its control of the key institutions: the churches, the legal system, the police force, and the press.

Production and censorship, then, were largely in the hands of the middle class. But though this inevitably had its effect on the ideological content of films, from a more narrowly political point of view Hollywood has been, on the whole, neutral (and therefore not representative, given that most Americans side with one party or another). It is true that on occasion it has lurched to the right, most notoriously during the campaign mounted by the studio heads in 1934 against Upton Sinclair's candidacy for the California Governorship, and in the blacklisting of Communists and 'fellowtravellers' in 1947. It is also true that from time to time some of the studio heads have openly thrown in their lot with one or other of the two major political parties. Louis B. Mayer, head of production for MGM from 1924 to 1951, was a friend of Herbert Hoover and a declared Republican. Jack Warner of Warner Bros. became very enthusiastic about Franklin D. Roosevelt (hence FDR's picture in *Footlight Parade*), though a bit less so about the Democratic Party. Dore Schary, variously head of production at RKO and MGM, was a well-known Democrat. And of course the party allegiances of actors such as John Wayne and Henry Fonda are well enough known. But far from such loyalties having a marked effect on the content of films, what is surely most obvious about politics in American movies is, firstly, how middle-of-the-road they are, and secondly how little there is of them. Perhaps what is most notable about the famous Hollywood Ten, at a distance of 30 years, is the very small amount of anything that could be called left-wing propaganda in their collected screen credits. Conversely, a film such as *I Married a Communist*, produced during the cold war period and deliberately intended to counter 'subversion', has in fact virtually nothing to say about politics. Communism is seen as a variety of gangsterism.

This is not to say that Hollywood tells us nothing about American politics. Indeed, this comparative absence of interest in political ideology has been seen from a European perspective as a fact not only about the movies but about American political life itself. But the equally notable absence of movies concerned, not so much with political ideas but with the political process, does not indicate a general lack of interest by Americans in political life. It stems, rather, from the fact that in the end one single factor controlled Hollywood production policy (even if, as I have argued, that control was not always direct); the box office. It has sometimes been supposed that because Hollywood was owned by big business (virtually all the big studios were in the hands of major financial interests) that it must support, in its production policies, the party of big business, namely the Republicans. But to do so would be to cut itself off from at least half the audience. For the same reason Hollywood was reluctant to involve itself in controversial subjects such as industrial relations or race. That most Hollywood pictures are about fairly safe subjects, then, does not mean that Americans preferred not to think about such problems, only that Hollywood did not think them commercial.

It is only very recently that Hollywood has started making movies for sections of the public rather than trying to find subjects that would appeal to virtually everybody. The notion of a single national consciousness, which historians, rather unhistorically, seem tempted to find in Hollywood movies, and which the film makers themselves seem to have believed in, has at last been abandoned. To say that Hollywood films have always embodied much that is personal and partial, however, is not to say that they are untypical of America; only that the influence of class and box office should be taken into account when assessing the extent to which they represent the country as a whole.

REFERENCES

1. S. Kracauer (1947) *From Caligari to Hitler*, Princeton University Press, 6.

2. A. Schlesinger Jr., When the movies really counted, *Show*, 77, (April 1963).

3. L. Rosten (1970) *Hollywood, the movie colony, the movie makers*, reprinted Arno Press, 387.

4. Rosten *Ibid.*, 390-393.

From October to 'October': the Soviet Political System in the 1920s and Its Films

Richard Taylor

'Things are going badly in the cinema': Stalin (Ref. 1).

Every society acquires, perhaps requires, its own political mythology. Eisenstein's *October* provides us with a useful illustration of the pitfalls involved in the treatment of film as documentary evidence, whether that film is a fictional feature, a quasi-documentary, or even a documentary film. Readers who are assiduous viewers of television programmes on the October Revolution or early Soviet life will be aware of these difficulties. In their desperate search for visual materials to illustrate these programmes producers are apt to use as documentary material feature films which attempt to re-create history. *October* is one of these films, and the scenes in it of Lenin's arrival at the Finland Station and of the storming of the Winter Palace are those most frequently abused in this manner. The difficulty for the programme maker, and indeed for the historian, is that no film exists, or ever existed, of the key events of the October Revolution. If we have no 'real' record of the Revolution, then it is left to people like Eisenstein to create an imaginative, perhaps largely fictionalised, and certainly propagandist version of reality for us. And so myth becomes reality. The storming of the Winter Palace in *October* has become documentary footage in many people's minds, just as the Odessa Steps sequence in *Battleship Potemkin* has become reality: in the one case the film maker has exaggerated, in the other he has invented. The poetic licence of the director carries his audience away on a wave of emotion, which reason can no longer resist, and a new reality is created. This factor is of fundamental importance when we attempt to understand the Soviet cinema of the 1920s, and the very need of the Bolsheviks to create for themselves a new past, a new historical legitimacy, led them to utilise the cinema as a propaganda weapon. If reality was not there it had to be invented: the myth had to be created. As Lenin (Ref. 2) said, 'Of all the arts for us the cinema is the most important'.

To understand fully the films made in the Soviet Union in the 1920s, it is also necessary for us to comprehend their political and historical context, and this of course includes that of the cinema industry itself. By the time of the Revolution the cinema was by far the most popular form of entertainment for the urban masses of the population, but it was still regarded by many people as little better than a fairground attraction and its political potential therefore remained unrealised. In

---

Dr Richard Taylor is Lecturer in the Department of Political Theory and Government, University College of Swansea.

1913 Nicholas II had written: 'I consider that the cinema is an empty, totally useless, and even harmful form of entertainment. Only an abnormal person could place this farcical business on a par with art. It is complete rubbish and no importance whatsoever should be attached to such stupidities' (Ref. 3). But under the pressures of war the old order came increasingly into question. New methods of retaining the loyalty of the population had to be explored and various suggestions were made for harnessing the cinema to the needs of the regime. Following a proposal in 1915 that cinemas should be run like a vast military operation (Ref. 4), the Ministry of the Interior established a commission of enquiry. A contemporary newspaper commented: '...the cinema, if it were ever established on a broader basis, could be used by the government to instil healthy political and social opinions among the populace. It could lessen the sharpened conflict between different classes and bring patriotic and monarchist ideas to the people. Government cinemas should be aimed largely at the lower classes of the nation' (Ref. 5). But, although the cinema's potential was now being realised in theory, it was not to be realised in practice until well after the Revolution.

It would be difficult to exaggerate the significance of agitation and propaganda in the history of the Russian labour movement. Even before Plekhanov's (Ref. 6) attempt to clarify a distinction between them in 1892, the role of the agitator-propagandist in circle work had been acknowledged. This was inevitable if a closely-knit, politically motivated minority group were ever to attain power. For these revolutionaries the media for such activity were the spoken word, the leaflet and the underground newspaper, in particular. By these means isolated incidents, demonstrations, strikes were to be given a broader historical meaning. By these means the working mass, or at least its political vanguard, would be made conscious, first of its existence and then of its needs, as a class. But in October 1917, when the Bolsheviks seized power in the name of that class, they initially seized only the commanding heights of the political machine, a machine which the strains of war and the uncertainties of the Provisional Government's interregnum had done much to undermine. The new rulers controlled only certain parts of the country and they did not have the support of large sections of the working mass whose interests they were supposed to represent. Propaganda therefore inevitably loomed even larger in their calculations, for through propaganda they could reindoctrinate the mass and bring the Revolution to it in a lasting sense. For this they used all the methods at the disposal of a modern state: posters, the theatre, the press, leaflets, street demonstrations, gramophone recordings, agitational lorries, trains and steamers (Ref. 7), and, of course, the cinema.

Why was the cinema so important to Bolshevik propaganda? One can detect many reasons. First, the member of the cinema audience is like a spectator in a football crowd: he is at the same time both alone and of the mass. He is therefore uniquely susceptible to mass emotional reactions. In the cinema his vulnerability is enhanced by the darkness which envelops him: he can all too easily be transported by the image flickering across the screen before him. The cinema was the first, and in many ways the only real, mass medium. Second, as already mentioned, the cinema was by 1917 the principal form of entertainment for the urban masses of the population. This meant that, in the towns at least, the audience did not have to be attracted in the first place, for it was already there. But it also meant that the cinema was held in high esteem by certain intellectuals precisely because it was a 'low' art form with which they could sweep away the remnants of previous cultures now designated both 'bourgeois' and 'decadent'. One critic wrote of the cinema: 'It is not yet the art of the present. The present is a transitional epoch in which the decrepit art of the theatre is writhing in terrible convulsions and fighting for its very existence, while the art of the cinema is growing triumphantly and becoming conscious of itself. The art of the cinema is all in the future' (Ref. 8). The cinema was also associated in the minds of such people with their new god, the machine. Not only did the machine represent progress and the new age (and here one may make comparisons with German Expressionism and Italian Futurism), but its mechanical capabilities made it a more reliable medium for propaganda than its rivals. The film could be produced and reproduced at the centre, and only at the centre, and the same film, at least in theory, shown simultaneously in all parts of the Soviet Union. The same critic remarked: 'The mechanical possibility of unending reproduction and distribution of the works of the cinema make it, as distinct from the other arts, the sole and exclusive expression of the era of the new culture' (Ref. 9).

The association in the popular mind of the cinema with the machine, and therefore with progress, combined with the essentially visual nature of the silent film to make it the ideal weapon for propaganda work in the Soviet countryside. Most peasants had never seen a moving picture before, and there is ample evidence to show that they were deeply moved by the experience (Ref. 10). Lenin himself wrote in 1922: 'Special attention should be paid to the organisation of cinemas in the villages and in the East, where they are novelties and where our propaganda will therefore be particularly successful' (Ref. 11). Equally important was the fact that, as a contemporary newspaper observed, 'The cinema is the only book that even the illiterate can read' (Ref. 12). In a country with 85% illiteracy this factor was of immense significance. So too was the fact that the cinema, by its visual nature, did not encounter the linguistic limitations of the leaflet, newspaper or the spoken word. The same film could be shown to a Russian-speaking audience in Petrograd, to a Georgian-speaking audience in Tiflis, and to an Uzbek-speaking audience in Tashkent. There were of course cultural differences which restricted the universality of a particular film's appeal or, in some cases, enhanced it: 'We recall a curious scene. In July 1923 we attended the opening of the Red Tea-House in Tashkent, on the edge of the Old City. The highlight of the evening was a film show. The room, or rather the garden, because the show took place in the open air, was packed with Uzbeks and Kirghiz and resounded with cries of delight. It was strange, in a temperature of 50°C, to see on the screen the icy winter of northern Russia, its wooden houses, etc.... The socialist newsreels of Petrograd and Moscow, which we in the capital view with boredom, were watched with a lively interest in distant Tashkent' (Ref. 13). Nonetheless, the cinema was the most suitable and universal, the only truly mass medium available to the Bolsheviks for their propaganda at that time.

There were of course many problems too. Not the least of these was the opposition of film producers, distributors and cinema owners not merely to the Bolshevik government and its ideology, but more particularly to the nationalisation of cinema enterprises, which one journal (Ref. 14) described as the 'sword of Damocles' hanging over the cinema. The major film producers moved their studios to areas still controlled by the White forces and later went into exile, taking much of their equipment and many of their staff with them (Ref. 15). Some cinema owners buried their entire stock of films in the hope that the Bolsheviks were nothing more than a passing unpleasantness from which they would soon be freed (Ref. 16). But most important was the chronic shortage of equipment and raw film stock that had a longer history. Russia had imported all her film stock and cinema equipment and so, like many other sections of Russian industry, the cinema was severely, and adversely, affected by the outbreak of the First World War. After the War, and the Revolution, the so-called bourgeois democracies were scarcely eager to supply the new régime with the essentials for its propaganda, and in any case the Soviet government was desperately short of the convertible currency with which to pay for them.

The cinema was eventually nationalised in August 1919 (Ref. 17) although the process was still not completed in the spring of 1920 (Ref. 18) and the complete reorganisation of the cinema along centralised lines was not attempted until December 1922 (Ref. 19). But neither nationalisation nor reorganisation in themselves offered a solution to the problems. Throughout the 1920s there were repeated calls for the cinema to be taken in hand. At the 13th Party Congress in May 1924, Stalin said:

'Things are going badly in the cinema. The cinema is the greatest means of mass agitation. The task is to take it into our own hands' (Ref. 20). A year earlier, in an article in *Pravda*, Trotsky had complained: 'The fact that we have so far, i.e. in nearly six years, not taken possession of the cinema shows how slow and uneducated we are, not to say, frankly, stupid. This weapon which cries out to be used, is the best instrument for propaganda, technical, educational and industrial propaganda, propaganda against alcohol, propaganda for sanitation, political propaganda, any kind of propaganda you please, a propaganda which is accessible to everyone, which is attractive, cuts into the memory and may be made a possible source of revenue' (Ref. 21). But this kind of exhortation, repeated at every Party Congress, was not enough. As one contemporary observer, writing under the pseudonym of 'Banquo's Ghost', remarked: 'Many people talk about the cinema, but few think about it' (Ref. 22). The general enthusiasm for the cinema appears to have been intermittent. The Party newspaper, *Pravda*, published no articles on the cinema at all between 1917 and 1921; then cinema information and film reviews were published under the general heading 'Theatre and Music' and the first article to appear under the 'Cinema' heading was not published until September 1923 (Ref. 23). What *Pravda* and other publications actually printed on the cinema was not necessarily what the Party wanted to see either. In June 1923 the back page of *Pravda* carried an advertisement for the American film *Sodom and Gomorrah*, announcing, 'A poem of human passions in two parts and fourteen reels...In the richness of its settings and in its techniques the picture surpasses everything hitherto seen on the screen' (Ref. 24).

In the absence of Soviet film production resulting from the shortage of materials, cinemas had to rely on films that had either been produced before the Revolution or imported then. Clearly most of these were not considered to be ideologically suitable. After 1924 the Soviet market came increasingly to be dominated by the Hollywood product: Mary Pickford, Charlie Chaplin, Buster Keaton and others were familiar figures in the pages of Soviet film journals. Despite his later protestations, Anatoly Lunacharsky, who as People's Commissar for Enlightenment had overall ministerial responsibility for the cinema, encouraged this tendency. He originated the screenplay, dedicated to Mary Pickford, of a film involving both her and Douglas Fairbanks and entitled *The Kiss of Mary Pickford*, which was released as late as September 1927 (Ref. 25). In the same year the Soviet public was still being kept informed of the intimate details of Chaplin's private life. When Chaplin's wife started divorce proceedings in the American courts, Lunacharsky penned an article for the Moscow evening newspaper under the title 'The Campaign against Charlie Chaplin' in March 1927 (Ref. 26).

Soviet film production did not get under way until 1924, and it was not until the 1927/28 season that box-office receipts from Soviet films exceeded those from imported films for the first time. We must not therefore fall into the trap of assuming that Soviet filmgoers in the 1920s existed on a diet of Eisenstein, Vertov and Pudovkin, or that they were necessarily profoundly influenced by *Battleship Potemkin*, *The Man with the Movie-Camera*, *The End of St Petersburg* or, for that matter, *October*.

In 1923 a special organisation, Proletkino, was established to encourage the growth of a cinema network in workers' clubs (Ref. 27). The workers were, after all, supposed to be in the vanguard of the Revolution. Although it is estimated that by 1925 three-quarters of the cinema installations in the Soviet Union were to be found in workers' clubs (Ref. 28), it is also known that 79% of the films shown in these clubs in that same year had been imported (Ref. 29). Bukharin lamented the lack of progress in developing a specifically proletarian cinema: 'Unfortunately very little has been done so far in this field. More words than actions. More "plans" and projects than living practice' (Ref. 30). How then was a film like *Battleship Potemkin* received? It was billed as 'the pride of the Soviet cinema' (Ref. 31) and was shown simultaneously at all Moscow's twelve first run cinemas (Ref. 32). The First Goskino cinema, where the premiere was held, was decorated so that it looked like a battleship and the staff were dressed as members of the crew (Ref. 33). Little effort was spared to popularise the film, but the authorities were obviously on the defensive; the journal *Kinogazeta* produced figures to show that, in a twelve-day period, 29,458 people had seen *Potemkin*, while only 21,281 had seen the American hit *Robin Hood*, starring Douglas Fairbanks, which had incidentally been banished to suburban cinemas for the duration (Ref. 34). These figures are open to question if only because they were produced to prove a point, namely that Soviet audiences wanted Soviet films. In addition, two weeks before the release of *Potemkin*, *Robin Hood* was showing at eleven of the twelve first-run cinemas (Ref. 35) and the advertisements proclaimed, 'All Moscow is watching *Robin Hood*' (Ref. 36). *Potemkin* was released on 18 January 1926 (Ref. 37) but taken off on 16 February (Ref. 38). Meanwhile, *The Bear's Wedding*, an adaptation by none other than Lunacharsky himself of a short story by Prosper Mérimée, had been seen by 64,000 people (Ref. 39) and was being hailed as 'the first hit of 1926' (Ref. 40). Clearly this was one Soviet film that Soviet audiences did want to see, although it was not the kind of Soviet film that the Party wanted them to see.

It was not until May that *Potemkin* became a *cause célèbre* because of its phenomenal success in Berlin and the attempts of the German authorities to ban the film (Ref. 41). *Pravda* quoted German press reviews of the film under the title 'The Victory of the "Battleship"' (Ref. 42). In June 1926 a leading film critic observed that it was easier to see *Potemkin* in Germany than in the Soviet Union: *'Battleship Potemkin* has also not been shown enough in the USSR. Until recently it had hardly been shown at all in the Ukraine, while abroad in Berlin it is showing successfully at 150 cinemas' (Ref. 43). Following the film's success in Germany it was re-released at the Second Goskino cinema on 15 June (Ref. 44) but was replaced after only a fortnight by Buster Keaton's *Our Hospitality* (Ref. 45) and, one week later, ironically enough, by yet another showing 'by public demand' of Douglas Fairbanks in *Robin Hood* (Ref. 46). Sovkino, which now controlled film distribution in the RSFSR, though not in the entire USSR, had to face the fact that, given a choice, Soviet audiences preferred foreign films. As one wag remarked: *'Potemkin* comes to the USSR as a foreign hit' (Ref. 47). The pull exerted by foreign films was reflected by contemporary advertising, even in papers such as *Pravda*: time and again a cinema would offer 'an American hit' (Ref. 48) or 'foreign attractions' (Ref. 49) and the foreignness was emphasised rather than disguised (Ref. 50). Perhaps there is some obscure significance in the fact that the cinema advertisements in *Pravda* were placed next to those for private clinics for the treatment of venereal disease.

Meanwhile important Soviet films like Dziga Vertov's *Forward, Soviet!* were held back for months from release. This particular film was reviewed in *Pravda* on 12 March 1926 but a correspondent complained on 16 May that it had still not been released. To quote again the critic previously cited: 'Our cinema screens, in summer even more than in winter, are hired out to the French bourgeoisie, to Italian beauties, to Piels, the tears of Veidt and other "trash"' (Ref. 51). If this was the situation at the centre, it may be imagined that the situation at the periphery was even worse. There were constant complaints about the kind of film made available to rural audiences and about the poor technical quality of the prints: 'Because of these worn films the countryside is turning not merely against Sovkino but also against Soviet power' (Ref. 52). Children were also not adequately catered for, although one source suggests that they comprised up to 30% of the evening cinema audiences in Leningrad (Ref. 53); in as far as films aimed specifically at children were available, they consisted of fairy tales involving kings and queens (Ref. 54). The situation was described as 'worse than desperate' (Ref. 55).

In an attempt to involve the mass of the audience more closely in the cinema the People's Commissariat for Internal Affairs established in 1925 an organisation known as ODSK (*Obshchestvo druzei sovetskogo kino*) or the Society of Friends of the Soviet Cinema (Ref. 56). Its first head was Feliks Dzerzhinsky, former head of Cheka, and its establishment was welcomed by cinema organisations such as Sovkino: 'We cannot have a situation in which the cinema organisation merely shows the film and the audience, our Soviet audience, merely watches. Intimate contact with the mass audience is necessary; they will help us to a successful fulfilment of the task we are trying to achieve, i.e. the construction of the Soviet cinema' (Ref. 57). At the same time the first efforts were being made to establish the Association of Revolutionary Cinematography (ARK), which was intended to be the cinema's equivalent of RAPP in the literary world (Ref. 58).

In these ways the Party was attempting to take control of the flesh of the Soviet cinema, rather than just its bones. But the decisive steps were not taken until after the First All-Russian Party Conference on the Cinema, held in March 1928. Here all the old grievances were aired anew. The aim of the conference was best summed up by the journal *Zhizn' iskusstva* the previous September: 'Although we all share Lenin's view that the cinema is the most important agitational and propaganda weapon for influencing the masses, we have nonetheless hitherto allowed this art form to drift on the Soviet sea "rudderless and without sails"... The forthcoming conference will work out a "single" platform for the "unification of the socialist state with the cinema on proletarian foundations"' (Ref. 59). Following the conference the same journal remarked: 'Now we are witnessing an organic transformation of our cinema, which is entering, one might say, the period of its reconstruction... Our cinema is still being constructed as a socialist art' (Ref. 60).

The immediate result of the conference was a reiteration of the usual exhortations to take the Soviet cinema in hand. But this time there were two more concrete results. In January 1929 the Central Committee of the Party issued a decree 'On the Strengthening of the Cadres of the Cinema': 'The heightening of the class struggle on the ideological front cannot fail to evoke from petit bourgeois groups the desire to influence the most important lever for the cultural improvement and education of the masses. The task of the Party is to use all measures to strengthen its leadership of the work of the cinema organisations and, by preserving the ideological consistency of the films produced, to combat decisively the attempts to bring the Soviet cinema nearer to the ideology of the non-proletarian strata... Party, trade union, social and scientific organisations should play a more active part in the work of the cinema' (Ref. 61). And in May 1929, speaking to the 14th Congress of Soviets, Lunacharsky (Ref. 62) remarked that, 'At last, great steps have been taken in the development of the cinema'. Sovkino, which had been subjected to so much criticism at the conference, was reorganised in 1930 into Soyuzkino, and the structure of the Soviet cinema which has largely survived until the present day was created.

This then was the background against which the most famous Soviet films of the 1920s were made. Writing in 1929, and conveniently summarising the gist of what I want to say, the critic Petrov-Bytov (Ref. 64) commented: 'When we talk of the Soviet cinema we wave a banner on which is written: *Strike, Battleship Potemkin, October, Mother, The End of St Petersburg*, and we have recently added *New Babylon, Zvenigora, Arsenal*. Do 120 million workers and peasants march beneath this banner? I know very well that they don't... The people who make the Soviet cinema are 95% alien, aesthetes or unprincipled... *You will not lead with 'Octobers' and 'New Babylons', simply because people do not want to watch these pictures. Before you lead the masses behind you, you must either be of the masses yourself, or have studied them thoroughly, and not just studied, but also experienced what the masses experience...* I repeat, we must speak in their own comprehensible, native language. Our heart and mind must be in it. We must not look down on the masses from above, but the artist himself must think and feel fundamentally and positively at one with the masses and be in the vanguard... *Every picture must be useful, comprehensible and familiar to the masses, otherwise neither it nor the artist who made it are worth twopence...* With the help of art which is not separated from the masses we shall fight all the base aspects of life, so that not only art but life itself shall become beautiful'. What better prologue to the artistic ideals of the Stalin era could one find?

The evidence that I have already cited confirms Petrov-Bytov's assertion that the films that we associate with the Soviet Union of the 1920s were not the films that the population either wanted to see, or did in fact see in large numbers. If we want to know what films the Soviet citizen enjoyed watching, if we wish to analyse his tastes and habits, then we must turn our eyes westwards to Hollywood. But, if we want to know what the Soviet government and Party wanted him to see, and what they wanted him to think, then we can look at Soviet films of the 1920s, for that is the value of the propaganda film for the historian.

We have returned to the central problem of the myth versus the reality. Clearly the reality was that Soviet audiences wanted films from the West but, equally clearly, a study of these films will tell us little about the Soviet political system in the 1920s. On the other hand Soviet films should tell us something about that system. If they attracted large audiences, they would tell us perhaps, though not necessarily, something of the way that people thought. But, regardless of the size of the audience, a film that obviously has the *imprimatur* of the Party will tell us very clearly what the Party wanted people to think. (I am of course talking here of 'revolutionary' films, and not of the kind of films previously mentioned, with which Lunacharsky had for instance been associated.)

Any propaganda machine must have three principal aims: it must convince its audience of the historical legitimacy of the system that it propagates; it must persuade people to tolerate present difficulties; it must mobilise them into active participation in projects to ensure a better future or, as a contemporary critic put it: 'In as far as the new way of life is still an abstract concept, we must show it in the process of creation. We must show the sprouting shoots of the new way of life, the new relationships between people. We must romanticise the struggle between the birth of the new and the death of the old' (Ref. 65). The regime acquired its historical legitimacy through the history of the workers' movement and the Revolution itself. This was reflected in a whole series of films: *Battleship Potemkin* and *October* obviously, but also *Strike*, Pudovkin's *Mother* and *The End of St Petersburg*, Dovzhenko's *Earth* and Room's *Bay of Death*, Protazanov's *White Eagle* and *The Forty-First*, Kozintsev and Trauberg's *SVD*, based on the Decembrist Uprising of 1825, and *New Babylon*, which dealt with the Paris Commune of 1871. These films all depicted various aspects of the workers' struggle to emancipate themselves from the yoke of capitalist exploitation. They produced stereotyped images of heroes and villains, workers and capitalists, peasants and landowners, the oppressed and the oppressors.

These stereotypes of the revolutionary struggle are also to be seen in films set outside the Soviet Union. Protazanov's *Aelita*, made in 1924, depicts a revolution on Mars in a society clearly divided along class lines. But there is a particularly good example of stereotypes in Room's *The Ghost That Never Returns* (Ref. 66). The film is set in Latin America and the opening sequence depicts a prison. We see first the mechanical perfection with which capitalism has refined its oppression of the workers, then we see the prisoners' revolt and the panic measures of the authorities to restore order. There is a clear-cut, if indirect, confrontation between the hero-revolutionary, José Real, who is bearded and strong, and the prison governor, ape-like, casting a shadow like the vampire in *Nosferatu*, and therefore really less than human. The hosing-down of the prisoners, which the governor orders to reassert his authority, acts as a purifying force on them and is directly followed by their liberation. The issue is stated, both literally and metaphorically, in black and white.

There is a similar series of stereotyped contrasts in Eisenstein's *Strike*: the workers are clean-limbed and strong, the managers are moustachioed and fat, their lackies thin and slimy. The workers live in a domestic idyll, the managers are alone, drinking furtively. This particular conflict, in *Strike*, ends with the symbolic slaughter of a calf, a sequence so horrifyingly effective that it was echoed in the anti-Semitic Nazi film *The Eternal Jew*. But then the Jew was to the Nazis what the capitalist was to the Bolsheviks, a subhuman exploiter of everything that was upright and noble, a necessary enemy and scapegoat.

The second and third groups of films that I have delineated, those dealing with the present and those dealing with the future, to some extent overlap, as the promise of a better future did much to make the unpleasant present more tolerable: films like Eisenstein's *The Old and the New* (originally *The General Line*, but the general line had changed), Dovzhenko's *Earth*, Ermler's *Fragment of Empire*, Yutkevich's *Lace*, Room's *Bed and Sofa* and of course the 'documentary' celebrations of Soviet power like Shub's *The Great Way*, Turin's *Turksib* and many of the productions of Dziga Vertov: his Cine-Eye newsreels, *The Man with the Movie-Camera*, *A Sixth Part of the World* and *Forward, Soviet!* But we must beware especially of documentaries. In 1925 the film *Images of Red Russia* was shown in Berlin for propaganda purposes, but it was accepted as depicting the long-awaited truth about Russia: 'On the first day that the film was shown, the theatre manager gave an introductory talk in which he observed, amongst other things, that "We have heard many things about the USSR which we were unable to confirm, but now the moving picture, which cannot lie, has the stage"' (Ref. 67). We of course know better: the camera can lie, and frequently does, especially in the hands of someone who believes in the importance of editing, as Vertov did. There was in fact an inherent and central contradiction in the film-making theories of Vertov (Ref. 68). On the one hand he claimed: 'We shoot only facts and bring them through the screen to the consciousness of the workers. We consider that to explain the world as it is is our principal task'. This was enshrined in the concept of 'zhizn' vrasplokh' or 'life as it is', but life as it is depends very much on how you choose to interpret it. Elsewhere, Vertov (Ref. 69) wrote: 'To see and show the world in the name of the world proletarian revolution - that is the simple formula of the Cine-Eye'. The journal *Novyi zritel'* said of Vertov's *The Man with the Movie-Camera* that it 'contrasts "life as it is" from the viewpoint of the eye armed with the camera *(the Cine-Eye)* with "life as it is" from the viewpoint of the imperfect *human eye*' (Ref. 70). In other words Vertov's documentary film, like Eisenstein's fiction film, aimed to improve upon reality (Ref. 71):

> 'I am the Cine-Eye, I create a man more perfect than Adam was created, I create thousands of different men according to different preliminary drafts and schemes.
> I am the Cine-Eye.
> I take the strongest and most agile hands from one man, the fastest and best proportioned legs from another, the most handsome and expressive head from a third and through montage I create a new, perfect man...
> I am the Cine-Eye. I am the mechanical eye.
> I, the machine, show you the world as only I can see it.'

The closing sequence of *The Man with the Movie-Camera*, even when shown at the correct silent film speed, is a dazzling example of Vertov's creation of a new reality through montage. In this instance we should give Vertov credit for nowhere trying to deceive us into thinking that he is showing us reality pure and simple, for the film abounds with reminders of the presence of the camera, and the very structure of the film is itself a reminder that this is 'life as it really is' through the Cine-Eye. The same cannot be said however either of Vertov's other films, or of other Soviet documentaries of the period.

Finally let us return to the beginning and *October*. The film opens with the toppling of the statue of the tsar, but it topples only hesitantly. This is a warning of things to come. It is toppled by the workers and peasants: it is their Revolution. The Provisional Government is immediately associated with those twin pillars of reaction, the Church and the bourgeoisie, so that we are left in no doubt as to the principal source of danger. The proletariat expect peace and lay down their arms and fraternise: the bourgeoisie continue the war. Soon the workers are queuing for bread, their rations steadily reduced, and Lenin arrives at the Finland Station to liberate them. In the tsar's apartments Kerensky struts about and is compared to a peacock and to Napoleon, traitor to an earlier revolution. The factory hooter sounds a warning: 'The Revolution is in danger!' The tsar's statue is restored by trick photography: the Revolution is betrayed and the October Revolution, epitomised for Eisenstein by the storming of the Winter Palace, is therefore justified.

October is then an exercise in historical legitimisation. Despite the film-makers' protestations that it was 'an experiment comprehensible to the millions' (Ref. 72), the film was criticised for being 'not easily accessible' (Ref. 73). Notwithstanding these strictures, regardless of the audiences it attracted, the film does show us what the Soviet authorities wanted their people to think of the events of 1917. *October* thus shows us not the documentary reality, but the propaganda myth, not 'life as it is' but 'life as it ought to be', and that surely is the genesis of socialist realism. In other words, in the cinema, as in so many other spheres of Soviet life, we can see in the relative freedom of the 1920s the seeds of what was to happen in the following decade.

REFERENCES

1. I.V. Stalin in (1924) *Trinadtsatyi s"ezd RKP(b). 23-31 maya 1924 goda. Stenograficheskii otchët*, 132, Moscow.

2. G. Boltyanskii (1925) *Lenin i kino*, 16-17, Moscow/Leningrad. (From a conversation between Lenin and Lunacharskii in 1922, recalled by the latter in 1925 in a letter to Boltyanskii.)

3. A note scribbled in the margin of a police report by Nicholas II in 1913; I.S. Zil'bershtein, Nikolai II o kino, *Sovetskii ekran 10*, (8 April 1927).

4. V.M. Dement'ev (1915) *Kinematograf kak pravitel'stvennaya regaliya*, Petrograd.

5. *Russkoe slovo* (5 October 1916).

6. G.V. Plekhanov (1892) *O zadachakh sotsialistov v bor'be s golodom v Rossii. (Pis'ma k molodym tovarishcham)*, 58, Geneva.

7. R. Taylor, A Medium for the Masses: Agitation in the Soviet Civil War, *Soviet Studies* 562-574 (1971)

8. G. Boltyanskii, Iskusstvo budushchego, *Kino 1-2*, 7 (1922).

9. G. Boltyanskii (1927) *Kul'tura kinooperatora*, 7, Moscow/Leningrad.

10. A. Katsigras, Kak organizovat' kinoperedvizhku v derevne, in *idem*. (ed.)(1925) *Kino-rabota v derevne*, Moscow. (See page 83 for instance).

11. V.I. Lenin (1922, 5th edition 1964) *Polnoe sobranie sochinenii 44*, 361, Moscow.

12. *Pskovskii nabat*, 3 July 1924; quoted in A. Goldobin (1924) *Kino na territorii SSSR. (Po materialam provintsial'noi pressy)*, 64, Moscow.

13. V. Vainshtok and D. Yakobzon (1926) *Kino i molodëzh'*, 62, Leningrad.

14. *Mir ekrana*, 1 (26 April 1918).

15. V. Listov, U istokov sovetskogo kino, *Iskusstvo kino*, 13 (March 1969).

16. L. Forest'e (1945) *'Velikii nemoi.' Vospominaniya kinooperatora*, 98, Moscow: and N.F. Preobrazhenskii, Vospominaniya o rabote VFKO, *Iz istorii kino 1*, 88 (1958).

17. *Izvestiya VTsIK*, (2 September 1919).

18. A.M. Gak (ed.) (1973) *Samoe vazhnoe iz vsekh iskusstv. Lenin o kino*, 52, Moscow.

19. V. Vishnevskii, Fakty i daty iz istorii otechestvennoi kinematografii (1921 - 1924), *Iz istorii kino 3*, 137 (1960).

20. I.V. Stalin, *loc. cit.*

21. L. Trotskii, Vodka, tserkov' i kinematograf, *Pravda* (12 July 1923).

22. 'Dukh Banko', 'Velikii' glukhonemoi, *Zhizn' iskusstva*, 21, (18 December 1923).

23. N. Lebedev, O Proletkino, *Pravda*, (8 May 1923); and *idem.*, Boevye dvadtsatye gody, *Iskusstvo kino*, 90, (December 1968).

24. *Pravda*, (19 June 1923).

25. *Sovetskie khudozhestvennye fil'my. Annotirovannyi katalog. Tom 1: Nemye fil'my (1918-1935)*, 219, Moscow (1961).

26. A.V. Lunacharskii, Pokhod protiv Charli Chaplin, *Vechernyaya Moskva*, (7 March 1927).

27. S. Syrtsov and A. Kurs (eds.) (1926) *Sovetskoe kino na pod"ëme*, 71-76, and R. Marchand and P. Weinstein (1927) *L'Art dans la Russie nouvelle: Le cinéma*, 71-74, Paris.

28. B. Filippov (1926) *Kino v rabochem klube*, 6, Moscow.

29. E.G. Lemberg (1930) *Kinopromyshlennost' SSSR: Ekonomika sovetskoi kinematografii*, 93, Moscow.

30. *Proletarskoe kino*, 1, (1 February 1925)

31. *Pravda*, (4 February 1926).

32. *Pravda*, (17 January 1926).

33. N.I. Kleiman and K.B. Levina (eds.) (1969) *Bronenosets Potemkin*, 210, Moscow.

34. *Kinogazeta*, (16 February 1926).

35. *Pravda*, (8 January 1926).

36. *Pravda*, (3 January 1926).

37. *Pravda*, (19 January 1926).

38. *Pravda*, (16 February 1926).

39. *Ibid*.

40. *Pravda*, (2 February 1926).

41. Kleiman and Levina, *op. cit.*, 223-248.

42. *Pravda*, (12 May 1926). (On 9 May *Pravda* reported that a special showing of the film had been arranged in Berlin for Douglas Fairbanks and Mary Pickford. Fairbanks had declared that *Potemkin* was 'the most powerful film he had ever seen', while his wife expressed herself 'profoundly moved by what she had seen'.)

43. Kh. Khersonskii, Kinointerventsiya, *Pravda*, (2 June 1926).

44. *Pravda*, (15 June 1926).

45. *Pravda*, (29 June 1926).

46. *Pravda*, (6 July 1926).

47. *Sovetskii ekran*, 5, (27 July 1926).

48. e.g. *Pravda*, (9 March 1926).

49. *Ibid*.

50. e.g. *Pravda*, (22 May 1926).

51. Khersonskii, *loc. cit.*

52. B.S. Ol'khovyi (ed.) (1929) *Puti kino. Pervoe Vsesoyuznoe partiinoe soveshchanie po kinematografii*, 74, Moscow.

53. Vainshtok and Yakobzon, *op. cit.*, 44.

54. N. Sats, Deti i kinematograf, *Novyi zritel'*, 8, (4 November 1924).

55. N. Sats, Deti zhdut svoyu fil'mu, *Zhizn' iskusstva*, 3, (9 March 1926).

56. L.M. Sukharebskii (1926) *Nauchnoe kino*, 45, Moscow.

57. I. Trainin (1925) *Kino-promyshlennost' i Sovkino*, 31, Moscow.

58. Yu. S. Kalashnikov *et al.* (eds.) (1956) *Ocherki istorii sovetskogo kino. Tom 1: 1917-1934*, 228, Moscow.

59. K predstoyashchemu kino-soveshchaniyu, *Zhizn' iskusstva*, 1 (27 September 1927).

60. A. Piotrovskii, Kino 1928 goda, *Zhizn' iskusstva*, 9 (4 November 1928).

61. Ob ukreplenii kadrov kino; reproduced in N.A. Lebedev (ed.) (1939) *Partiya o kino*, 82, Moscow.

62. *XIV Vserossiskii s"ezd sovetov. Stenograficheskii otchët*, (1929), part *12*, 11, Moscow.

63. V. Vishnevskii and P.V. Fionov (eds.) (1973) *Sovetskoe kino v datakh i faktakh, Spravochnik*, 58, Moscow.

64. P. Petrov-Bytov, U nas net sovetskoi kinematografii, *Zhizn' iskusstva*, 8 (21 April 1929).

65. V. Nedobrovo, Romantika byta v kino, *Zhizn' iskusstva*, 5 (14 December 1926).

66. Both the entire film and the relevant study extract are available for hire on 16 mm from the British Film Institute.

67. Kino-propaganda, *Zhizn' iskusstva*, 1 (3 November 1925).

68. D. Vertov, Otvet na pyat' voprosov, *Kino-gazeta*, (21 October 1924).

69. D. Vertov, Kino-glaz, *Pravda*, (19 July 1924).

70. Fil'me grozit opasnost'. Beseda s Dzigoi Vertovym, *Novyi zritel'*, 13, (27 January 1929).

71. D. Vertov, Kinoki. Perevorot, *Lef 3*, 140-141 (1923).

72. Cf. S. Eizenshtein, G. Aleksandrov, Eksperiment, ponyatnyi millionam, *Sovetskii ekran 6-7*, (5 February 1929).

73. T. Rokotov, Pochemu malodostupen *Oktyabr'?*, *Zhizn'iskusstva*, 17 (10 April 1928).

SECTION II
Relationships Between the Academic User and Producer

Section I examined the background to film and television production in terms of its influence on the media available for public or academic use. A related but distinct set of constraints applies to the academic who becomes directly involved in the production stage itself. In this situation an additional set of problems will arise both for the individual academic concerned, and for other users who have the task of assessing the relationship between the academic, the producer and the finished product. Although this applies to only a small proportion of total media output it may be relevant to a significant part of the material of interest to some academic users.

Two fundamentally separate contexts require our attention. The first, exemplified in Nicholas Pronay's discussion, concerns the classic but complex relationship between the academic (dedicated to content, as assessed by criteria such as truth, completeness, balance, depth and clarity) and the producer (committed to 'good film' or 'good television', as assessed by criteria such as impact, pace, audience enjoyment or filmic elegance and creativity). These two sets of criteria are rarely compatible, so that any production is likely to represent a compromise. The discerning user thus has the task of evaluating to what extent the academic priorities have been compromised in the process - an extension of the general critical basis of media use introduced in Section I.

Stig Hornshøj-Møller examines the very different situation in which the academic (or team of academics) acts as producer also. At first sight this might appear to remove any possible conflict, but his paper demonstrates that the underlying balance between academic and production priorities must still be resolved. The degree of purity of the end-product is seen to depend on the extent of technical facilities and time available: any limit on these immediately increases the demand for production decisions on coverage and pace, which in turn may impinge upon sequence, balance and depth. In practice, the circle appears unbreakable, so that we return to the great importance of the user being given, or evaluating for himself, a clear picture of the production priorities and conventions that have been used.

Television Based History Teaching in the Context of the Traditional University

Nicholas Pronay

The hopes and expectations surrounding the introduction of Television Services into British universities have remained largely unfulfilled. Although a decade has passed since the first six 'High Activity' University Television Services were established, at Leeds and elsewhere, there are still virtually no examples of television being used as the *central* element of any major British university degree course in the Arts and Social Sciences, very few in the Sciences and regular use can only be found in certain specialised areas of medical teaching. Although a number of enthusiastic individuals have over the years made film and television programmes with the facilities, technical and personnel, of the Audio-Visual Services, the great majority of these productions were 'extras' designed merely to add to or to enrich existing courses. Television has failed either to make a significant contribution to relieving increasingly heavy teaching burdens as far as university departments were concerned or to the development 'towards independence in learning' as far as the students were concerned. The only area within the Arts and Social Sciences where it is possible today to find any courses at all which can be said to 'depend' on television are those actually concerned with television as a medium, either as part of some English/Drama degree schemes or in courses specifically concerned with the impact of television/film in a political, historical or sociological context. Reviewing the position of usefulness reached by the University Television Services a decade after the Brynmor Jones Report which led to the massive investment involved in establishing them, C.F. Page and John Kitching in a publication for the Society for Research into Higher Education reported: 'The general picture of scale and use has not changed; it remains patchy and low' (Ref. 1).

Failure to utilise the considerable investment of public money represented by the facilities provided by the forty-odd Television/Audio-Visual Services of one kind or another which exist now in the field of higher education, should not be put down to the innate conservatism of the British academic - as is commonly done by the staffs of the Television Services. Extensive research carried out into the use of television by American universities shows not only the same situation as here but worse. Many American institutions whose administrations made substantial efforts to 'push' the utilisation of their expensive investment in audio-visual technology by effectively forcing departments to try developing courses based on television teaching, a power fortunately not possessed by anyone within British university structures, have since reduced or even abandoned their commitment even to the maintenance of Tele-

---

Nicholas Pronay is Senior Lecturer in the School of History, University of Leeds and Chairman of the InterUniversity History Film Consortium.

vision/Audio-Visual Services. In practice such a process of withdrawal has also begun to happen in Britain. In the course of the enforced financial stringency of the mid-1970s, universities with the longest established Television Services, such as Leeds, have decided upon the evidence of internal enquiries, that so far from television having proved itself popular with members of the teaching staff and a medium capable of quantitatively assisting in the teaching process, the opposite was the case. It was proved to have been (apart from Medicine) an expensive and peripheral extra. Accordingly, the original development plans for the building up of Television Services were drastically cut back and opportunities offered by staff movements were avidly taken up in order to actually reduce the existing establishments.

The crux of the internal enquiries into the contribution of the Television Services was the inability either to find courses where television has already played an essential role in the teaching of a subject, or the inability to find departments which, even after years of co-existence with the facilities and personnel of these services on their doorstep, were prepared to express faith in the future utility of television for their own area, in terms which went beyond the occasional, specialized or personal use. In brief, very few university departments, practically none outside the medical schools, have found sufficient reasons after many years of being offered the use of the medium, to assign any priority to the maintenance or development of Audio-Visual Services on account of their ability to contribute effectively to the solution of their teaching problems, even in a period of constricted resources. The internal University enquiries bore out only too well the belief of J. Cowan, in surveying the position of Television Services from the inside, in 1974: 'It is time for educational technologists to realise that they are making a minimal impact in higher education. Despite vast expensure of UGC funds on Audio-Visual units backed by the forceful promotion of workshops for lecturers...' (Ref. 2).

The purpose of this article is to argue that in order to make use of television as a central element of a major undergraduate course leading to real and substantial savings in staff time, without the dilution of academic control over the material which reaches the students through the screens and without loss of academic standards, all that is primarily required is a re-appraisal of the relative roles of academics and television producers within the process of production. Secondly, to argue that the invention of video cassette systems to be used by students themselves in place of 'piped' or broadcast television programmes, has made it much easier to evolve a new relationship between academics and the television screen, as well as emancipated television as a medium from those disadvantages which made academics justly doubtful about its comparability with books or lectures as a suitable medium for high level study. In the third part of this article we will describe the application of these ideas in practice which led to the introduction, as a compulsory element of the syllabus, of a course in the School of History, Leeds University, where television provides the whole of the formal tuition of the students. The course has since proved to be able to effect a very substantial saving of staff time, as well as being entirely accepted by the students and has provided excellent standards of performance.

The view that a re-appraisal of the relationship between academics and television producers is an essential prerequisite to the utilisation of the potential of Television Services can hardly be described either as startlingly original or unique to the position in Britain. Drawing together the threads of many specialist investigations into a decade of the use of television in American universities, Evans and Leppmann reported in 1968 that 'a large majority of staff were hostile to television either because it seemed to represent a threat to their existence or because they thought it a plaything irrelevant to a serious academic education'. They also found that 'most staff thought that while television might be useful for some other subject, it was useless in their own'. They were also: 'Impressed with the apparent consistency of attitudes towards television, regardless of an institution's size, its urban or rural location, its sponsorship or even its past experience or inexperience with television as an instructional device' (Ref. 3). Relating to the position in Britain in 1975-6, Dr J.R. Moss of Leeds University Television Service and Dr David Clark of the University of London Audio-Visual Centre, while they were diametrically opposed about the solution of the problem, agreed that: 'The main difficulty in educational television (is) the critical relationship between the academic (or teacher or lecturer) and the producer' (Ref. 4). Looking at the position from within the academic circle the impression is the same. Distrust of the 'media men's' willingness to produce just what the academic wants, the prospect of 'endless and futile arguments', of 'unconscionable expenditure' of the academic's time and of the tedium of being 'guided' in how one should profess one's own subject, are the common coin of currency in virtually all conversations about 'media services' within the four walls of academic common rooms. Few comments have found greater general approval amongst academic readers in the compendium *The Historian and Film* than the brusque advice of Professor D.C. Watt that the historian should either keep clear of television productions or if financial rewards make that stance too puritanical, he should see to it that his name does not appear in the credits (Ref. 5). These may indeed be subjective impressions derived only from within some English university departments in the Humanities. The description by an outsider however, Mr Peter Coltman, a producer at the large Audio-Visual Service at Glasgow University, bears out strikingly these impressions from the context of not only a Scottish university but also of a Science Department. The passage deserves quotation in full: 'The current dissatisfaction of educational technologists working in university services is matched only by the suspicion in which they are often held by members of academic staff. The academics feel that they are competent to teach their specialised subject without the advice of 'communications specialists', 'media men' or whatever the current jargon dubs them - a multiplicity and confusion of terminology reveals how poorly their role is understood. Some teachers are repelled by the aura of show business which they feel attaches to the mass media and they suspect that educational values may be subordinated to technical gimmickry. The technologists on the other hand are critical of the archaic teaching methods which seem to them to cope inadequately with the growing student population and they feel frustrated that the possibilities offered by educational technology of streamlining these methods are poorly exploited. The basis of the problem is that academics and technologists have no common ground' (Ref. 6).

The first step therefore for an academic department wishing to make full use of the facilities provided by the Television Service of their own university is to understand the ideas motivating the people in charge of it. Without a full understanding of these ideas right from the outset, effective and practical co-operation, without which these facilities cannot be utilised, is bound to break down. The difference between our concept of our role in relation to teaching and their view of it is too great to expect it to evaporate in practice. As far as academics are concerned the point comes down to the view held by the majority of Audio-Visual Services today, that television producers are not merely technicians whose job it is to 'realise' the expository intentions of the academic as precisely and as effectively as the technology permits it, but that they are to be accepted as the ultimate experts on how best to teach students. Mr C.F. Page of Bradford University, a prolific author on the subject of educational technology in higher education, has asserted: 'The (audio-visual) expert who knows merely about machinery cannot give the kind of advice and help that teachers need. The audio-visual expert must also be an educational expert to be of real use' (Ref. 7). What this principle means in relationship to the academic's use of television has been expressed with admirable lucidity in a strongly-argued article by Dr Moss of Leeds University Television Service. He scornfully rejected the idea that the producer in a university television production should act merely as a 'sort of amanuensis to the blind sage', helping the academic to 'express his own views in an unfamiliar medium' (Ref. 8). He noted that 'the teaching tradition in Britain is thoroughly private, personal, individual' but he regarded the view that therefore 'the role of educational technology is merely to act as handmaid to academic individuality' as a 'council of despair' (Ref. 9). As for the whole question of whether the academic or producer should be in ultimate control of what appears on the screen and is to be studied by the academic's own students, he wrote that much educational television or film 'has been distorted by the prejudice of the academic or teacher that he or she must retain ultimate authority over content *and* structure' (Ref. 10). Expressions of similar views could be quoted from the majority of producers or educational technologists working in our universities today, but it should be recorded that there is a growing minority who are abandoning these views, such as Dr David Clark working at the University of London.

What these views can mean in practice - and therefore why they are of more than 'theological' importance for academics wishing to use Television Services - may be illustrated by Mr Coltman's description of the making of a film designed to introduce biology students to the organisms of Loch Lomond. The academic having approached the Television Service with a demand that he needed an audio-visual production for his own students, the procedure is thus described by Mr Coltman: 'The producer (Peter Coltman) was totally ignorant of the subject matter of the film. It was suggested that (the lecturer) should write notes on what he expected to be said and seen on the film with no guidance being given on how to organise the material. The document which emerged was useful because it presented all the information which might have been included in the film, but it was not a suitable basis for a shooting script for two reasons. First it contained a great deal of information which could not be visualised in any way: second the pattern of the summary was a logical verbal pattern. There was no visual thread to the script....Most teaching is verbal and the compactness of a logical ratiocinative train of thought which one may expect to reduce to concise note form cannot be reproduced on the screen' (Ref. 11). So much for universities being principally about the training of young minds in 'logical ratiocinative' thinking and the verbal expression of it.

The producer having decided that what was needed instead was a film depicting a 'walk around the lake', the academic was instructed to produce another 'treatment' from which the *producer* was to write a shooting script which listed the shots *he* expected to take, in the final order in which they would be seen, and the actual shooting then started. The academic's role in a film for his own students was to be strictly limited during the actual production of the visual elements: 'During the shooting the lecturer must take a secondary role; he still maintains his strong advisory capacity, but once the pattern of the film has been well-established - and the detailed planning which this requires cannot be too much emphasised - he is under the direction of his colleague. There may be a temptation for academics to aim at a degree of intellectual honesty which can greatly complicate the filming process and make co-operation with the producer difficult but not important to the teaching process' (Ref. 12). So much for that, 'intellectual honesty' and all.

The editing of the film - i.e. the crucial process of 'writing with images' - was to be done by the producer with the deliberate exclusion of the lecturer: 'It is only when the film has reached the stage of fine-cut that the lecturer will be asked to view it for his comments and criticisms'. The reason given is that the inexperienced academic may be appalled at what appears on the cutting bench (Ref. 13).

May it be, then, that the academic would be able to *say* at least verbally if not any longer in pictures, what *he* wanted to say about *his* own subject to *his* own students? Not a bit of it: 'Writing for film is an art, for it requires words and pictures to follow each other exactly: For this reason although the content will be at the discretion of the lecturer the wording is a task which must be undertaken in conjunction with the producer.' (Ref. 14).

Since the producer ('totally ignorant of the subject') has already cut the film without the presence of the academic, thus determining not only the visual language and content of the film but also the amount of time, the number of words, the lecturer could actually say about each topic which he had hoped to cover in his film, the result in terms of precision, qualifications and 'intellectual honesty' is already a foregone conclusion, a lost cause.

Little wonder then that American researchers have found a most uncharacteristic reluctance on the part of academics to let their peers or senior colleagues 'read' their publications in the medium of film or television (Ref. 15) - or at Professor Watt's advice that one should not even admit to having been in any way responsible for them.

Clearly, to contemplate the making of television programmes or films on the basis of a relationship with the production process even remotely like this and of co-operation with 'educational experts'/producers imbued with such views, is simply out of the question for any scholar wishing to profess his subject in an audio-visual medium. Especially is this so when a department is contemplating the making of television programmes or film designed to form the basis of a student's tuition and not merely a pleasant but strictly peripheral introduction to the real expositions to follow - in ratiocinative verbal patterns - remembering the awesome responsibility that a student's examinations and therefore his results and his subsequent career may depend on it.   Yet it is to be realised that the rationale of the views which we saw expressed in general terms above by our educational television producers, leads inexorably to a conduct which may be less brutally expressed in practice in milder climates than Glasgow, would nevertheless result in an insoluble confrontation, between the responsibility of the academic towards his subject and students and the ideals of those whose co-operation is essential for the production of television or film. No wonder that Dr David Clark should have written, after rehearsing the origins of views held by producers about their role *vis à vis* the academics: 'This leaves the perplexing problem of how it is that academic television gets made at all. There is a body of opinion which suggests that from a utilitarian point of view none does get made.' (Ref. 16).

The starting point of any project by a department envisaging *substantive* teaching by the medium of television must be a full and clear understanding of the views which are likely to be held honestly, almost religiously, by their would-be television collaborators. To paraphrase the slogan of a campaign launched by the Ministry of Information in 1940: 'Know Your Enemy', it is essential to 'Know your TV Allies'. Since these views usually strike academics as such utter nonsense that they are unwilling to accept that anyone can possibly mean them in practice, particularly such earnest and nice people, it might even be useful to read some of the many printed expressions of their views to be found in audio-visual literature, a small proportion of which have been quoted before - and above all to realise that not only are these views held with deep conviction but that their rejection by the academic body is viewed with incomprehension by most Television Service staff.

The next stage is to organise the project from the outset so that there can be no doubts left in the minds of the Television Service that the Department intends precisely that the academic should 'retain ultimate authority over content and structure' and, to paraphrase Dr Moss, intends so 'to distort educational film or television' that it becomes History or Politics, or Sociology expressed through the medium of a screen and ceases to be 'film' or 'television' *per se*. In practice this means to involve actively the Television Service only after the academics concerned with the development of the television-based course have thoroughly thrashed out within the four walls of their own Department what they want to do and what they want their students to see and hear through the television screens which means having written the 'script' of the videotapes. Of course it is advisable to notify the Television Service that such and such a number of television programmes of such and such a length and format - i.e. video cassettes, - will be required and agree on the setting aside of suitable blocks of time well in advance, preferably at least a year ahead. Offers by the Television Service, likely to be made at their first hearing of the project, for the setting up of 'a course team' for 'planning the curriculum', 'deciding which media to use' and above all for the 'definition of educational objectives' by the Department to be submitted to the 'educational technologists' for 'advice' upon the best ways of achieving them, should be politely but uncompromisingly refused. Nothing comes from entering into such arrangements except endless meetings characterised by fruitless discussions between people operating from entirely different premises, held by each to be axiomatic, reminiscent of the disputations for composing their differences organised by the Emperor Charles V, between Lutheran and Catholic Divines. Time for *fruitful* discussions, and indeed the more the better, will come later when the production process has actually started on the basis of the scripts written already and when the questions will be on the nature of the lighting, framing, animating, camera movements etc. best suited to the realisation, as faithfully and precisely as possible, of the academic's script. It is then that the fund of specialised knowledge and genuine enthusiasm which does exist within most Television Services, can be tapped for the benefit of all concerned, especially for the academic purpose and the interests of the students.

But can an 'academic' write a 'script'? Not merely 'an outline treatment of his ideas' to be transmogrified into the end-product by the producer as in the example quoted before - but produce a script of both what the student should see, in the order and form desired, and what he should hear juxtaposed to the visuals, particularly if the academic has never done that sort of thing before? Is there no reality in the arguments put forward by the audio-visual fraternity as well as by the exponents of the 'art of film-making' and other forms of audio-visual montage, concerning the particular spatial and time relationships of audio-visual perception? It is indeed a very large and specialised subject. But for *our* purposes - as academics primarily concerned with the provision of specific information and precisely formulated interpretations and ideas, to a specific and pre-prepared audience receiving the audio-visual expression within the usual context of reading lists, lectures and other forms of teaching - these problems are of much less significance. Nevertheless, to communicate through an audio-visual medium which has to convey the intentions of its maker through the specialised experience involved in viewing a film in a darkened auditorium or a normal television screen, does call for a certain degree of specialised knowledge as well as aptitudes not commonly or necessarily possessed by a scholar. As academics, we have been trained to communicate primarily through the medium of writing and the essence of academic writing is that the reader, student or fellow scholar, should be able, and can be expected, to *study* the text provided by us. It does not have to yield its information and ideas through a single hearing. Many academics have therefore not only been justifiably doubtful of their ability to communicate through an audio-visual medium which flits through a screen, small or large, but have also doubted whether a medium which can only be viewed and not studied, unlike books, can ever be legitimately employed in the scholarly training process of university education. To use such media for creating interest, kindling enthusiasm and involvement has long been accepted but to rely on them as much as one would rely on books, that is a very different matter. Some of the same doubts incidentally have always been attached to lectures as a medium of scholarly education, which has led in more recent years, as scholarship became more exact and exacting, for lectures to be relegated to being 'optional' in many universities, such as Leeds; a view reinforced by the belief that no student should be penalised for the absence of any materials in his examination scripts which were only presented to him in the form of lectures.

It is in this central and crucial respect that the recent introduction of 'self-access' video equipment has made a fundamental difference of far-reaching significance. Self-access television simply means that a television programme is not offered to the student merely as a single experience which he is obliged to view from begining to end, but is given to him in the form of an actual video tape encapsulated in a cassette or cartridge, which he can replay for himself through a machine, controlled by himself. He can therefore stop the tape at any particular point, repeat any part of it as often as he feels he needs it for full understanding or for the purpose of taking notes. In short, he can use it for the purposes of *studying* with the same facilities he has for studying books. Since it is not difficult to impose on the video tape numbers and since he can stop the tape at any particular point, accompanying sheets of paper can also provide as full footnotes and references as may be desired. But the most essential element of the video cassette system is that it changes the relationship between the material on the tape and the student. Instead of having to rely on the specialised and in fact ill-understood 'black art' of montage in order that the message may appear within the mind of the viewer, through the complicated effect mechanism of sound and visual impulses and with the time and spatial relationships of a single experience, the student can now *study* the material much like working with a book, in his own time and at his own pace. Montage, time and spatial effects do not operate where the tape is constantly stopped, replayed, 'frozen' or held.

The invention of the 'self-access video cassette system' has therefore removed from the academic use of television, the two main intellectual and interrelated-technological, difficulties. The academic need no longer think of the formidable problems of having to translate into an uncertain and unfamiliar medium, the exact and rational thought processes of his vocation. At the same time he need not be concerned over the appropriateness of the impact of the emotionally and psychologically complex, and essentially unscholarly 'viewing situation' upon the prime aim of university teaching, which is precisely the training of minds in exact, analytical and rational modes of thought. He can therefore use the 'self-access video cassette system' as a direct and straight-forward extension of his teaching, an immediately comparable alternative to both lectures and written expositions. If he chooses a subject which is not liable to constant revision in the light of current research - as for example we have chosen to deal with the basic source material for History in our course - he will find that the extra work involved in putting his exposition of the subject on video cassettes a genuinely labour-saving device in subsequent years when the cassette can go on delivering it as long as it is required. Because he can now rely on the student being able to study the material with the same facility with which he can study books, footnotes and all, he can legitimately and fairly make a course based on video cassettes a central part of the curriculum. Above all, because the academic need no longer be baffled and worried by either the large volume of gobble-degook or the small kernel of reality in the arguments about the special nature and requirements of audio-visual perception, he can set out with confidence to write his script, both visual and aural, of what *he* wishes *his* students to study through a video cassette machine, relying on his own well-tested techniques as a lecturer and academic author. He need not brook any nonsense about this or that not being 'effective television' because the end product is not going to be 'viewed' as television anyway. The only thing he needs to make sure is that students are told right at the beginning that they are not expected to sit through the tape like Coronation Street on the television set - or for that matter as they have to sit through an Open University programme - but on the contrary they are expected to stop and start and take notes, just as if they were reading a book.

Finally, in subjects such as History or Politics or Sociology, which are essentially verbal and which lead to students being examined through the written/verbal exposition of their knowledge and understanding, the academic teacher need not cast around frantically in order to find some 'relevant' visual material to put on the screen. He need only put a pictorial representation on the screen where that is directly relevant to the point he is making. If he wishes to quote from a book or wishes to talk about statistics, in a video cassette relationship such things are perfectly suitable fill the screen. Where the point he wishes to make is a purely verbal one, where a visual would in fact be distracting from the train of thought, there is no reason why in such a system there should be anything else on the screen except the academic himself, as he would be in a lecture or tutorial. On the other hand where visual materials in the nature of moving images whether they are quotations from the film evidence of the past, or specially-made material about living conditions or topographical information, the video cassette provides all the opportunities of an ordinary television set with the enormous further advantage that the student and academic can make a detailed examination, if necessary shot by shot, of such material as an integral part of the students 'reading'.

In 1974 the School of History at Leeds University decided to embark on an experiment in the use of self-access television technology. After a good deal of discussion and drawing upon the collective experience of several members of the School in the use of audio-visual media, we proposed to develop a course with the following objectives:

1. Formal tuition should be conducted entirely through the medium of specially produced video cartridges, together with accompanying folders of written materials, in place of both lectures and tutorials.

2. The course should require no day to day disciplinary supervision by members of the School, once in operation.

3. The course should be so devised that day to day educational supervision, including the marking of the weekly written work required of students, may be carried out by a single postgraduate tutor within the permitted weekly work load of postgraduate tutors, i.e. four 'tutorial hours', amounting to twelve hours per week.

4. The course should allow students to reach academic standards of written work broadly comparable to their other courses, to be assessed by a terminal essay chosen from a list of titles, each marked by the member of staff in whose area the particular subject lay, irrespective of whether or not he has been involved in the production of the video cartridges.

5. The course should enable students to monitor their own progress and adjust the tuition-time provided by the video cartridges to their own individual needs.

6. The production process of the video cartridges should be so organised as to place no excessive burden on the teaching staff of the School, to keep to the minimum the amount of time necessarily spent working with the Television Service; the work to be accomplishable in one academic year without relief from normal teaching duties.

7. The course should be produced as a pilot project in the first instance: all members of the School should be invited to satisfy themselves of the workings and standards of the course by personal observation, discussion with their tutees and by access to the evidence gathered by an extensive monitoring of students' progress and views.

8. After members of the School have satisfied themselves on these points the course should become compulsory for all History Single Honours students. It would in fact be the only compulsory course taken by all students within a syllabus structure based on a free choice and would thus provide the one common foundation element; it would provide the whole of a term's work in their first year.

9. The course should provide an introduction to the uses of historical evidence. It would cover the principal sources from which historians work from the ancient period to the twentieth century. Such a subject would ensure that the course in its final form would remain usable for a number of years.

Clearly, although the word experimental can be legitimately applied to our course, it was an experiment only in the large-scale adaptation of ideas and experience which we have already gained in the course of much earlier exploratory experimentation with the use of audio-visual media and of the forms of co-operation with Television Services. In our case, the School of History had, collectively speaking, several years of such experimentation to draw upon by 1974. In 1966 the School had founded the InterUniversity History Film Consortium which by this time had provided eight years of experience in how historians can use the medium of moving images for teaching undergraduates, what it can and cannot do, and above all by what means the historian can communicate his particular art through a medium which instead of a solitary pen requires the commanding of the skills of a team of technicians. Since 1971, the School has also been offering a course, *Communications and Politics in the 20th Century*, in which video cassettes, to be studied by students individually in the library like books, formed an integral part of the compulsory 'reading matter' of the course. We have therefore also had experience already of how students react to using self-access video cassettes, of their ability and willingness to handle the associated machinery themselves. We were therefore able to approach the ambitious undertaking involved in this course with a good deal of experience and above all with confidence in our ability to obtain, within a reasonable time and without the expenditure of too much time or mental wear and tear, what *we* would regard as suitable for *our* students working through the medium of television.

Having decided on these objectives we formed a committee of the School under the Chairman of the School for establishing *modus operandi*. After a good deal of discussion we agreed on the following four principles:

1. No single historian could possibly have command of all the sources and techniques of the subjects and periods covered by the course and any kind of authoritarian central planning approach would be inappropriate. Instead we should choose the most experienced and senior members of the School, irrespective of whether or not they had any television experience, as solely responsible for the video cassette dealing with their own particular period/subject and leave it to that person to design how best it should be taught.

2. We would appoint a single person with such experience to be responsible for the sorting out of all the day to day problems of timetabling, of dealing with the Television Service and the library etc. rather than have a permanent committee in action, or burden individual authors with more than the basic minimum of contact necessary for the realisation of their scripts through the production process of the cartridges. The person in charge we called the Co-ordinator and he took over the chairmanship of the committee.

3. We would in all cases of doubt act on the principle that we regard the use of video cartridges - to be studied by students individually - as a self-teaching form and extension of our normal history teaching rather than as an exercise 'in television'. The criteria to be applied to any 'problems' would be analogous to those applicable to an extensively illustrated lecture by historians rather than those applicable to a television programme.

4. We aim at evolving a course which would emphasise the individuality and creative nature of the work of the historian: as being the result of the personal interaction of individual historians with the vast range of evidence left behind by the past. Just as we would not impose any common pattern of approach on the subjects covered by our authors, so we would not permit the imposition of a common pattern of television presentation or format, regarding the role of the medium as a communicator of the individuality of the historian and his work.

It took only a remarkably short (and sweet) discussion to decide on the titles and subjects of the eight video cartridges which were to form the core of the course. General ideas by any member of the group as to what might be covered partly or wholly by a unit prepared by another colleague were freely expressed and the checking of scripts to avoid accidents of duplication of material was delegated to the 'co-ordinator' of the course, but each author remained entirely sovereign in the treatment of his own particular area.

The eight units of the course with their authors are as follows:

UNIT NO.	UNIT TITLE	UNIT AUTHOR
1	The Records of Ancient History	H.B. Mattingly, Professor of Ancient History
2	Medieval History: Administrative Records	Dr W. Childs, Lecturer in Medieval History
3	Early Modern History: Central Records	Dr C.E. Challis, Senior Lecturer in Modern History
4	The Records of Local History	G.C.F. Forster, Senior Lecturer in Modern History
5	Nineteenth Century Political Records	Dr E.D. Steele, Lecturer in Modern History
6	Nineteenth Century Diplomatic Records	Dr F.R. Bridge, Reader in International History
7a	The Records of Twentieth Century International History	D.N. Dilks, Professor of International History
7b	The Records of Contemporary History	K.G.M. Ross, Lecturer in International History
8	The Records of Public Opinion	N. Pronay, Senior Lecturer in Modern History

Owing to a sabbatical year involving the Co-ordinator, a year elapsed between the decision to go ahead with the planning and production of this course and the commencement of the actual work. This allowed us to provide the Television Service with ample warning to prepare sufficient time and production facilities for the period April 1975-April 1976 which was the year set aside for the production of the course. The Nuffield Foundation, under their newly-announced Small Grants Scheme, gave us the initial impetus and additional financial resources. The money so provided was principally used towards the salary of a Teaching Fellow. The task of the Teaching Fellow, in the event, was to take no part in the production of the tapes themselves but to assist in the preparation, in co-operation with the Library, of the 'paper packages' or 'folders' accompanying each video cassette; the organisation of the necessary timetabling of sixty-two students so that each should have a fixed weekly period in which he could study the particular week's video cassette; to assist in the devising and then the marking of the weekly written work of the students so that they should in fact be suitable for a postgraduate tutor such as the Teaching Fellow himself; finally it was his task to take a major part in the laborious and extensive testing and reporting process upon the working of the course for the first time.

The detailed working out of these ideas and of the general approach adopted by us, in terms of the educational achievements of this course, lies beyond the scope of this article. Briefly we have to report, however, that the course has succeeded in achieving all its objectives: it has proved possible to produce all the video cartridges within the time allocated without unreasonable strain on the nine members of staff involved. The great majority of students took to the course happily, most of them with extra enthusiasm. Remarkably, there have not been any disciplinary problems. In fact the rate of attendance has been markedly better than in other courses - not a single student actually missed a single video cartridge session in two years, although many students made their own arrangements for 'swapping' periods when unable to attend for reasons of illness or other causes. The weekly written work proved to be within the capacity of postgraduate tutors to handle, although it has become clear that the man selected for the task needs to be a person of potential university teacher calibre, with experience already in tutoring. The standards of the terminal essays in both years have proved higher than expected: they not only met our initial requirement for 'being broadly comparable' with standards reached by the same student in other 'orthodox' courses, they were in the majority as high and in a significant proportion of cases, higher in standard. Clearly, the self-teach principle can produce as high standards of both motivation and achievement as personal tuition can. The experiment has manifestly succeeded for, insofar as the severest critics of any course are the colleagues not involved in it, the fact that by resolution of the School this course has now been made compulsory for all single-subject honours students, proves that point beyond reasonable doubt. This does not mean of course that the experiment is at an end: an elaborate evaluation procedure - including a large-scale and confidential programme of student interviews - will continue for a third year; two additional units representing slightly different approaches are currently planned; the logistic problems of extending the course to other students, taking International History and Politics, are being explored. We are only partly satisfied with the weekly written work requirement where the balance between offering the students a means for testing their own progress and comprehension on the one hand, and on the other hand providing a vehicle giving sufficient scope to those who are particularly interested in any one of the units, requires further adjustment. In terms, however, of 'the practical testing of a hypothesis', the course is no longer an 'experiment'.

It is also beyond the scope of this article to discuss in detail the working out of our ideas and general approach in respect of collaborating with our Television Service in the production of our course. It will not have escaped the notice of the reader that the author of some of the most uncompromising statements quoted earlier about the role of the producer as being anything but a mere 'amanuensis to the blind sage' or of being an audio-visual technician at the command of the academic, were expressed by our own Director of Television, who also took personal charge of their side of the production process. He had put to us politely but with clarity and vigour all his views about the need to form 'a course team' with him and so forth, which we politely but with equal conviction rejected. The Television Service had to work both from a course-concept and from scripts in the preparation of which they had no hand, and they had in the last resort to 'realise' just what was in the script whether they regarded it as unvisual or not, although suggestions were gratefully received and sometimes incorporated. There was one exception to this rule which we made precisely in order to test our own views. In the case of the Ancient History Unit, Dr Moss was given an entirely free hand to deal with the author of that cartridge, the Professor of Ancient History, H.B. Mattingly, from the scripting stage onwards. There was another reason for this: Dr Moss is a man of wide accomplishments which include a Ph.D. and publications together with tutoring experience in Ancient History, as well as being Director of the Television Service. It is perhaps not without significance (as well as an element of humour) having to record, as the opinion freely expressed by students as well as my own, that if there is one single cartridge which can be said to reflect the personality and highly individual approach of a single historian more than others, it is the Ancient History cartridge.

As for the further details of this story, it should suffice to say that while 'co-operation' was not without its moments at times, the cartridges did get produced on time and were deemed by their authors to say and show what they wanted. In some cases, the Television Service has put in so much effort to persuade an author to use various materials and devices that he had not originally thought of at the expense of concentrating on such mundane details as ensuring that things and speakers were 'produced' in *technically* the best possible manner. An element of dissatisfaction with the technical quality of the cartridges, as well as a certain amount of grumbling about their having had to undergo more argument than we had intended, is fairly widely expressed by the authors. The cartridges have since worked for the students, however, perfectly well and the whole production procedure had therefore manifestly succeeded, despite the warning given at the outset by the Television Service that unless their approach to the production of an academic television course be adopted - 'course-team' etc. - 'it would fail'. The general point of significance for any other Department in an orthodox university which may wish to use the video cassette technology in the way we did is simply, that whatever may be the views of the local Television Service, provided the academics in the Department stick to their guns, in the last resort they can get their tapes produced as they want them. The plain fact is that in an orthodox university where no Department, or individual academic by the terms of his contract, is obliged to make any use whatever of the Television Service, while the latter depends utterly on academics bringing work to them, the academic Department has the last word. One should add of course that, as in any other co-operative activity whatever the relative position of the partners involved may be, in dealing with a Television Service it is essential that the academics, individually and departmentally, should behave towards them with the courtesy which should be accorded to people who sincerely hold views with which one disagrees.

More fundamentally, our experience has shown that, individually and collectively, the audio-visual services are comprised of people not only with skills but also with a rare measure of idealism and an overwhelming desire to produce programmes, especially those which can make a *central* contribution to the teaching of an academic department. It should be placed on record that while it is difficult to conceive a Television Service more strongly opposed to the principles which we held and to which we stuck about the respective roles of television producers and academics, of Television Services and academic Departments, we received nothing but the best of which they were capable - alongside of course a flow of arguments, memoranda and even examples to make us see the error of our ways. We could have done without the latter during a busy teaching term, but could not do without their dedication and hard work. The example of the successful conclusion, within a single academic year, of our new course involving the scripting, preparation and actual recording of some eight hours of television and the fact that the result was accepted as being sufficiently scholarly, accurate and 'history' *sui generis* to be made the compulsory common element for the students of a large School of History, by the verdict of the members of the School as a whole, proves, we feel, our point. By adopting a new approach to the relationship between the academics and the Television Services, by affirming that technology should indeed be the electronic handmaid of academic individuality, it is possible to fulfil some of the hopes and expectations on the basis of which the public purse has given us both the technology and the human resources for improving and extending in quality and quantity the teaching of our subjects - even in these days of constrained resources and large demands in the Humanities.

NOTES AND REFERENCES

1. C.F. Page and J. Kitching (2nd ed. 1976) *Technical Aids to Teaching in Higher Education*, Society for Research into Higher Education, Guildford.

2. J. Cowan in *The Times Higher Education Supplement*, quoted in C.F. Page and J. Kitching, *ibid*.

3. R.I. Evans and P.K. Leppmann (1968) *Resistance to Innovation in Higher Education*, Jossey-Bass, San Francisco, quoted in C.F. Page and J. Kitching, *op. cit*.

4. J.R. Moss, The Academic and the Producer, *University Vision 14*, 36 (1976) and D.R. Clark, The Producer in Academic Television, *University Vision 13*, (1975).

5. D.C. Watt in P. Smith (ed.)(1976) *The Historian and Film* Cambridge University Press. See, in addition to Professor Watt's discussion of problems of the relative roles of the producer *vis à vis* the academic historian, also the article by J. Kuehl on the role of the producer and the historian in broadcasting and J.A.S. Grenville's article discussing the work of the InterUniversity History Film Consortium.

6. P. Coltman, Making an Educational Film: The Roles of Teacher and Producer, *University Vision 9*, 19 (1972).

7. C.F. Page and J. Kitching, *op.cit.*, 34.

8. J.R. Moss, *op.cit.*, 37.

9. *Ibid.*, 38.

10. *Ibid.*, 37.

11. P. Coltman, *op.cit.*, 20-1

12. *Ibid.*, 22.

13. *Ibid.*, 23.

14. *Ibid.*, 24.

15. R.F. Evans and P.K. Leppmann, *op. cit.*

16. D.R. Clark, *op.cit.*, 24.

APPENDIX

A clear impression of the practical basis on which historians of the School of History, most of whom have had no previous experience in writing television scripts approached that task may be best gained from the text of the circular letter which was sent to each author to confirm in writing the substance of the discussion which I had with them, as the co-ordinator of the course, concerning the practicalities of script writing. It was explained to each first-time author of a video cassette that all he needed to do was to write down the text of the 'lecture' which he would normally give to students about the subject concerned, assuming that he would also be able to show them all the documents, monuments, coins or whatever evidentiary material he was discussing. The only difference from the normal texts of such a lecture is that he should clearly indicate what he would want students to be looking at at each point in time in the course of the exposition.

> May I remind you that we agreed to produce our scripts for the first year (Nuffield) Sources of History course by the end of the Easter vacation. It does not matter at this stage whether the script is handwritten, dictated into the tape recorder or typed, as they will all be typed up in a different format - the only thing which does matter is that they should be ready in time. There is no need to polish the words at this stage either, because there will be ample opportunity for doing so when you actually come to read it into the microphone.

> Although the scripts will be eventually transmitted to the students through a

television receiver you should feel under no constraints in writing your script. Television is an *audio*-visual medium, even if this is sometimes overlooked in entertainment television, therefore anything which you would regard as fit to be spoken in a lecture to a small audience, is fit to be said over a television receiver. *You* know the subject, *you* have experience in teaching first year students both through lectures and tutorials; all that is going to be different is that this time the student will hear you, see you or see what you want him to be looking at at a particular time, via a television set.

What is wanted therefore is simply a text of the talk which you would give to a group of students, about three to half dozen in size, if you were talking to them in front of a table on which every document, artefact or picture, to which you may want to point, has been laid. If you think there is nothing to be gained by showing what the type of evidence, the value of which you may be discussing, actually looks like, or even more, if you feel that it would be a distraction from the argument, there is absolutely no reason why the screen should have to have some pictures on it in preference to yourself or a general background shot if you prefer it. On the other hand, of course, you may wish to avail yourself of the opportunity to direct your students' eyes to precisely what you want them to be looking at, at a particular point in your talk.

The length of the talk is to be about a lecture-hour, 50 minutes. Please indicate what you *want* to show on the screen at all appropriate points, but there is no need, unless you feel like it, to give detailed instructions at this stage. The point is to distinguish what may be a metaphor ('Now consider Hansard...') from what may involve a fortnight's work for the studio ('Now consider Hansard pp. 1-25, each page to be slowly filmed from top to bottom...') If there is nothing specific which you want to be on the screen during a passage, we will assume this from the absence of indications for the screen in your script.

After your script has been typed, work can begin on the preparation of a shooting script and studio work. The producer will come to consult you at that stage about the details of the materials which you want to show and the way you want them shown. Thereafter you will not have to be involved in any more work until the recording in the autumn. Nothing, however, can be done until the arrival of your script.

The Political Scientist as Film-maker: Some Reflections Concerning a German Filmic Documentation Project on Election Campaigning

Stig Hornshøj-Møller

One of the fundamental human traits is the ability and will to make meaningful contact with other human beings. This can be done in many different ways: by gesticulation, by oral expression or in writing. Common to most forms of communication is the use of either the auditory sense or the visual power, perhaps both of them. Only rarely do the other senses play a significant role. Thus, with the aid of audio-visual media which theoretically involve the sense of hearing as well as the visual power, contemporary man is placed in a kind of 'eye-witness' situation in spite of disparities in time and place. In particular, one can maintain that film and television are the best and most perfect instruments so far available to communicate and recreate 'reality' in its outward manifestation. In actual practice, this assertion meets with strong opposition among scientists who stress the subjective element in the audio-visual medium. This criticism is levelled particularly against the selection of the picture coverage which takes place, and against the way in which the different shots are later joined to form a 'new' whole.

However, in my opinion it is clear that the often justified attacks on the pragmatic use of the medium (e.g. television) do not shake the fundamental validity of considering the audio-visual medium as a splendid instrument of research. Instead of rejecting its use in humanities, one must ask the question: Why does not practice square with theory? To what extent is this apparent disparity attributable to actual insufficiencies of a technical nature within the medium itself, and to what extent due to human flaws, including lack of experience and method in the practical use of the medium?

In judging existing material one must not forget the strong demand for actuality, technical perfection and economic considerations that are experienced by media producers. The present election campaign project was conceived to evaluate these

---

Stig Hornshøj-Møller is currently working at the National Museum, Copenhagen. This paper (which was translated by Anna Le Steen Hansen) contains some of the central points in the analysis which he has made of the election campaign project which was implemented in 1972 by the Institute for Scientific Film (the IWF) in Göttingen, directed by the then head of the Department of History, now Professor Karl Friedrich Reimers. The preliminary results were presented in Göttingen 1973 and in London 1976. The final analysis is now available as a paper in Danish which was presented to the University of Copenhagen in June 1977.

factors in an idealized case without the demand for actuality and the associated production deadlines. The initiator and leader of the project, Professor Karl Friedrich Reimers wanted to test the optimum possibilities of the audio-visual medium as a means of documentation and analysis in humanities.

POLITICAL-SCIENTIFIC BACKGROUND

Most investigations of elections and campaigns in Western Germany have concentrated on general sociological-deterministic explanations of movements of the electorate, primarily on a federal level. Only few have dealt with the significance of the regional election campaign, yet it is on the local level that the individual voter has the possibility of having a political influence which exceeds the acclamation of giving a party his vote. But to what extent is this theoretical possibility real? And to what extent are his possibilities predetermined by party strategists who by the aid of demoscopics and political propaganda have carefully fixed the themes for political discussion? According to the West German constitution it is the duty of the political parties to participate actively in the creation of political public opinion. To fulfil this duty the different parties receive a Government grant to run their election campaign. Most of this grant, which is given in proportion to the number of votes achieved by the parties, is used on the regional level for the distribution of folders, for advertising, for posters etc.

What function does this offer of information from the parties have in the creation of public opinion, and how is it used by the individual voters in the public debate? Theoretically the ordinary voter has the best opportunity to exert influence when he participates actively in the various meetings arranged during the election campaign. Politicians often refer to this kind of immediate contact with the voters, to which they assign great importance. But is it so 'immediate', and who is present at these local election meetings? What is the underlying strategy of these meetings, and which function do they really have in the modern 'democracy of the television'? How do the politicians and the voters argue? What is the importance of the image or of the personality of the individual politician? Do the politicians answer the questions put by the ordinary voters, and are these answers given in a language which the voters can understand? These were some of the questions of a political-scientific nature which we hoped would be elucidated through the project.

By the application of film to an election campaign, we took up a theme, related to the field of activity within which the historical department of the Institute for Scientific Film* had been working for several years. The department had been interested in the use of film in the late period of the Weimar Republic and the beginning of the National Socialist State. The most significant example is 'Hitlers Aufruf an das deutsche Volk' (Ref. 1), Hitler's first public speech after becoming Chancellor of the Reich. Almost the whole speech was filmed and quickly distributed as a propaganda film so that it could act on the millions who had not been present. Today this film is a document of inestimable importance, because, contrary to most other film sources for Hitler's speeches, this one is preserved in almost complete form, which

---

*The Institute re-issues old political films and news-reels with a scientific commentary, which is also published in the Institute's serial publication: Publikationen zu wissenschaftlichen Filmen. Sektion Geschichte, Pädagogik, Publizistik. See K.F. Reimers: 'Audio-visuelle Dokumente in der Forschung und Hochschule: Die "Filmdokumente zur Zeitgeschichte" des Instituts fur den Wissenschaftlichen Film (IWF), Göttingen' in G. Moltmann & K.F. Reimers (ed.): 'Zeitgeschichte im Film- und Tondokument' (Göttingen 1970) pp. 109-142.

enables us to apprehend his rhetorical manner and gestures. It also enables us to
understand how he could create the mass psychosis he did when speaking. Only by
seeing this film is one able to grasp now how he could end the speech by saying
'Amen', and how it is in fact the only suitable word for an ending!

METHODOLOGICAL BACKGROUND

The whole project was conceived within the scientific philosophy and ideology which
the Institute for Scientific Film represents. The Institute has set itself the tasks
of assisting with filming in areas where science considers the film medium as the
best instrument of cognition, and building up an 'Encyclopaedia Cinematographica'
comprising scientific films of approved quality (Ref. 2). A basic principle is that
the film medium must be employed as an objectifying, demonstrating instrument of
observation in which the camera must not interpret by using filmic tricks. This
extremely puristic and positivistic view of science has developed within the Natural
Sciences where disruption by the camera only rarely matters. However, within
Humanities this has produced the result that the ethnographic films made (which are
the most comparable with our election campaign films) primarily treat simple working
processes like bread- and pottery-making. Already in connection with more complicated
actions such as religious rituals and dances there are current methodological con-
troversies within the Institute itself (Refs. 3 and 4). There is a general demand
that such rituals should be watched repeatedly by the producer before he proceeds to
take a film of what goes on. In this context, it will be appreciated that a major
difficulty of filming the campaign events was that they were not repeated, although
there were certain established standards. On the other hand (and this is probably
the reason why the project received the Institute's blessing, money and production
capacity), the Institute now stresses the documentation of rituals in its selection
of themes, because rituals include a strong visual element which could not have been
made the object of scientific research in any other way. A strong argument was a
reference to the work of Professor Konrad Lorenz who was carrying out a significant
part of his studies of 'ritualized fighting-behaviour' with the aid of films produced
by the Institute (Ref. 5). And what is an election campaign other than a ritualized
way of fighting within the frame of modern, democratic society?

In the implementation of the project, discussion of ethnological method was of practical significance, as the filming was realised by a team of cameramen and sound
technicians who usually produced ethnological films. As a result they worked mainly
with long and medium shots and only a few real close-ups, few cuts and some panning
shots in an attempt to relate the participants in the 'ritual' (that is, the election
meetings) to each other. Thus, our principle of documentation differed in several
important respects from the way in which television usually treats political meetings.
As the television coverage is limited in time, the reporter responsible receives a
copy of the speech before the meeting indicating the most important points. During
these periods, the camera is pointed at the politician, and the cameraman takes
supplementary picture-coverage of the surroundings and the audience during the less
important parts. At the cutting-table this material is edited to fit the well-known
scheme: panning-shot of the hall; the speaker; the audience; the speaker; perhaps a commentary from the reporter. In such cases it is essential to stress that
only the shots of the synchronously-speaking politician can be called 'documentary'
in the sense of Niels Skyum-Nielsen*.

---

*Professor Niels Skyum-Nielsen, Historical Institute, University of Copenhagen, was
the initiator of research in the field of history and film in Denmark and has summed
up his methodological considerations in the book 'Film og kildekritik' (Copenhagen
1972). He advocates a very narrow definition of the concept of 'documentary' in
history, which he calls 'documentality', cf. the paper of K. Fledelius p. 105.

To sum up, we can characterize the differences between our project and the usual form of television coverage as follows:

TELEVISION	INSTITUTE CAMPAIGN PROJECT
Conscious pre-selection of 'the central' (according to the politician or/and the political journalist). Little concern with local candidates.	'Completeness' as far as possible.
Partial synchroneity between sound and picture.	Total synchroneity between sound and picture.
Many close-ups and extensive cutting.	Many long and distant shots, few close-ups and little cutting.
Selection of themes of major topical interest for the public.	Selection of themes according to a strict plan regardless of public interest.
Official distribution through a current mass medium.	Primary function to be an instrument of social psychological cognition, with a didactic function as secondary priority.

CRITERIA FOR SELECTING THE THEMES FOR DOCUMENTATION

For logistic reasons we chose constituency number 49 of Göttingen as the location for the project, but luckily the election sociological investigations of the constituency later showed that in many respects it could be considered as a 'typical' West German constituency. The tight economy of the project* and the small size of the camera group called for a strong prior selection of themes to be documented. This was done in cooperation with the three biggest political parties. Initial approaches to Party organisers and politicians were met with some suspicion as the parties feared that their political opponents would get important internal information through the project group, but later Professor Reimers succeeded in convincing them of the absolute impartiality and scientific interest of the group, and they realized that they would be interested in having documentation which could be used later for internal discussions of their tactics. The result was that from the beginning of the hot phase of the election campaign in October there was extremely good cooperation with the three main parties CDU (Christian Democrats), SPD (Social Democrats) and FDP (Free Democrats). There was more superficial contact with the DKP (Communist Party), and no satisfactory contact could be established with the NPD (National Democrats). The reason why the DKP was not very cooperative might be that they were suspicious of the Institute as a kind of state institution. However, there was no problem in getting admission to film the party's public meetings.

The documentation group decided to choose the themes according to two main principles: the three big parties should be treated equally and the documentation of events with a single party should be characterized by the party itself as typical for it. The two largest parties sought the stabilization and mobilization of their own voter potential by arranging 'Grosskundgebungen' (huge mass meetings with prominent federal party politicians), by holding their own party meetings with the local candidates in areas of support, and finally by participating in meetings held by friendly professional and industrial bodies. Instances of this are the SPD 'Grosskundgebung' with

---

*A realistic guess at the total costs of the project (including materials, development, wages etc.) is about 300,000 D-marks.

the Federal Chancellor Willy Brandt (film number 17), the three DGB meetings of the United Trade Unions (film numbers 2, 3 and 19), and the children's party arranged by the Social Democratic Voters' initiative (film number 13). The Willy Brandt film is interesting because it succeeds in capturing how he was virtually idolized during the election campaign. In spite of bad weather, fifteen thousand people stood for hours to listen to his speech, and his supporters enthusiastically cried: 'Willy, Willy!' every time he aimed a blow at those groups who tried to disturb his presentation. Likewise, for the CDU it is worth mentioning the 'Grosskundgebung' with Dr Gerhard Stoltenberg, prime minister of the constituent state of Schleswig-Holstein (tape-recording number 7), the meeting with Dr Herbert Hupka, (film number 12) and the event with guests from the university and the industry (tape recording number 15). In this connection the Hupka film should be singled out as an 'historical document', witnessing to what a degree his inflammatory speech agitated the audience of elderly people whose homes now lie in the East Bloc and called up associations with the above-mentioned Hitler-Aufruf.

Common to both of the largest parties was the relatively small importance they attached to open debate at panel discussions, in which they only participated from a sense of duty and because their absence would have made a bad impression. This was not the case with the FDP. They made a point of participating in such meetings, where they could manifest themselves as a possible compromise party. In its campaign strategy the FDP laid particular stress on discussing with the individual voter who happened to pass by the information stand in the market square (film number 16), or whom the party came across when canvassing in the surroundings of Göttingen (film number 21).

The communist party, the DKP, who mainly used students as campaign members, first and foremost made a point of manifesting themselves in panel discussions - no matter whether they were officially invited (films numbers 1 and 2), participated as critical voices from the audience (films numbers 6 and 19), or forced through their participation in the panel at the last minute (film number 18). The party arranged only few meetings (film number 11) but made more of inviting passers-by to discuss politics (film number 16). The national democratic party, the NPD, did not run a direct election campaign and participated in only one panel discussion, where potential voters could be supposed to be present. This was at the Federal Border Defence School in Duderstadt where, on the other hand, the DKP failed to attend although they were invited (film number 14).

In West Germany there is a compulsory subject on the school curriculum called 'politische Bildung' (political education). The idea of this is to breed 'responsible citizens' who are capable of taking rational decisions on politics and thereby create a really functioning democracy. Meetings arranged by youth organizations for young voters were given a high priority by the project in an attempt to estimate the value of political education (film numbers 1, 6 and 18).

Towards the end of the election campaign it was possible for us to make more analytically-oriented records of the strategical-tactical considerations of individual parties at the planning of the election campaign. This was done with the aid of interviews with the candidates and their campaign leaders. As a natural conclusion, we followed the three main candidates on the evening when the final results of the election were announced. In this connection we had their immediate reaction with a backward look at the regional campaign and its importance for the results.

The selection of events was further determined by several structural factors. Meetings which were held outside the big cities could not be filmed because of electricity supply problems. As the Institute had other current productions we did not always have the whole production group at our disposal. This obstructed, for example, a planned documentation of a SPD and a CDU propaganda tour.

PRINCIPLES OF DOCUMENTATION

Roughly formulated, one can say that our ideal was to film the 'reality' of the political meetings as objectively as possible. One of the main aims was to find out what happens when the scientist himself produces his own audio-visual material. Clearly, 'true recording of reality' is an impossible ideal, for what is 'reality' and what is 'true'? It is just as evident that an objective recording of events is impractical, for any recording with a camera lens and tape recorder is inevitably subjective. However, the medium is used daily by the television companies as if the requirements of objectivity were fulfilled, so what happens when you do try to record what happens at a political meeting without bias and as openly as possible?

A brief account of how we tried to put this into practice will now be given. First of all it is necessary to carry through a source-critical analysis of the genesis of a source before it can be interpreted in a relevant way. Furthermore, as one who has worked on the film-producing as well as the film-analysing level, I have found that this is the very point where even experienced researchers fail. To a large extent their source criticism remains on a theoretical plane and is not applied rigorously to exclusively film sources. It will also become clear through such a description to what extent answers to the above-stated questions were found.

We frequently found that technology defeated science. Often the very best scientific intentions simply could not be carried out because of technical difficulties. Our material was 16 mm film - black and white, as that was much less expensive than colour and because we considered it to be more important to shoot as much as possible instead of amplifying the information content by using colour, which would also have demanded more light. The sound was recorded synchronously on a tape recorder.

When we had decided to document a campaign event the whole team comprising two or three cameramen, two or three sound technicians, a light technician, Professor Reimers and myself would survey the place. We would discuss with the leader of the meeting the plan for the event, and would then jointly decide which principle of documentation we would follow. We distinguished between two approaches.

1. The 'chronologische Protokollfilm' (the 'chronological fact film')

2. The 'charakterisierende Situationsdokumentation' (the 'characterising documentation of a situation').

The 'chronological fact film' can be defined as a film which reproduces a chronological audio-visual record of an event, conditioned by scientific interest and knowledge: in brief, passive at the recording, passive at the montage. This kind of film is not directed. The documenting team keeps in the background as far as possible. The discussion at a meeting writes the script in the same way as the football at a live-transmission of a match. This was the underlying principle where the situation could be said to be reasonably well defined by a fairly rigid programme with few centres of auditory and visual action.

On the other hand, where several centres of action could emerge simultaneously, and where the technical possibilities of recording could not therefore be considered methodologically safe enough for a chronological fact film, we would use the alternative principle. The 'characterising documentation of a situation' can be defined as a film which communicates for subsequent analysis a characterisation of an event by means of recorded audio-visual material: in brief, passive at the recording, active at the montage (but at the same time making clear the criteria used in editing).

Accordingly we found out where the politicians were to sit, where the microphones were placed on the platform and where in the room the audience could put questions. Taking this into account, we would then select camera and microphone positions and set up the lighting (always a major problem as a great deal of light was needed, which sometimes led to difficulties of electricity supplies). When these practical problems were solved, we determined our strategy of recording as far as possible. For this it would have been ideal to have worked with an OB-van, so that we could have selected the right camera during recording. As this was not possible, advance discussion of strategy became the more important. Another factor was that we had to use the film sparingly, so we would make every effort to have only one camera shooting at a time. As the film cassette of a 16 mm camera has to be changed every 11 minutes, we had to use pre-arranged signals to avoid blanks in the picture coverage. We then decided on the use of framing, zoom, panning shots etc. As mentioned above, particular stress was laid on carrying through a quiet and puristic direction of the camera without the extremes often seen on television.

To secure synchroneity, each camera was wired to a tape recorder. The synchronising bleeps later caused trouble at the editing stage when they had to be cut out. The cameramen tried to start shooting in pauses in the speech, but when they failed the editor would be faced with difficulties. After processing and dubbing, the picture and sound synchroneity for each camera was reconstructed on the cutting-table, and only then was editing started. In most cases the cutting was obvious, because as one camera stopped another had to take over. Here we would as far as possible make a soft cut in a pause in the speech, hopefully without any visual disturbances. Only in few places were artificial manipulations necessary because communication during shooting had failed. Where picture synchroneity was lacking substitute visual coverage was supplied by insert shots of the audience. These cutaway shots of the audience were, of course, taken at another time and they are therefore not entirely authentic, especially because a positive or negative attitude in the audience used consciously or unconsciously at the editing stage may evaluate the contents of the speech. The total amount of material used for the project was approximately 20,000 metres of 16 mm negative film, of which 9,939 metres were retained in the edited films, that is 15 hours and 6 minutes screen time. Apart from this we had two supplementary sound documentations lasting 1 hour 19 minutes, and four documentations which were only on tape lasting for 7 hours 33 minutes.

THE RECEPTION OF THE DOCUMENTS BY THOSE WHO HAD BEEN DOCUMENTED

In an attempt to establish the objectivity of the documentation we showed the edited films to several groups. The screening of the films to the politicians was naturally the most interesting. In the course of two days they saw most of the material. No-one raised objections to the way in which the films had been made. On the contrary the screening (which unfortunately could not take place until the summer of 1974) provoked a very open debate about the tactics which had been used during the election campaign in terms of the tactics of discussion, forms of argument, political significance of election meetings etc. Films numbers 1 ('School of Commerce') and 6 ('The Youth Organizations of Göttingen') were shown to the groups who formed the audience in these films. These groups did not object to the form of the documentation, but the films started a violent debate about the relations between the voter and the politician as regards rhetoric, plus a more concrete discussion of the promises which the various politicians had made during the meeting. The critical attitude towards tactics was especially prevalent among the pupils of the School of Commerce, but could also be found in a control group from a secondary school who had seen the film. The students of the School of Commerce were aware that they had made a tactical mistake by one-sidedly attacking the CDU-representative Professor Gamillscheg who had been rhetorically superior to them. Thereby they had blocked the other politicians from getting an opportunity to speak in support of the views that they wished to disseminate by way of their questions to Professor Gamillscheg. In these groups, the screenings and the ensuing discussions functioned as a piece of political education.

Perhaps the most informative of all the films is the so-called 'Marktplatz-Film' (film number 16)*. In this we tried to find out how the ordinary citizen in the Market Square in Göttingen reacted to the information offered by the politicians. We tried to investigate how political discussions would arise and end, how an ordinary shopping tour was politicized for a short while, and to what extent a dialogue between the politicians and the electorate actually took place. In this case we could not develop a strategy of documentation beforehand. We could only seek out the places in the square where something was happening and try to record these situations because many discussions broke down when the participants caught sight of the camera. However, not everybody was negatively influenced by the presence of the camera. For example, the FDP candidate was always 'better' when he was filmed. Unlike a television programme where such 'unsuccessful' scenes would have been cut out, we have tried to draw attention to this methodological problem by leaving some such scenes in the film. This film is also an example of our second principle of documentation. At the editing stage where one hour's coverage was reduced to half an hour, we partially structured the scenes according to where they had taken place in the square. First there are general long shots, then the DKP, FDP, CDU and the SPD, and finally a longer separate discussion which actually took place at the stand of the DKP.

The film was hotly discussed and criticized when it was shown in 1973 at the international conference 'Past and Present in the Audiovisual Media'** in Göttingen. The representatives of the political parties, who were actually only present as guests, took over the debate and all dissociated themselves from the picture which the film gave of their respective parties. For example, the CDU complained that the transition to their stand was made by showing the poster on the side of the bus from which they had handed out propaganda. This poster showed a naked girl who is running away between sand-hills with the text 'Do as the prices do. Run away from the SPD'. Their arguments were that the poster had been intended as a joke and only a limited number had been printed. We argued that this was simply the way in which the CDU on that particular occasion had attracted attention and made people come to their bus. Similarly the SPD complained of a Young Socialist who had recruited 'customers' to a poster of Franz Josef Strauss. He is standing behind a newspaper whose headlines are 'Young Socialist bites Defenceless Child', and below as commentary: 'there is always a brainy fellow who pulls the wires'. The Young Socialist had among other things said: 'It is only 6 DM - is there really nobody who wants to buy Strauss for 6 DM? You can always stick him up in the bog!' When the politicians had overcome their first negative reactions and accepted that it actually was a valid documentation, then the SPD politician who was both lord mayor of Göttingen and teacher of political schooling at the Pedagogical High School, stated that in that case the film was a classic example of how the objects pursued in political schooling had not been reached.

FILM ANALYSIS THROUGH 'ANALYSIS-FILM'?

At the above mentioned international congress in Gottingen in 1973 where the election campaign project was presented for the first time, I suggested provocatively that the concept of 'analysis-film' should be accepted as a scientific term for an analytic way in which to work with audio-visual sources in the medium itself. Apart from conscious work with the editing (which is usually considered to be negative in a

---

*This film ('Offene diskussionen auf dem Göttingen Marktplatz, 11/11, 1972') is the only one available on hire from the IWF, under the number W1144. The others are only available in the original cutting copy and can, therefore, only be seen in the IWF with special permission.

**Unfortunately, the proceedings have never been published but are filed in the IWF together with tapes of the discussions.

source-critical sense), the scientist could use his justified selection and commentary to communicate his research results through film 'tricks' like stills and zoom-in on relevant details as a means of documenting his assertions. In this connection it should be stressed that this filmic form of 'scientific publication' can only be employed in connection with subjects which contain a strong visual component. On that occasion I defined an analysis-film as a film which gives a characterising analysis of a certain theme by drawing upon the available material of chronological fact films and documentations of situations through conscious use of the possibilities of editing. Furthermore, it is imperative that the material used has been subject to a source-critical 'filtration' and that the criteria according to which the films have been cut are available to the audience.

If one produced a short 'survey film' as an introduction to our election campaign project, it could be formulated as an analysis-film. The theme could be: how does the publicity which a politician makes for himself and his party at a panel discussion differ from the publicity he uses at discussions in the streets or at mass meetings? Other aspects which could be demonstrated include the political commitment and form of argumentation of the youth, or the activities of the voters' initiatives. A critical title for such a film could be: 'Is Democracy a Reality in the Federal Republic of Germany? Experiences from the Regional Election Campaign in Göttingen 1972'. In the selection of the sequences, the correct chronological order should be kept as far as possible, so that no logical inconsistencies would occur in the statements which the persons in the films made. The central theme of the film should be an emphasis on the structural difference which exists in the case between politicians and non-politicians, which has a strongly restrictive influence on a really democratic process.

CONCLUSION

The main purpose of the project was an initial practical attempt to find out the analytical possibilities of the audio-visual medium. The conclusion of my analysis is that the value of the recordings lies not so much in the results which a scientific evaluation of them can give in the traditional sense. Their value lies in the documentation itself and the ability of the audio-visual medium to communicate - to create publicity. Only by virtue of the documentation is it possible to create a relevant basis of discussion and to criticise in an objectifying way the function of the regional election campaign in the democratic process. Only in this way is it possible to make the politicians as well as the voters aware of the discrepancy which exists between the theoretical and the real function.

It is important to underline the didactic aspect. The use of the different filmed themes as a basis for political education (where the pupils were given, for example, the task of producing analysis-films as an answer to problems of a more general theoretically-democratic or structural nature) would result in a more critical attitude to the audio-visual medium (television), and would also recognize the significance of direct, personal communication, for the development and articulation of the political opinion of the individual citizen. Such a use of the project would relate it to the critical attitude towards democracy represented by Jurgen Habermas among others.

I have tried to argue above in favour of the recognition of the audio-visual medium as an instrument of analysis in political science on condition that its character as a medium with only qualitative statements is consciously recognized. In my opinion it is a brilliant instrument of analysis in connection with situations and structures with a significant visual component, as it can document and communicate elements which no written analysis could incorporate. My suggestion for an analysis of such themes is simply 'film analysis through analysis-film'; first you should try to document a situation as openly as possible, and then elucidate through conscious editing (by using the special 'grammar' of the language of film) the results you have reached in your analysis by way of either comments from a speaker or a written commentary.

Here, critics could raise the objection that in this case it would not differ from the journalistic way in which television works with the same material. But would this matter? Where is the borderline between science and popular science? Cannot one characterize syntheses which attempt to give an overall picture and thereby provoke new investigations as science? Such an argument against film and television would be both dangerous and mistaken. Although we have little experience with the use of the medium, and although this could lead to misunderstandings between sender and receiver, it does not mean that it cannot be used at all. In my opinion it would be the same as rejecting beforehand everything which was written in German because you just happened not to know German. On the contrary it should mean that we ought to continue to experiment with similar projects to develop if possible a particular practical technique of recording which could be accepted in a scientific context as a means of analysis.

SURVEY OF THE THEMES OF DOCUMENTATION

No.	Title	Date
1	Discussion between party representatives from the CDU, DKP, FDP, SPD and students of the School of Commerce of Göttingen (film).	10/10
2	Presentation of the trade union orientated candidates from the DKP and the SPD by the Trade Union of Göttingen (film).	18/10
3	Presentation of the trade union orientated SPD candidate in a solidarity meeting for women strikers and wives of strikers from the abrasives industry (film).	19/10
4	Penalty kick competition of the candidates of the CDU, FDP and SPD (film).	22/10
5	Attempt at an interview with pickets in Hannoversch Münden (film).	24/10
6	Discussion between the candidates of the CDU, (DKP), FDP, SPD and groups from the non-political youth organisations of Göttingen (film).	25/10
7	CDU mass meeting and discussion with the prime minister of Schleswig-Holstein, Dr. Gerhard Stoltenberg (only sound recorded).	27/10
8	FDP party meeting following the party conference in Freiburg (film).	27/10
9	FDP mass meeting and discussion with Werner Maihofer and Rudolf Augstein (only sound recorded).	31/10
10	Regional election meeting of the CDU at Reinhausen (only sound recorded).	1/11
11	Election meeting of the DKP in Hannoversch Münden (film).	2/11
12	CDU meeting and discussion between refugees and Dr. Herbert Hupka (film).	4/11
13	Children's party arranged by a social democratic voters' initiative in cooperation with the 'Young Theatre', Göttingen (film).	4/11
14	Discussion between representatives of the CDU, FDP, NPD and SPD and officers of the Federal Border Police, Duderstadt (film).	6/11

15	Discussion between the CDU and invited guests from the university and industry of Göttingen (only sound recorded).	9/11
16	Open discussions in the Market Square of Göttingen (film).	11/11
17	SPD mass meeting with the Federal Chancellor Willy Brandt in Göttingen (film)	12/11
18	'Pop and Politics' - discussion evening with the political youth organisations of Göttingen (film).	12/11
19	Presentation of the candidates of the CDU, (DKP), FDP and SPD by the Trade Union of Duderstadt (film).	13/11
20	The anticipation of the CDU (film).	15/11
21	The anticipation of the SPD (film).	16/11
22	FDP propaganda tour in the neighbourhood of Göttingen (film).	17/11
23	The anticipation of the FDP (film).	17/11
24	Polling Day (film).	19/11

REFERENCES

1. K.F. Reimers et al. (1971) *Hitlers Aufruf an das deutsche Volk*, Edition G 126. Publikationen zu Wissenschaftlichen Filmen (Göttingen), Sektion Geschichte, Pädagogik, Publizistik: Bd II, 157-281.

2. G. Wolf (1976) *The Scientific Film in the Federal Republic of Germany*, Bonn-Bad Godesberg.

3. F. Simon, Der etnographische Film (Technik und Wahrheitsgehalt), in *Premier Congrès Internationale d'Ethnologie Européenne, Paris 24-28 Août 1971*, Résumés des communications.

4. E. Schlesier (1972) *Ethnologisches Filmen und ethnologisches Feldforschung*, Göttingen.

5. K.F. Reimers (1975) *Konrad Lorenz spricht über 'ritualisiertes Kampfverhalten'*, Edition G 119, Göttingen.

SECTION III
The Message Received —
a User Perspective

Having established some of the constraints on media production it is instructive to consider related problems from the point of view of the user. The range of possible applications of media study in political science and history is very wide, and the four studies published here have been selected to emphasize this range rather than to attempt either overall coverage or definition of main uses.

Jay Blumler's review of recent studies on the intervention of television in British politics typifies an interest in the media as political instruments. The academic is concerned here both with the result of the intervention and with the nature of the process involved. The breadth of literature surveyed indicates that this is far from being a minority interest, and given its obvious applicability to the current political scene it is relevant to consider how far such analysis might be extended to a study of the role of the media in the political life of past periods. This is one of the themes developed by Paul Smith in his examination of an historian's use of readily-available film material relating to Neville Chamberlain. In this example, both teaching and research applications are apparent. It is also worth noting that a similar theme could be developed from some of Nicholas Pronay's discussion in Section II.

Political interest is by no means confined to media with overt political content, as was demonstrated in Section I. It is interesting to assess the role of feature film as a source of political and historical analysis - a complex but practicable task provided that a clear and critical awareness of the production context is maintained. Philip Davies indicates the potential for such a use of feature material in which both the material and the teaching application have their roots in North America.

As a final indication of user potential, it is appropriate to turn to analytical methods designed to strengthen the basis of film study for academic purposes. Although it is clear that there is scope for rigorous academic application of audio-visual media, many academics remain deeply sceptical of the value of such sources as compared with traditional literary material. Karsten Fledelius offers an admirable counter to this view in his meticulous demonstration of the possibility of applying equally rigorous analytical methods to film - in this case using a structural approach. Taken in conjunction with the foregoing examples of academic use retaining a firmly critical and constructive basis, his paper goes far towards dispelling any remnant of the suggestion that film is merely an 'expensive frill'.

An Overview of Recent Research into the Impact of Broadcasting in Democratic Politics

Jay G. Blumler

The significance of communication content in any field may be assessed from several angles. One reason why it could matter concerns the influence it may exert on receivers. This paper presents an interpretation of the 'effects potential' of political broadcasting that emerges from much recent research. Although British evidence is cited where relevant and available, illuminating work undertaken elsewhere (notably in the United States, France, Germany and Scandinavia) is also taken into account. The discussion is not confined to the impact of electronic media on the political outlook of audience members, however, since a view of television effects cannot be developed in isolation from wider considerations about the persuasive power of political messages as such.

Interested laymen sometimes experience frustration and irritation when following accounts of research into communication effects. Such difficulties are due only in part to scholars' excessive reliance on technical jargon. They may also arise from a failure fully to appreciate that the empirical research road to truth is just as hazardous, pitfall-strewn and problematic as is any other attempt to accumulate knowledge. It is noticeable that in paragraph 42 of its report the Pilkington Committee (Ref. 1) stated that, 'So far there is little conclusive evidence on the effects of television on values and moral attitudes.' Yet no professional researcher could claim to provide *conclusive* evidence on any topic within his domain. The best he can offer is carefully sifted data derived from methodologically self-conscious attempts to test well-stated hypotheses. He and his colleagues cannot even present a united front to the layman. Since the virtues of rival theories and methodologies are perpetually in dispute, only banal and uninteresting propositions are likely to be accepted with unanimity. Finally, the research worker is an inveterate qualifier. He cannot commit himself to sweeping statements of high generalisability - as if trying to demonstrate that in some respect or other television exerts a massive and indiscriminate influence on the views of all exposed to it. As the Social Morality Council stressed in its report on *The Future of Broadcasting* (Ref. 2): '... one

---

This contribution is a shortened version of a research paper originally submitted to the Committee on the Future of Broadcasting and is reproduced by permission of HMSO. Crown Copyright Reserved.

Professor J.G. Blumler is Research Director, Centre for Television Research, University of Leeds.

conclusion that may safely be drawn from the body of existing research is that broadcast content will often affect different people in different ways, depending partly on the variety of other circumstances in which they are placed'.

THE REINFORCEMENT DOCTRINE OF POLITICAL COMMUNICATION EFFECTS

The political communication literature aptly illustrates how academic perspectives on a common problem may diverge radically from each other. Not long ago many students of mass persuasion asserted that exposure to mass media messages was unlikely to make much difference to the political thinking of audience members. This 'minimal effects' position arose largely from a series of studies, conducted in the 1940s and 1950s, first in the United States and later in Britain, of the role of communication in election campaigns, in which the central focus of investigation was either a comparison of people's early voting intentions with their recorded votes (in the context of how they had followed a campaign in the mass media) or the development of people's attitudes towards the competing parties and leaders over the period of a campaign (in relation to their exposure to election content in the mass media). The main impressions conveyed by the published outcomes of these early election studies were, first, that measured campaign change was limited in magnitude and inconsistent in direction, and second, that communication factors had played very little part in bringing about those changes that did occur. In their study of the British General Election of 1959, for example, Trenaman and McQuail (Ref. 3) reported changes of voting intention among less than a quarter of the members of a Yorkshire sample and, further, that no single party had benefited appreciably from those changes that did take place. It is true that attitudes (as distinct from votes) had shifted in favour of the Conservative Party during the campaign, but no measurable association could be traced between this movement and how the voters had followed the election, either through television or in any other medium.

Such investigators of campaign communication did not stop short at presenting their findings of little or no communication influence on votes, party attitudes and leader attitudes. They also sought to explain why the data so often took this negative form. That explanation embraced a network of related ideas - about what the typical outcome of audience exposure to political messages was, about the spirit in which the standard voter attended to such messages, about the mechanisms that often filtered mass media exposure, and also about a certain underlying disposition that normally shielded people from the persuasive force of political communications unleashed on them.

A widely accepted view of the typical outcome of the communication experience was succinctly expressed by Joseph Klapper (Ref. 4): 'Persuasive communication functions far more frequently as an agent of reinforcement than as an agent of change'. In other words, Klapper concluded, when people are exposed to mass media coverage of political affairs, they are more likely to be confirmed in their existing ideas, whatever they might be, than to be fitted out with new or modified ones. The spirit in which most voters supposedly attended to political material was vividly characterised in this passage, which appeared in the book that presented the results of the first American election communication study (Lazarsfeld, et al, Ref. 5): 'Arguments enter the final stage of decision more as indicators than as influences. They point out, like signboards along the road, the way to turn in order to reach a destination which is already predetermined. So, in a sense, it is for votes at this ... stage. The political predispositions and group allegiances set the goal; all that is read and heard becomes helpful and effective insofar as it guides the voter toward his already "chosen" destination. The clinching argument thus does not have the function of persuading the voter to act. He furnishes the motive power himself. The argument has the function of identifying for him the way of thinking and acting which he is already half-aware of wanting. Campaigning for votes is not writing on a public *tabula rasa*; it is showing men and women that their votes are a normal and logical and more or less inevitable expression of tendencies with which each has already aligned himself'.

Consequently, certain mechanisms of audience response to political messages were invoked as operating sufficiently often to serve the reinforcement function. Given such labels as selective exposure, selective interpretation and selective recall, their linking thread was the idea that many people used their prior beliefs like compasses for charting their course through the turbulent sea of political messages - accepting more speeches, ideas and reports from the side they initially supported, while also counter-arguing, *sub voce*, against any alien and opposing opinion that might happen to penetrate the front line of their defensive screens. Of course it was recognised that there was a group of floating voters whose prior political anchorages were not firm enough to conform to this reinforcement model of electoral behaviour. Nevertheless, the findings of early research were also drawn on to suggest that political communication was virtually irrelevant to many such floaters. Because they tended to be less interested in political affairs, they were also less likely to be reached by political messages. In short, as Greenstein (Ref. 6) concluded, mass communication was 'an inefficient technique for changing beliefs and behavior', not only because 'the message tends largely to be received by those who are already sympathetic to it and therefore least in need of change' but also because 'for the remainder of the population the message is ignored, "crowded out", by other more potent communications'.

Finally, a key lynch-pin of this edifice of interpretation may be identified. This concerned the role of party loyalty in mass electoral psychology. It was assumed that most voters could be counted on to be tuned in to political affairs through some underlying party allegiance. Typically, this would be acquired early; persist throughout the citizen's lifetime; be echoed among many of his family members, workmates, friends and social acquaintances; and serve as a 'beacon light' (Mackelprang, et al. Ref. 7), guiding the vast majority of the electorate through the maze of issues and events that appear on the political stage, helping them to learn what the appropriate views and feelings to adopt on a host of other political questions might be.

Latterly, however, some of the most active workers in the political communication field have with increasing insistency been signalling their conviction that this framework of data and interpretation is no longer so valid and acceptable as had previously seemed the case. According to Kraus and Davis (Ref. 8), for example, 'It is unwise to continue to use classical studies of the influence of the mass media upon election campaigns as reference points'; the book on political communication effects must not be regarded as closed. That is why the recent literature is ripe with ever-more frequent reference to a 'new look in political communication research' (Blumler and McLeod, Ref. 9), to 'new strategies for reconsidering media effects' (Clarke and Kline, Ref. 10) and even to a 'return to the concept of powerful mass media' (Noelle-Neumann, Ref. 11). There are at least four main sources of this shift of emphasis, each capturable in a phrase: new environment, new media, new models, and new evidence.

NEW ENVIRONMENT

The reinforcement doctrine of political communication impact was part and parcel of an overall *weltanschauung* that placed far more emphasis on the underlying stability of the world of politics than on its flux. Most voters had prior loyalties and stuck to them. In the characteristic words of one of the first students of campaign communication (Lazarsfeld et al., Ref. 12): 'The subjects in our study tended to vote as they always had, in fact as their families always had'. Today, however, the political environment no longer appears so stable to researchers as it did to their predecessors. Political scientists in one democratic country after another are documenting evidence of accelerating rates of electoral volatility. In the United States, Dreyer's (Ref. 13) analysis of a steady and steep downward trend across five successive Presidential elections since 1952 in the capacity of party identification (a measure of electors' underlying, long-term loyalties) to predict voting direction graphically illustrates the transformation. Danish scholars have reported a doubling of voter mobility rates between the elections of 1971 and 1973, with that of 1975 sustaining the high volatility of its predecessor (Thomsen and Sauerberg, Ref. 14). Similar trends have been reported from Germany, Norway, Sweden, Belgium and Holland, often coupled with splinter-party inroads into the past dominance of two or three traditional parties. For Britain, Butler and Stokes (Ref. 15) have assembled an impressive array of evidence indicative of 'far greater volatility of party support' in the 1960s than in the earlier post-war years - as witnessed by more violent between-election fluctuations in party opinion poll ratings, bigger swing margins between one victor and another at successive elections, and the recent dramatic increases in Liberal and Nationalist strength. As they point out, 'Electoral change is not due (any longer) to a limited group of "floating" voters but to a very broad segment of British electors'. In fact, when the votes cast by a Leeds panel of young electors in 1970 (when they first came onto the electoral register) and February 1974 were compared, it was found that as many as 54% had behaved differently at their second election. In this case at least, the provocative observation of Himmelweit and Bond (Ref. 16) is well-supported by the evidence: 'The consistent voter is the exception; the floating voter is the rule'.

A related environmental feature, which suggests that higher volatility rates may be no passing phenomenon, is a gradual erosion of some of the sub-surface props of past electoral stability. For example, the power of social class to predict the ultimate destination of voters' ballots seems to be on the wane in Britain. Consequently, people are less likely to encounter a consistent and consistently reinforcing pattern of party loyalties in the particular social and work circles in which they move. Similarly, family socialisation processes may no longer be capable of transmitting life-long partisan affiliations from parents to children so effectively as had been supposed in the past. For example, only 60% of the previously mentioned Leeds sample of first-time electors intended to vote in 1970 for the parties their fathers supported; of those with non-party fathers as many as two thirds had acquired party preferences of their own. Moreover, the incongruent youngsters (those with preferences different from their parents) were far more likely to change allegiance during the 1970 campaign than those young people who had entered into their first election situation in partisan agreement with their parents. In fact the greater instability of this initially incongruent group proved surprisingly long-lasting, persisting when the point of comparison was change from the 1970 vote to the February 1974 pre-campaign voting intention and even when change was measured across the period of the 1974 campaign itself.

The implications of these environmental trends for communication roles in politics are tolerably clear. First, as traditional party ties lose their salience for people, and as their social situations become politically less homogeneous, the potential for mass communication to exert an influence correspondingly widens. Secondly, the enlarged body of floating voters can no longer be regarded as consisting mainly of people who have opted out of the political communication market. For example, a recent American analysis of floating voters concluded that '... electoral outcomes depend as much on floating by high media attentives as the low media attentives' (Dobson and St. Angelo, Ref. 17). And those Leeds first-time voters of 1970 who had switched to a different party in February 1974 actually saw more political programmes on television during the latter campaign than did the more stable voters in the same sample. Thirdly, there is reason to suspect that in this era of more widespread electoral volatility, issue outlook and policy preferences may tend to displace long-term party allegiances as a prime determinant of voting behaviour. Although relevant British data are not yet available, recent American research strongly suggests that this is happening in the United States at present (Miller and Miller, Ref. 18). The logic underlying this trend is well-stated by Himmelweit and Bond (Ref. 19): 'Where choice becomes less a matter of habit or tradition, one would expect that an individual's cognitions would play an increasingly important role in determining not only how but also whether he will vote'. It follows that how the mass media frame and project national issue agendas could also become more critical for the workings of the political process in this period.

A NEW MEDIUM

In audience terms the intervention of television into politics has been dramatic. Reliance on it to follow political arguments and events is particularly heavy and widespread at election time. In June 1970, for example, two Leeds samples - one of first-time voters, aged 18-24, and another of older voters, aged 25+ - replied as follows when asked which medium they had found 'most helpful' for following the campaign:

TABLE 1 Medium Preference of Leeds Voters, 1970

	Younger voters %	Older voters %
Television	70	68
Newspapers	15	16
Radio	6	7
Other/Don't know	9	9
	100	100

A different indicator of audience dependence on television stems from a two-stage line of questioning in which voters were first asked to indicate their reasons for following an election campaign and then requested to designate a medium as best suited to cater for the need concerned. When questioned in this manner during the General Election of October 1974, a majority of the members of a national sample invariably gave the nod to television:

TABLE 2 Medium preference of Leeds Voters, 1974

	Best medium				
	Television	Press	Radio	Other people	None
To judge what leaders are like	76	8	6	7	2 = 100%
To help make up my mind how to vote	60	14	6	9	11
To remind me of my party's strong points	55	19	6	14	5
To use as ammunition in argument with others	53	22	10	10	4

When the same questions were administered to a French sample during the Presidential election campaign of 1974, pro-television responses ranging from 41% to 74% were also elicited - a result which the investigator concerned published under the title, *La victoire de la télévision* (Cayrol, Ref. 20).

More important than its overall dominance, however, is how the coming of television has helped to re-structure the audience for political information in two respects that are essentially at odds with the reinforcement thesis of propaganda impact. First, television has penetrated with a regular supply of political materials a sector of the electorate that was previously more difficult to reach and less heavily exposed to message flows. In Katz' (Ref. 21) words, 'Large numbers of people are watching election broadcasts not because they are interested in politics but because they like viewing television'. This observation is amply documented by a Leeds survey of election broadcasting that was fielded during the General Election of 1964 (Blumler and McQuail, Ref. 22), showing that both motivation to follow the campaign and customary viewing habits had independently determined how many party broadcasts the viewers saw:

TABLE 3 Average Number of Party Election Broadcasts Seen: by Customary Weight of Viewing and by Strength of Motivation for Following the Campaign

	Motivation				
	Very Strong	Moderately Strong	Medium	Moderately Weak	Very Weak
Heavy viewers	5.6	6.6	5.3	6.2	3.6
Medium viewers	6.0	5.4	4.8	4.0	2.9
Light viewers	4.0	4.3	3.9	2.6	1.9

Katz supposed that the forging of a special relationship between television and the less politically minded electors was largely beneficial: 'Television has "activated" them: they have political opinions and talk to others about them. It can be demonstrated that they have learned something - even when their viewing was due more to lack of alternatives than to choice'. His judgement is also supported by a finding of Noelle-Neumann (Ref. 23), who compared trends between 1967 and 1968 in expressions of political interest among the members of a German sample of new set-owners and a matched sample of more long-established viewers. If the average development of interest in the latter group over the study period was set at 100, then the rising curve of interest among the new viewers attained a figure of 131. But a more potent feature of television's extensive audience reach may lie in its creation of a new setting for persuasion. Since lukewarm viewers tend to be the least informed, and the least politically formed, part of the electorate, their internal defenses against persuasion are liable to be relatively frail. Hence the dichotomy of audience structure that earlier writers took for granted - between a body of interested/ partisan voters seeking reinforcement and a body of indifferent voters unlikely to be exposed to much political material - is no longer so valid as it used to be.

A second consequence of the coming of television has been a reduction in the frequency of selective patterns of exposure to party propaganda. A medium which is constitutionally obliged to deal impartially with all recognised standpoints, and which offers favourable time slots for the screening of the parties' own broadcasts, affords little scope for viewers consistently to tune in to their own side of the argument. Although the figures presented below, which are drawn from two Leeds-based election surveys, show that viewers with prior party preferences did receive somewhat more propaganda on average from their own party than from its principal opponent, the differences are slight and are overridden by the fact that each party support group was exposed to more materials from the other two main parties combined than from its own side of the political fence.

TABLE 4 Party Direction of Election Broadcast Viewing by Respondent Vote in Two British Campaigns

Average Number of Party Broadcasts Seen

Originating Party	In 1964 by: Con. voters	Lab. voters	Lib. voters	In 1970 by: Con. voters Young	Old	Lab. voters Young	Old	Lib. voters Young	Old
Conservative	1.8	1.8	1.9	1.9	1.9	1.5	1.6	1.7	1.6
Labour	1.4	2.2	1.6	1.7	1.5	1.7	2.1	1.6	2.0
Liberal	0.9	1.1	1.2	0.8	1.0	0.8	0.9	1.1	1.3

It is true that the reinforcement interpretation of campaign communication effects never depended on the prop of selective exposure alone. Reinforcement could ensue, even in the face of many-sided communication, from a selective interpretation by voters of the messages that came their way. But the effectiveness of such a second line of defense presupposes that the initial partisanship of voters will be sufficiently strong to shape their responses to contrary communications, and that the messages received are not subversive of the very principle of partisanship itself. The first of these conditions has been weakened by the aforementioned trend of increasing electoral volatility. And how television - which is wedded not to the principle of partisanship but to norms of fairness and impartiality instead - stands in relation to the second condition is at least an open question. The overall implication of this facet of television is aptly epitomised by Noelle-Neumann's summary proposition (Ref. 24): 'The smaller the possibility of selection, the greater the potential of the mass media to change attitudes'.

NEW MODELS

Another major impulse feeding the current revival of interest in the impact of the mass media has been a change in the conceptual underpinnings of political effects enquiry. In the earlier post-war period political communication research was regarded as virtually co-terminous with persuasion research; investigators were chiefly concerned with associations between communication and attitudes underlying the direction of voting decisions. Now it is more fully realised that the political influence of the mass media may be channelled along a wide variety of other paths.

At least four themes recur in this shift of emphasis. One concerns the nature of political content in the mass media. As Becker et al. (Ref. 25) have pointed out, 'Most of the resources of newspapers and news-staffs of television and radio stations are devoted to information transmittal, not persuasion'.

This observation accords, secondly, with a certain feature of audience psychology. Where overt persuasion is recognised, its guard may tend to be raised. But mass media content may be received in a less sceptical spirit if it purports to shed an informative light on political events and how these could impinge on voters' personal circumstances. Certainly a so-called 'surveillance' reason for following election campaigns ('to see what some party will do if it gets into power') has invariably received more numerous endorsements from voters than has any other motive on the five different occasions since the 1964 election when British surveys have collected data on this point.

Thirdly, the newer approaches reflect a heightened interest among research workers in charting the likely cognitive effects of exposure to mass media materials. Wade (Ref. 26), for example, has referred to the ability of the media 'to create images of social reality by which the public may structure their views of the world'. And Kraus and Davis (Ref. 27) maintain that '... in many crucial and diverse ways, the mass media "create reality" - defining activities and events, moulding and shaping a variety of images for us'. Thus, more emphasis is now being placed on how the media project definitions of the situations that political actors must cope with than on attitudes towards those actors themselves. It should be noted here that this emphasis tallies in turn with the results of many institutional and content studies, purporting to demonstrate the maintenance of a strong strain to consonance in media reporting about certain prominent problem areas - e.g. the industrial relations scene, the race relations field, the Vietnam war, or the incidence of deviance of various kinds. Moreover, certain characteristics of television news bulletins suggest that they could play a special part in helping to disseminate stereotypical impressions of newsworthy situations and the groups involved in them since, in comparison with press reports, they have a lower informational capacity, hence encouraging the provision of a more concentrated dose of whatever is making the headlines at a given moment; they depend on holding the attention of a mass audience throughout the programme, thereby generating pressure to ensure that each item is of interest to as many viewers as possible; and they include a pictorial component, thereby creating a demand for exciting and conflict-laden visuals.

Finally, it is assumed that in the long run the influence of the propagation of such images and perceptions will not be confined to the cognitive realm alone. Reputable psychological theory would predict that when an individual's attitudinal orientation conflicts with a view of the world that is constantly being projected by a trusted communication source, the former will eventually be modified to adjust to the latter. Thus, even research in this more cognitive vein is ultimately likely to concern itself with communication influences bearing at least indirectly on electors' attitudinal dispositions, party preferences and voting tendencies. Thus, Becker and McLeod (Ref. 28) have recently argued for what they term a three-step model of communication effects, 'beginning with the impact of the environment on the media, moving to the cognitions ... of the electorate, and ending with the effect of these cognitions ... on such things as voting behavior and political activity'.

To prevent misunderstanding, however, three *caveats* must be entered at this stage. Although the theoretical tendencies described in the preceding paragraphs are quite widely shared, they have not yet resulted in the formation of anything so cohesive as a 'school'. This is evidenced by the variety of perspectives that investigators have actually adopted when trying to measure political media effects (see examples below). Secondly, although persuasion research of the conventional kind has been to some extent submerged by these newer cognitive emphases, it is by no means extinct. Finally, none of the more recent research models has yet been subjected to a full programme of empirical testing. Although sufficient evidence has been produced by now to suggest that a turning point really has been reached in the field of political communication research, exploration of all the newly laid-out avenues of enquiry is far from complete.

NEW EVIDENCE

The results of recent investigations of political communication effects tally more often with the newer analytical models than with the reinforcement theory that preceded them. From six selected examples of recent work, some impression can be formed both of the main lines of enquiry that are currently being pursued and of the insights they are beginning to yield.

'The Press as King-maker' is the provocative title of an article by John P. Robinson (Ref. 29), which flouts conventional wisdom by suggesting that American newspaper endorsements of Presidential candidates can affect readers' voting behaviour after all. Reanalysing survey data from five Presidential elections between 1956 and 1972, Robinson detected a voting differential according to the editorial preferences of the newspapers people read, amounting typically to something like 10-13%, invariably among party independents (voters professing neither a Democratic nor a Republican affiliation) and in landslide election years also among individuals initially identifying with the losing party. This level of differentiation persisted after controls had been applied for the influence of 12 other possibly confounding variables, including pre-campaign voting intention. In interpreting the results, Robinson suggests that a press which is free to editorialise and to slant headlines and comment in favour of preferred candidates, has a stronger persuasive potential than television which 'seldom offers its own message to the voters on how they ought to cast their ballots'. If, however, we stress as central to his data the greater and more consistent susceptibility to press influence of independents and undecided voters, then a link may be forged to other studies where television effects have been detected.

One such study is the Leeds-based election survey of 1964 in which a statistically significant association was found between an improvement in public attitudes towards the Liberal Party and levels of viewer exposure to political programmes on television (Blumler and McQuail, Ref. 30). Moreover, a splitting of the respondents by strength of prior motivation to follow the campaign showed that this effect was concentrated among the 60% of the sample members whose election interest had been rated in advance as only moderate or weak:

TABLE 5 Average Shift in Liberal Party Attitude Score

Strongly Motivated Viewers				Medium to Weak in Motivation			
No. of Liberal Broadcasts Seen				No. of Liberal Broadcasts Seen			
0	1	2	3	0	1	2	3
0.23	-0.06	0.76	0.20	0.23	0.72	0.94	1.30

In short, television had helped to promote the Liberal cause chiefly among those viewers whose presence in the audience was due less to a keen political interest than to devotion to their television sets.

Another major British study focused on turnout effects during the General Election campaign of 1970 (Blumler and McLeod, Ref. 31). A first glance at data comparing pre-campaign voting intentions and Polling Day voting, in both a first-time voter sample and a control sample of older adults, suggested that the campaign might have deterred people from voting instead of encouraging them to go to the polls. Abstention rates had risen in the former case from 15% to 26% and in the latter from 9% to 19%. A detailed multi-variate analysis was designed with two main features. First, turnout effects were assessed by comparing like with like so far as possible - that is, by seeing how those individuals with a prior intention to vote who had not eventually voted compared with those individuals with a prior intention who in fact had cast a vote. Secondly, communication influences were measured after the impact of a large number of other potentially confounding variables was taken into account. The results showed that communication factors had independently affected the turnout propensities of young voters in particular. In fact a block of such variables accounted for 13% of the total variation in the turnout rates of the original Labour supporters and 28% of that for the original Conservatives. Thus, when election participation behaviours were examined dynamically, and particularly among politically less-formed citizens eligible to vote for the first time, communication mattered just as much as any other factor deployed in the analysis did.

The contribution of communication factors in this analysis proved far more complex than any single image of how they might be related to voting behaviour could adequately convey. Three main communication roles in turnout were detected. One was directly *quantitative*, showing itself in a 'more-the-more' relationship, whereby higher exposure rates helped to produce higher voting rates. Interestingly, the most powerful communication prop of turnout in this quantitative sense proved to be not a mass media measure but an interpersonal discussion variable - how often voters had talked about the election at home with other family members. A second communication role was termed *relational*, because it stemmed from a congruent or incongruent relationship between the party leaning of an individual elector and that which inhered in one of his regularly received sources of messages. Thus, some of the young voter 'drop-outs' were readers of newspapers backing parties different from those the respondents had initially supported. But a third and quite intriguing form of communication influence embedded in the findings was *qualitative* in character. This was reflected in the fact that abstention, particularly among initial Labour supporters, was predicted by unfavourable opinions about how the politicians had waged the 1970 campaign itself. This suggests that at election time some voters may not only be receiving the discrete bits of information about issues, policies and candidates that happen to come their way; at the same time they may also be forming, sustaining or modifying impressions of politicians in their roles as campaigners and of the campaign itself as a typical example of the country's political processes. Evidently such perceptions may vary in favourability, and at some point the creation of a positive or negative impression may strengthen or weaken the individual's inclination to vote.

This complex process of effect was not confined to the decision to turn out or abstain on Polling Day in 1970. Follow-up analysis over a longer-term period showed that this decision, and some of the communication influences that had nourished it, were significantly related to the subsequent growth of a sense of duty to vote among the younger respondents when they were contacted again some 18 months later (Blumler, McQuail and Nossiter, Ref. 32).

It is true that television exposure measures did not feature prominently among the direct sources of these effects. Even so, an important indirect contribution by television could not be ruled out. For one thing, the powerful participation-sustaining measure of family-based political discussion was strongly related to measures of political viewing during the campaign. This is consistent with a conception of television as a domestic medium that can inject political materials into the family circle which may then be further aired and sifted in informal conversation. For another, many of the qualitatively favourable and unfavourable impressions that voters formed of politicians as campaigners probably derived from what they saw of them on their television screens - in party broadcasts, clips from hustings speeches in the news, and in appearances in broadcast interviews and debates.

A different relationship between interpersonal and mass communication influences is currently being traced by Professor Noelle-Neumann in Germany, who has formulated a so-called 'spiral of silence hypothesis' (Ref. 33). Her point of departure is the proposition that the direct influence of the media is not exerted so much on people's own attitudes on a topic as on their perception of the opinions that other members of their society hold about it - perceptions, then, of the views predominant or becoming more prevalent in their social environment. This theory implies that the mass media function like surrogate opinion polls, giving viewers, readers and listeners impressions of what the prevailing views on various issues are and which ones are becoming more fashionable. Such a thesis is neither naive nor trivial. For example, it does not imply that, band-wagon-like, some voters simply take over as their own what they suppose to be the majority sentiment. But it does predict that a person's willingness to express and defend his ideas in public will be affected by these perceptions. Thus, beliefs imagined to be in the ascendant will be aired more often in interpersonal exchanges, while those believed to be on the way out will be voiced less often. In the long run such a mechanism could prove highly influential, since interpersonal communication has always been credited with a stronger power to penetrate people's attitudinal defenses than mass communication. So far, data collection guided by this framework has given it uneven support. Impressive confirmation has been obtained of a tendency for voters who believe themselves to be in a minority position to be less willing to stand up for their convictions in conversations with other people. This tallies with survey evidence from the United States documenting the greater reluctance of Nixon supporters to speak up for their beleaguered leader during the Watergate scandals (O'Keefe and Mendelsohn, Ref. 34). How exactly the mass media may be used by people to build up maps of the public opinion terrain, however, has not yet been clarified by this line of investigation.

Another recent study has illustrated the possibility of linking cognitive communication effects with persuasion outcomes. During the 1972 Presidential election in the United States, McClure and Patterson (Ref. 35) examined the impact on voters of spot political commercials broadcast over television. Certain Nixon advertisements were found to have helped to implant beliefs in exposed viewers about some of the policy positions that his opponent, McGovern, favoured (e.g. that he wanted to cut defense spending). In line with some of the other studies described above, this effect was greater among viewers of moderate and low political interest than among the more heavily interested audience members. The significance of this result arises from its connection with one style of communication strategy that is open to a political party waging a campaign, namely to try to project belief messages linking itself in voters' minds with political objectives that the public values and opposing parties with ones the public dislikes. If 'issue-voting' is seen to be on the increase, the appeal of such a strategy to party publicists could also become greater.

One of the currently most active products of the cognitive reorientation of political communication research can be found in a host of attempts - largely American so far - to study the so-called 'agenda-setting function' of the mass media. These aim to explore what it means to have a media system 'that determines which issues among a whole series of possibilities are presented to the electorate' for attention (Becker and McLeod, Ref. 36). This particular research perspective is exceptionally rich, for it embraces attempts: (a) to test the assumption that the issues selected for prominent and frequent display in newspaper columns and broadcast news bulletins are the ones that individual voters will think are important to them personally or to the country at large; (b) to identify those variables which may differentiate audience members in terms of a greater or lesser receptivity to the issue agendas set out in the media organs they patronise; (c) to assess how far campaign agenda items derive respectively from voters' prior concerns, politicians' speeches and pronouncements, and the issues that professional journalists think are important; and (d) to measure the impact of agenda-setting on voting behaviour as such. On all these matters a certain amount of interesting evidence has already been published, more data are being collected, further hypotheses are being generated, and theories about the agenda-setting process are being elaborated. The variety of findings and interpretations virtually defy generalisation at this stage. Nevertheless, more often than not these studies have found a correspondence between electoral issue concerns and issue themes projected in mass media content in at least some definable sub-group of the audience. Consequently much of the thrust of this work is now being directed towards a specification of those conditions under which an agenda-setting effect is most likely to be exerted.

THE LESSONS OF RESEARCH: A PROVISIONAL SUMMING-UP

Much of the above material has inevitably taken on the flavour of an interim report. Clearly the political communication research field is undergoing a vigorous rebirth. It is once again permissible to assume that communication processes may yield important outcomes, and many promising paths of enquiry have been identified and are under intensive exploration. It would be premature to try to predict at this stage, however, the ultimate shape of the findings that the present surge of activity will produce. Nevertheless, at least three overall impressions can be derived from the work already undertaken and the insights thus far gained.

One concerns the fate of the reinforcement doctrine of political communication effects that until recently dominated the field. Despite the attacks of many writers cited in these pages, it should not be supposed that this has been exploded or firmly displaced. It would be more accurate to conclude that its range of application has been sharply reduced. It is not denied that in response to political communications the convictions of individuals with strong views and deep-seated commitments are more likely to be reinforced than changed. But it is argued that on many political questions the proportion of the electorate in this frame of mind is probably declining, and in particular that party loyalty is less often being used by citizens as a peg on which to hang a cluster of other beliefs and attitudes to be reinforced. Perhaps the British General Election of February 1974 affords a useful illustration of the waning power of political communication to uphold prior beliefs. On the face of it that campaign was well-placed to reinstate the reinforcement doctrine. The postures of the major parties seemed designed to activate the basic loyalties of their most keen supporters, while persuading floating voters that a choice had to be made between one or the other side. In fact, writing before the campaign started, Professor Richard Rose (Ref. 37) put forward the hypothesis that 'a crisis choice will lead voters to ignore Liberal and Nationalist alternatives' in favour of Labour and Conservative candidates. Yet in the event the two major parties combined secured a lower percentage of the popular vote than at any previous postwar election and less support on Polling Day than the opinion polls had recorded for them at the start of the campaign (Blumler, Ref. 38).

This observation leads to a second summary impression: the context of democratic political communication has been transformed by the increasing instability of electoral behaviour. It should be pointed out in this connection that some analysts are increasingly voicing their suspicion that one of the factors responsible for this development may be the intervention of television into modern politics. Miller (Ref. 39), for example, deplores the fact that until recently 'the impact of television on mass political partisanship has been badly underestimated'. O'Keefe (Ref. 40) argues that 'television has ... reduced the salience of parties as a political force within our society overall'. And, so far as British conditions are concerned, Butler and Stokes (Ref. 41) conclude, 'It should occasion no surprise that the years just after television had completed its conquest of the national audience were the years in which the electoral tide began to run more freely'.

There are several reasons for regarding television as a medium that is suited to shaking up previously firm political loyalties. It is, for example, eminently a mass medium, one that has a greater reach in conveying political materials to essentially apolitical men and women than any previous communication vehicle has commanded. Thus, in penetrating this electoral element with more, and more varied, political stimuli than it was ever previously exposed to, it may have encouraged people who, in former times, would have supported the parties they were virtually born into more or less uncritically, to wear their votes on their sleeves more often now. In addition, there is the unique position of television as a public medium, one which has a corresponding obligation, then, to give some access and attention to all the main contenders for electoral support and not to let the traditional major parties monopolise the limelight and the argument to themselves. Thus, television has in many countries made a critical difference to the recognition-gaining chances and the persuasion opportunities open to certain minor party challengers, which are taken more seriously than they might otherwise have been and are given lines of contact to less politically minded people who might be more open to their appeals.

Finally, there is television's unavoidable above-the-battle relationship to party political conflict. Since broadcasting may not support individual parties, it is obliged to stand instead for a string of such non-partisan - perhaps even anti-partisan - standards as fairness, impartiality, neutrality and measured choice - at the expense, then, of such alternative values as commitment, consistent loyalty and a forthright readiness to take sides. Thus, television may tend to put staunch partisans on the defensive, help to legitimise the less certain attitudes of those who feel that a conditional and wary commitment is the outlook most appropriate to a model citizen, and even set up pressures on other communication organs, such as newspapers, increasingly to hedge their endorsements around with various qualifications, riders and reservations, rather than invariably to sound off to do battle on the side of a single supposed set of political angels.

Meanwhile, increasing electoral volatility seems to be posing problems of exceptional subtlety and difficulty for all involved in the communication system. To the voter it has made political communication at one and the same time more important and potentially more frustrating. So far as the political parties are concerned, it has undermined that part of the rationale of electioneering which supposed that the prime function of a campaign was to reinforce pre-existing attitudes and allegiances. It has also increased the already weighty responsibilities of professionals working in television and radio, since electors whose votes are dictated less and less by traditional habits and allegiances will be looking for comparative information, which is more likely to be available in the broadcast media. Overall, it may be a partial cause of the more frenetic and disconnected style of latter-day British campaigns - that is, their seemingly greater preoccupation with short-term events and exchanges (the so-called 'issue-a-day' approach) at the expense of a more leisurely and sustained handling of a few dominant themes. Thus, in this new political climate it becomes both more urgent and more difficult to try to solve some of the inherent problems of political coverage by radio and television.

Finally, the potential significance of the cognitive thrust of many recent effects studies in the political communication field should be underlined. In following this path researchers may be nearing the heart of the competition-through-communication that is waged in a democratic pluralist society. We have seen that issue opinions may be playing a more central part in the formation of electoral judgements than in previous times. In designing their publicity strategies, political parties are often concerned to command the current issue terrain. Meanwhile, newsmen in the several mass media are engaged in propagating images of political reality that few people can challenge for lack of first-hand experience. And insofar as reporting of news topics achieves a consonance that excludes alternative perspectives, to that extent is the chance increased that an influence will be exerted on how audience members think about them. Although the returns are not yet fully in from the more cognitive lines of political communication research, when they are available for consultation, they should help to refresh the perennial debate about the quality of the news and current affairs services that are provided by television and the other mass media.

REFERENCES

1. Pilkington Committee (1962) *Report of the Committee on Broadcasting, 1960*, Cmnd. 1753, H.M.S.O., London.

2. Social Morality Council (1974) *The Future of Broadcasting*, Eyre Methuen, London.

3. J. Trenaman and D. McQuail (1961) *Television and the Political Image*, Methuen, London.

4. J.T. Klapper (1960) *The Effects of Mass Communication*, The Free Press, New York.

5. P.F. Lazarsfeld, B.R. Berelson and H. Gaudet (1944, 2nd edition 1948) *The People's Choice: How the Voter Makes up his Mind in a Presidential Campaign*, Columbia University Press, New York.

6. F.I. Greenstein (1965) *Children and Politics*, Yale University Press, New Haven.

7. A.J. Mackelprang, B. Grefman and T.N. Keith, Electoral Change and Stability: Some New Perspectives, *American Politics Quarterly 3*, 315-339 (1975).

8. S. Kraus and D. Davis (1976) *The Effects of Mass Communication on Political Behavior*, Pennsylvania State University Press, Philadelphia.

9. J.G. Blumler and J.M. McLeod, Communication and Voter Turnout in Britain, in T. Leggett (ed.) (1974) *Sociological Theory and Survey Research*, Sage, London.

10. P. Clarke and F.G. Kline, Media Effects Reconsidered: Some New Strategies for Communication Research, *Communication Research 1*, 224-240 (1974).

11. E. Noelle-Neumann, The Spiral of Silence: A Theory of Public Opinion, *J. of Communication 24*, 43-51 (1974).

12. Lazarsfeld et al., *loc. cit*.

13. E.C. Dreyer, Media Use and Electoral Choices: Some Consequences of Information Exposure, *Public Opinion Quarterly 35*, 544-553 (1971-2).

14. N. Thomsen and S. Sauerberg (1975) *The Political Role of Mass Communication*, AEI Seminar on Recent Scandinavian Political Development, Washington.

15. D. Butler and D. Stokes (1969, 2nd edition 1974) *Political Change in Britain*, Macmillan, London.

16. H.T. Himmelweit and R. Bond (1974) *Social and Political Attitudes: Voting Stability and Change*, Report to the Social Science Research Council.

17. D. Dobson and D. St. Angelo, Party Identification and the Floating Vote: Some Dynamics, *American Political Science Review 69*, 481-490 (1975).

18. A.H. Miller and W.E. Miller, Issues, Candidates and Partisan Divisions in the 1972 American Presidential Election, *British J. of Political Science 5*, 393-434 (1975).

19. Himmelweit and Bond, *loc. cit*.

20. R. Cayrol, La Victoire de la Television, *Le Nouvel Observateur 21-26*, 32-33 (1974).

21. E. Katz, Platforms and Windows: Reflections on the Role of Broadcasting in Election Campaigns, *Journalism Quarterly 48*, 304-314 (1971).

22. J.G. Blumler and D. McQuail (1968) *Television in Politics: Its Uses and Influence*, Fabers, London.

23. E. Noelle-Neumann (1974) *Voting Behaviour in the Television Age: A Sociopsychological Interpretation of the 1972 Federal Election*, mimeo, Institut für Demoskopie, Allensbach.

24. E. Noelle-Neumann (1974) The Influence of the Mass Media on the Quasistatistic Perception of the Opinion Climate, Salzburg Talks on Humanism.

25. L.B. Becker, McCombs, E. Maxwell and J.M. McLeod, The Development of Political Cognition, in S.H. Chaffee (ed.) (1975) *Political Communication*, Sage, Beverley Hills.

26. S. Wade, Media Effects on Changes in Attitudes Towards the Rights of Young People, *Journalism Quarterly 50*, 292-296 (1973).

27. Kraus and David, *loc. cit.*

28. L.B. Becker and J.M. McLeod (1975) *Political Consequences of Agenda-Setting*, mimeo, University of Wisconsin.

29. J.P. Robinson, The Press as King-maker: What Surveys from Last Five Campaigns Show, *Journalism Quarterly 51*, 587-594 (1974).

30. Blumler and McQuail, *loc. cit.*

31. Blumler and McLeod, *loc. cit.*

32. J.G. Blumler, D. McQuail and T.J. Nossiter (1975) *Political Communication and the Young Voter*, Report to the Social Science Research Council.

33. Noelle-Neumann, *loc. cit.* (Ref. 11).

34. G.J. O'Keefe and H. Mendelsohn, Voter Sensitivity, Partisanship and the Challenge of Watergate, *Communication Research 1*, 345-367 (1974).

35. R.D. McClure and T.E. Patterson, Television News and Political Advertising: The Impact of Exposure on Voter Beliefs, *Communication Research 1*, 3-31 (1974).

36. Becker and McLeod, *loc. cit.*

37. R. Rose, An Election to Revive the Political Campaign, *The Times*, 8 February 1974.

38. J.G. Blumler, Mass Media Roles and Reactions in the February Election, in H.R. Penniman (ed.) (1974) *Britain at the Polls: The Parliamentary Election of February 1974*, American Enterprise Institute for Public Policy Research, Washington.

39. W.E. Miller, The Challenges of Electoral Research, *American Politics Quarterly 3*, 340-345 (1975).

40. G.J. O'Keefe, Political Campaigns and Mass Communication Research, in S.H. Chaffee (ed.) (1975) *Political Communication*, Sage, Beverley Hills.

41. Butler and Stokes, *loc. cit.*

Political Style on Film: Neville Chamberlain

Paul Smith

As soon as we enter the era of modern mass communications, film and then television become vital sources for political studies, because they provide two of the most important media in which certain aspects of politics are embodied, transmitted, and, of course, recorded for posterity. Politics gratefully - if often tardily - embraced the new technology of the moving picture because of its bearing on what was perhaps the central problem facing politicians from the late nineteenth century onwards, that of the politicisation and political mobilisation of the masses. Personalities, programmes, and ideas had to be projected to the new mass electorates, which had to be organised and set in motion for party and, especially in wartime, for public purposes. Film and, later, television, like radio, offered new means of approaching the most delicate of all political tasks, communication, and thus became not merely passive agents for recording politics but important instruments for practising them.

Of all the elements of politics, style is perhaps the one best conveyed and recorded by film, because of its very large visual content. Far from being a purely verbal activity - in which case, the study of visual sources would be almost irrelevant - politics possess a visual dimension whose importance is not necessarily of a merely secondary order. From certain viewpoints, indeed, it takes on a primary significance; for example, if one examines politics as theatre. The idea of politics and other forms of social activity as theatre, if old, is frequently renewed. Most recently, Lyman and Scott have reasserted from a sociological standpoint the notion that social reality is best understood in terms of drama, and Maurice Cranston has discussed performance in the theatrical sense as an indispensable ingredient of politics (Ref. 1). This is not the place to deal with the substantial problems involved in the use of such a metaphor. It suffices to note that it has been employed with some effect in studying politics. If its most fruitful application is perhaps to obviously theatrical figures like Napoleon III or Mussolini, and to movements of a highly theatrical character, like fascism (Ref. 2), it can also be used in relation to the more subdued and discreet performances of parliamentary politics in the British mode. British party politics, at Westminster and on the hustings, can well be regarded in one sense as theatre, a theatre of stylised and ritualised tribal conflict - the aspect perhaps most keenly seized by *Private Eye*'s 'Eric Buttock' in his reports on the dust-ups between Tories House and Labour House. The metaphor of theatre has been quite commonly applied: the image of the actor-manager is a familiar one in regard to politicians from Disraeli to Harold Wilson, and Professor John Vincent (Ref. 3) has

---

Paul Smith is Professor of Modern History at the University of Southampton

even chosen to describe the nature and function of Gladstonian liberalism by writing that 'Gladstone created a national theatre for England as Verdi did for nineteenth-century Italy'.

To the extent that politics are, or may be seen as analogous to, theatre, their visual element is of central rather than merely peripheral significance, and style among their most important features. The use of visual media is a major part of the political process, and their value as a record of it correspondingly great, not least where style is in question. Yet the evaluation of the evidence supplied by the visual, or audio-visual, record is a complex matter. The film and television material available for the study of political style has to be examined in at least three principal aspects:

1. As a record of styles of political discourse and deportment - both general styles and their variations in individual politicians and movements ('discourse' is here used in a broad sense, to include not only verbal discourse, but discourse through image, symbol, etc.).

2. Where made for public showing, as a record of the particular forms in which that discourse and that deportment reached the public through the medium of the screen. Films are seen here as operative factors in politics, helping to determine the nature of public understanding and to condition public response.

3. As a record of how film and television as media, by virtue of their special characteristics as media, have influenced the form and perhaps the content (if the two are separable) of that discourse and deportment, and the manner of its reception. Film as a medium like other media of expression and communication, may have properties which affect the content of what is expressed and communicated, both by influencing its presentation and by influencing its reception. Furthermore, any particular film, unlike an article or a speech, is a co-operative product, influenced by the organisation and processes necessary to create it; and in the sphere of reception its impact is significantly influenced by the circumstances in which it is viewed. In short, we are obliged to ask how film as medium and the conditions of film production and reception have affected political communication.

Film arrived when the conditions of politics were being drastically changed in Europe by the coming of manhood suffrage and the beginnings of mass political participation or mobilisation. The problem for politicians was not simply that a much larger audience had to be reached but that it was different in kind, less sophisticated than the old, limited political nation, sometimes, even, largely illiterate. Not only, therefore, had the scale of effort to be enlarged, but new techniques might need to be adopted and new styles devised. The mere physical task of diffusing political messages could to some degree be met by organisation: hence the development of the modern party machine and the mass movement. But it was also expedient to devise new styles of political presentation, based partly on the manipulation of visual imagery and spectacle, styles of which in the post-1917 era communism and fascism furnished the most striking exemplars.

In this situation, technological innovation in the means of communication - the coming of wireless, film, and ultimately television - had an immense impact. First, obviously, the technical possibilities of the dissemination of political messages to mass audiences were greatly enlarged. Second, the use of auditory and audio-visual media in addition to print and the platform speech meant that the range of effects that could be conveyed, especially to the illiterate and near-illiterate, was significantly expanded, and the projection of political style thus much facilitated. This was true even of the projection of individual personalities: if something was lost in immediacy of impact in the transition from the live appearance before an audience to the broadcasting or film medium, the latter nonetheless permitted in some ways a closer, more intimate experience of the politician's voice, visage, and gestures than was often possible to the individual spectator in a crowded hall. The politician and his quarry could be brought into something much more like a one-to-one relationship than had previously been attainable. But, and here was an additional advantage of the new media, it was a relationship susceptible of a certain degree of control from the politician's side, at least where his own organisation or a friendly source produced the material. For the material could be manipulated and edited to eliminate undesirable effects and furnish desirable ones: the public could be presented with a carefully-contrived product of rehearsal and technical adjustment. The illusion of intimacy, immediacy, and truth could be combined with the reality of distance and skilful arrangement. Moreover, with film shown to cinema audiences, the circumstances of reception were up to a point controlled, and the spectator's attention artificially focussed on the moving image in front of him, with its accompanying sounds, in the context of a degree of abstraction from external, competing influences difficult to achieve elsewhere. Yet if these were advantages, there were also some dangers: for instance, that growing recognition of contrivance and manipulation would eventually produce cynicism, and that, despite contrivance and manipulation, the new media would prove unintentionally revealing - that the message would in part escape the control of the emitting agency.

For their most effective utilisation, moreover, the new media required a new style of political discourse and deportment, taking into account their special characteristics and the conditions of audience reception, which it was often difficult for politicians to grasp. Men trained to the parliamentary tribune or debating chamber and the platform did not find it simple to adjust to the microphone, the camera, and the studio. It is not surprising that the adoption of the new media was often slow, and that initially they were frequently employed merely to record politicians doing what they had traditionally done in the way in which they had customarily done it. The camera, for example, was simply pointed at the platform speaker, rather as in the early filming of theatrical productions it was used just as a static recorder of a conventional stage performance not in the least adapted to the new medium.

Used as a vehicle of propaganda in Britain at least as early as 1903 (Ref. 4), film was extensively employed for mass communication during the First World War and after, proving its worth especially in conveying political messages to largely illiterate populations, but its potential was restricted as long as it remained mute. It was at the beginning of the 1930s, with the advent of sound, that it became a major medium of political communication and leading politicians started to use it as a matter of course. The old conventions died hard in their early essays with film: it is not uncommon to find them giving what are essentially platform speeches, complete with the old-fashioned rhetorical devices but without the platform. Abandoning the platform style, they tended to take refuge behind a desk, which easily lent itself to a rather static and wooden performance, in the worst cases dependent on a script on the desk-top. Gradually, however, attempts at a more relaxed and informal approach appear, with a conversational tone substituted for declamation or script-reading, little oratorical gesture, and much use of close-up. These points are well illustrated in film of such British politicians of the thirties as Baldwin, Beaverbrook, Lansbury, and Ramsay MacDonald (Ref. 5), and a recent production for the Archive series of the Inter-University History Film Consortium (Ref. 6) gives us a particularly good opportunity of seeing how another leading figure of the period, Neville Chamberlain, sought to come to terms with the film medium and to utilise it for the calculated projection of his political style. The film consists of eight unedited newsreel items showing Chamberlain at various times between 1931 and 1940. The material represents the first phase, at least in Britain, of the serious exploitation of film for party political purposes.

The Conservative party was well to the fore in the application of film to politics, not merely because it could better afford the cost than its rivals, but as a natural result of its readiness to try innovations which might improve its chances. It had been quick to take the necessary steps to enter the era of democratic politics in the late nineteenth century, preceding its opponents in the field of mass organisation, and had early developed its propaganda techniques, including the use of largely visual material. Well before the First World War, the London Municipal Society (the Conservative organisation for L.C.C. elections) was using poster advertising in preference to newspapers and even to platform speeches. One of its officials declared: 'You see exactly the same thing in electioneering that you are, of course, familiar with in business ... all the paraphernalia of salesmanship or electioneering, as the case may be. The big advertiser calls in the aid of professional experts ... The electioneer, if he is to secure the greatest efficiency for his campaign, must do the same' (Ref. 7). A party so interested in efficient publicity by the most modern methods took readily to wireless and film. Baldwin was one of the first politicians to master radio, and in the late twenties the party was quick to interest itself in the emergence of sound film. Its chairman, J.C.C. Davidson, secured a concession in 1927 for the use of the 'phonofilm', and already the use of travelling cinema vans was under consideration (Ref. 8).

Sound film was perhaps particularly important to the Conservative party in the facility it provided for the projection of leadership images. The Conservatives survived and prospered as a party in the democratic era partly through the defence of a particular principle of social organisation which they attempted to render not simply tolerable but attractive to the mass electorate in the form of 'Tory Democracy' - an outlook which regarded a stratified society, vertically integrated by reciprocal obligation and headed by a specialised governing élite, as not only the most natural but the most efficient form of social organisation. The validation of the social and political authority of the ruling élite as not merely a natural growth but a functional necessity was a prime task of Conservative propaganda, and it involved *inter alia* a good deal of what one might call ceremonial presentation of the élite to its followers. That presentation, hitherto done in print and still pictures, and from the platform, could now be done in moving pictures, and with the very voices of the gods. The main technical problem was to present the bearers of authority in such a way as to combine effective personal appeal and the illusion of a more or less intimate personal contact with the maintenance of their necessary hierarchic aloofness. That was, of course, a problem of conventional platform politics, too, but it was perhaps intensified by the degree of apparent intimacy permitted by the new radio and film media, which posed dangers. Still, compared with the intimacy of the public meeting, that of radio or film was at least a fundamentally one-way intimacy. If the politician lost the stimulus of a live audience and could not commune with his auditors as men like Gladstone had been able to do, nevertheless, he could not be directly heckled, or interrupted, or lynched. The path of timid men with small voices was made smoother.

In the film *Neville Chamberlain*, we have an opportunity to see a politician feeling for the right style to suit the film medium, trying himself out in an unfamiliar context. As chairman of the Conservative party and its Research Department from 1930, Chamberlain had direct responsibility for party propaganda, and was quick to appreciate the use of film. 'When he decided to explain the purpose and outlines of his first budget directly to the people through the newsreels, he not only initiated a practice which soon became a tradition but may also be said to have inaugurated a process of change in the relationship between the government and the governed which has not yet run its course' (Ref. 9).

The first two film items, Chamberlain on the Labour budget of 1931 and on his 1932 tariff bill, are very early examples of the politician grappling with sound film. The first piece was made a few months after the introduction of sound newsreels into Britain; the second 'is thought to have been the first occasion upon which a Chancellor of the Exchequer explained in a newsreel a financial measure of first-class importance, and is in that sense the forerunner of the televised ministerial broadcasts now familiar to us' (Ref. 10). Both show Chamberlain's unfamiliarity with the medium, seeming very stiff and static. The contrast introduced by his budget talk of 1936 is quite remarkable. Here is a distinctly theatrical, contrived performance, with the contrivance aiming to produce an effect of informality. There is greater bodily and facial mobility, and an effort at a direct, chatty approach, rounded off by the mixed mateyness and patrician condescension of the final 'it isn't such a bad budget after all'.

How much of this was Chamberlain and how much the 'producers'? It is hard to say. Certainly, Conservative politicians could usually rely on sympathetic production from the newsreel companies, especially Movietone and British Gaumont. Movietone's British chiefs, Sanger, Craig, and Campbell, were of Conservative inclination, and the company co-operated with the Conservative Central Office in many ways, including the provision of projection personnel for Conservative election candidates. Item seven in the film, the National Government rally at Cardiff, 1939, made by Movietone, was intended for use by Central Office in the mobile cinema vans (Ref. 11). Nevertheless, Chamberlain was not necessarily safe from a bad production job, as his talk on public health, etc., in item four reveals. This 1937 piece is stylistically a marked retrogression from the 1936 budget talk, showing Chamberlain in the more formal style derived from the platform, doing a very self-conscious set-piece, gazing up as though the script were written on the ceiling or something nasty were emerging from the chandelier. At least, however, the film does have the interest of contrasting, even if crudely, Chamberlain's political style with that of Franco, Mussolini, and Hitler. He did not much care for his own performance when he saw it: 'My voice appeared to me to be so distorted as to be unrecognisable and if I had not previously seen the person who addressed us from the screen I should call him pompous, insufferably slow in diction and unspeakably repellent in person!' (Ref. 12).

If we try to separate from the general characteristics of political style in the 1930s and its projection via film the special qualities of Chamberlain himself, what comes out most clearly is perhaps his difficulty in self-projection to the democracy, his shyness and lack of facility in adopting the common touch. One sees what his biographer, Iain Macleod (Ref. 13), meant in writing: 'His mastery of facts, his incisive intelligence, and the tough austerity and confidence of his bearing, were apparent enough. But lack of colour, or *panache*, or even eccentricity, and a temperamental inability to project very deep emotions or appeal to the heart or rouse a rabble, gave the impression of an altogether plainer and bleaker man than is remembered by his family or the few friends who knew him best'. The film gives us the public, not the private man, and the attempts at relaxation are not always happy. But one receives a formidable impression of energy and will from a man already sixty-seven at the time of the 1936 budget talk.

The fact that what we are seeing is the public image emphasises the importance of the material as a record of how Chamberlain was presented to the cinema-going public, at a time when the newsreels were possibly the most effective means of reaching a mass audience. At this period, there were some eighteen to twenty million cinema admissions weekly. Just how much attention cinema audiences paid to newsreels, except at moments of crisis, is arguable, but clearly the newsreel was potentially an important influence on public opinion. The most striking case in the film of the deliberate use of the newsreel to influence public reactions is item five, the special post-Munich issue of Gaumont British News, which works strenuously to put over the image of Chamberlain the peacemaker. This represented very much the official line: when Paramount sought to put out a newsreel issue critical of the Munich settlement, strong pressure was brought to bear by the government to stop it. But one might well also see in the Gaumont British reel and in the scenes it depicts additional evidence for the existence of a widespread sense of public relief and gratitude to Chamberlain in October 1938.

How far the film presentation modified or, alternatively, reinforced Chamberlain's public image it is hard to estimate in the absence of contemporary study of audience response. It may have done something to render him less cold and remote. Apparently, the 1936 talk won some applause in the cinemas, and led one newspaper to compare him to Groucho Marx, which stimulated him to find out who that gentleman was (Ref. 14). But the claim of the makers of the film is rightly cautious: 'It is more than possible that Chamberlain's careful use, indeed cultivation, of this penetrating medium, his directness and simplicity, helped to convey his sincere concern for social reform and for international peace and thus contributed to the powerful public support which he received in 1938' (Ref. 15).

The tentative nature of such a statement points up the difficulties of studying film as an operative factor in politics, influencing the content and reception of political messages and acting as a presumptively powerful determinant of public opinion. The analysis of political style and its communication on film cannot be a simple matter; but a consideration of *Neville Chamberlain* helps both to illustrate the sort of material available for such an analysis and to suggest some of the ways in which it can be approached. It is very much to be hoped that the corpus of film material readily accessible to researchers and teachers for the study of the evolution of modern political forms will be progressively enlarged, so that the visual dimension can receive the attention from political scientists which some models, at least, of political process would seem to require.

NOTES AND REFERENCES

1. S.M. Lyman and M.B. Scott (1975) *The Drama of Social Reality*, New York; and M. Cranston (12 November 1976) *The Theatre of Politics*, B.B.C. Radio 3 Programme.

2. For a recent treatment of the theatrical element in the new political style developed by German National Socialism, see G.L. Mosse (1975) *The Nationalization of the Masses: Political Symbolism and Mass Movements in Germany from the Napoleonic Wars through the Third Reich*, New York.

3. J.R. Vincent (1967) *Pollbooks: How Victorians Voted*, 47, Cambridge.

4. See the tariff reform sketch, *John Bull's Hearth* (1903), available from the Higher Education Film Library on the same reel as the 1931 Conservative party cartoon, *The Right Spirit*.

5. See, for example, the extracts of all four assembled on the reel *Personalities of the 30's* (Higher Education Film Library).

6. Alan Beattie, David Dilks, and Nicholas Pronay (1975) *Neville Chamberlain* (with accompanying booklet), Inter-University History Film Consortium, Archive series no. 1. Among comparable efforts by historians and political scientists to assemble film material for the study of politics and politicians may be noted the film documents of the Weimar period edited by the Institut für den Wissenschaftlichen Film, Göttingen, and Dr. R.L. Schuursma's (1966) *Anton Mussert*, Stichting Film en Wetenschap and Universitaire Film, Utrecht. The writer has not seen J.-N. Jeanneney's *Le discours et la cravate: Image et comportement des hommes politiques à la Télévision Française* (Institut National de l'Audio-Visuel). The work on the West German election of 1972 described in this volume by Stig Hornshøj-Møller represents a further step, the deliberate creation of film records for the purposes of political studies.

7. P. Thompson (1967) *Socialists, Liberals and Labour: the Struggle for London 1885-1914*, 77, London.

8. Beattie, Dilks and Pronay, *op. cit.*, 4. (Booklet)

9. *Ibid.*, 5.

10. *Ibid.*, 8

11. *Ibid.*, 19; and N. Pronay, The Newsreels: the illusion of actuality, in P. Smith (Ed.) (1976) *The Historian and Film*, 118, n. 24, Cambridge.

12. Beattie, Dilks and Pronay, *op. cit.*, 12.

13. I. Macleod (1961) *Neville Chamberlain*, 202, London.

14. Beattie, Dilks and Pronay, *op. cit.*, 10-11.

15. *Ibid.*, 5.

Film as a Teaching Resource: the Possibilities of Using Film in American Government and Politics Courses

Philip J. Davies

The use of feature films in a syllabus has generally been restricted to examination of their artistic merit. Acting, photography and directing are examined minutely by students in Arts Faculties. At the same time use of feature films in non-Arts subjects often meets with opposition. Many social scientists see such 'fiction' as being in no way part of their data set, and some artists contend that films may only be understood after intimate study of genre, directorial style, and frame-by-frame analysis. Given this scepticism, as well as the problems of financing a film-based course, the opportunities to experiment with such a form of teaching have not been widespread. However, a course using feature films in Government and Politics teaching has been offered at the University of Maryland (College Park), USA since 1974 and a workshop 'Film and Politics/Politics and the Cinema' has been repeated annually since 1974 under the direction of its originator, Dr James Glass (Ref. 1).

The workshop course offered at Maryland University was concerned with the use of films as a way of speaking and thinking about political theory and philosophy. The course lasted for three weeks of the summer school session, with one film being shown each day. After each film the participants took a short break, subsequently meeting in discussion groups of fifteen to eighteen persons, each being led by a teaching assistant. The teaching assistant's function consisted of facilitating discussion and not in 'telling' the students which 'messages' appeared in the film. Each of the teaching assistants had some background in political theory, generally as part of their current M.A. and Ph.D. programmes. The discussions were timetabled to last for one hour, but frequently went beyond this time as the groups were sometimes eager to explore the ideas stimulated by the film and discussion at greater length.

The course relied completely on commercial, feature-length productions. One propaganda 'documentary', *The Truth About Communism*, an extreme right wing analysis introduced by A.F. Kerensky, and narrated by Ronald Reagan, was the only departure from the feature film format. This film elicited little response and has been dropped in later courses. The films shown were:-

1974	1975
Mickey One	The Prime of Miss Jean Brodie
Cries and Whispers	They Shoot Horses, Don't They?

Philip J. Davies is Lecturer in the Department of American Studies, University of Manchester, UK. This paper was presented in slightly different form at the 1977 annual meeting of the American Politics Group of the Political Studies Association.

Rock Around the Clock
The Truth About Communism
Weekend
The Life of Emile Zola
Z
Nothing But A Man
Lord of the Flies
The Prime of Miss Jean Brodie
They Shoot Horses, Don't They?
Burn (Queimada)
The Liberation of L.B. Jones
The Conformist
Marat/Sade
The Music Lovers

Burn (Queimada)
The Liberation of L.B. Jones
The Conformist
Marat/Sade
The Music Lovers
If
The Picture of Dorian Gray
Midnight Cowboy
Trial
The Discreet Charm of the Bourgeoisie
The Autobiography of Miss Jane Pittman
Clockwork Orange
Love and Anarchy
Deliverance
The Exterminating Angel
King of Hearts
Devils

Since the three school weeks available for the course only allowed fifteen 'film slots' some of the above were shown in the evening as 'optional extras'.

On the 1974 course the students could be registered for varying amounts of credit. Assessment was by a final essay examination at the end of the course, and a term paper due three weeks after the end of the course. Three books were set for the course: *Marat/Sade* by Peter Weiss; *The Balcony* by Jean Genet; *Collected Short Stories* by Franz Kafka. According to the 1974 syllabus, 'each (book) embod(ies) a symbology of political and interpersonal relationships, presented through dramatic or highly symbolic content....The readings should complement the films and give an additional dimension to the discussions'. For extra credit a longer paper with reference to a variety of other books was required. In 1975 'an informal oral examination' was added (Ref. 2). No specific essay topics were set. Students were encouraged to develop themes and ideas in consultation with their teaching assistants, based on their own involvement with the films and discussions.

The workshop was in some ways an attempt to provide experiential stimuli to the participants, encouraging them to structure the received symbols and information into some comprehensive conceptual form. An attempt was consciously being made to break away from conventional lecturing techniques, which inhibit participation, and from behavioural-quantitative approaches, which were the dominant teaching form. Gerald Hopple (Ref. 3) says, 'Behavioral-quantitative teaching approaches are limited by their inability to transcend the constraints which are imposed by dominant paradigms and frameworks. The social scientific perspective provides data and tools for analysis but almost invariably fails to confront the questions which are not susceptible to precise measurement. Furthermore, conventional pedagogic techniques transform the student into a passive subject and do not encourage genuine dialogue'. The aims of the pedagogic form then, though unusual, were not spectacularly so. Many colleges offer courses relating politics and the novel, with similar aims in mind, and one has seen an increasing introduction of tangential literature in standard 'modern political thought' courses (e.g. Sigmund Freud, Marquis de Sade, R.D. Laing). In the United States the prolonged debate over the significance of Thomas Kuhn (Ref. 4) *The Structure of Scientific Revolutions* is fuelled by such approaches. The proponents of such courses often agree with Kuhn that the current paradigms of political science will almost inevitably be supported by tests conducted along the methodological lines acceptable within the terms of those paradigms, and that a conscious effort must therefore be made to advance political thought by means of alternative methodologies. In the United Kingdom it might be more fashionable to rely upon Edward de Bono's theories of lateral thinking, which again advocate the employment of unusual stimuli to confront familiar problems. Certainly a case can be made that the use of film in this way, though unconventional, is an extension of existing techniques and theories.

The experiential nature of the film workshop was preferred by J.M. Glass and G. Steuernagel (Ref. 5) especially as a method designed to pursue their own interests in the possible connections between Psychoanalytic Theory and Political Theory. Basing their model on the precepts of Jungian psychology, these two leading members of the teaching team explore the problems of the communication of symbols - a process they see as needing sensual stimuli interracting with the unconscious. This Jungian 'methodology' is called by J.M. Glass 'Political Theory as Recovery of Unconscious Archetypes', and in his paper he explores the contrasts between this proposed form of investigation as the development of awareness, and the rationalist approach which 'lacks awareness but is highly competent in technique' (Ref. 6). 'Images "open up" the self, the *gestalt* effect of the film "loosens" awareness and the students become receptive to those symbolizations of experience evident through representation in images. When the students therefore "feel" the concept, when it is internalised as an association rooted in the self-structure, it makes sense. It is not just cognitively apprehended; it is not an exercise in a classroom, but an activity in the world, in the student's experience' (Ref. 7).

This statement of the film's powerful sensory impression in no way depends on J.M. Glass and G. Steuernagel's psychoanalytic theory. It expresses a similar belief to that of Marshall McLuhan (Ref. 8) when he says he considers the cinema to be 'a hot medium, high definition, and concentrated'. I.C. Jarvie (Ref. 9), in his book *Movies and Society* goes on, 'The cinema, I believe, is a total environment medium, and the wider the screen and louder the sound, the more the sense one has of being swallowed up in it. It is a medium in which we talk of identifying with those who appear, and what happens to them on the screen.' In the same vein Ralph Stephenson and J.R. Debrix in their book *The Cinema as Art* say, '(film) brings us face to face with reality, or with something that looks like reality, in a compulsive, actual way' (Ref. 10). 'When we watch a film, it is just something that is happening - now.... The immediacy of what a film shows consequently surpasses anything in other arts, and it can have a tenseness and pace that literature cannot match' (Ref. 11). They do point out that film also presents the new problem of 'film literacy'. Films of a different country may seem too slow, or too fast, or too stylised to an audience unused to the particular conventions. In using American films the problem of cultural difference is reduced, but there may still be difficulties when using the films of a previous generation. Changes in convention may produce a sense of unreality. It would seem best to avoid such films unless they are directly relevant to the course. On the other hand the regular use of film would probably 'innoculate' the audience against the temptation to laugh at unfamiliar conventions as media literacy developed. At the same time a familiarised audience will be increasingly able to recognise and comprehend the use of the wide variety of film techniques that allow the development of useful and telling visual metaphors.

There have always been commentators who have believed films to have considerable impact on the audiences, although the fears expressed by Donald Ramsey Young in 1922 were more to do with the social situation of the cinema-going than with the films' content: 'Social standards are influenced by motion pictures ... and ... by the fact that the audience, often young boys and girls, are packed in narrow seats, close together, in a darkened room' (Ref. 12). Exactly twenty years later U.E. Harding was even more vehement: 'We are defaming our morals, corrupting our youth, inflaming our young people, exciting passion, debauching our children, making prostitutes and criminals through picture-going!' (Ref. 13). However, there is little contemporary research on the educational use of feature films. The work of F. Fearing has suggested that some significant effects may result from viewing films, but he was, as were most experimenters, concerned primarily with a variety of 'training' or 'propaganda' films. One 1954 article (Ref. 14) does claim that perception of the media is an 'active' response, whereby the audience seeks to place their experience in a cognitive framework. Furthermore, since all communication content is to some extent ambiguous, clear and direct messages, as in propaganda, and perhaps educational films, may be stolidly rejected.

In the absence of a comprehensive body of research I have to return to the Maryland course. The teaching team with which I worked agreed that the discussion groups were of a very high standard, with over 80% attendance, and almost all students became involved in the discussions at some time. G. Steuernagel (Ref. 15) also points out that 'At the very least ... the "I didn't get a chance to read it" excuse is eliminated', a fact which is really not so trivial, since it encouraged the groups to discuss the piece of literature which they knew they had all shared. This spontaneity of response may have been in part due to the fact that the discussions followed immediately after the films, rather than on a later day. A film course taught at Lanchester Polytechnic, where timetabling put the film and discussion a week apart, did not produce the same heights of involvement. Nevertheless the Lanchester course (Ref. 16) was well attended (both at the films and the week later discussions), and appeared to increase the amount of student involvement in discussions.

Gerald Hopple conducted a questionnaire study of the 1974 and 1975 Maryland courses, as well as reading a selection of the students essays. The latter, he says: '... did tend to show that the film medium can be an effective technique for eliciting reactions to pervasive political themes, such as the meaning of freedom, the role of choices in politics, the impact of estrangement from self and society, the clash between inner and external-political realities, and the relationship between objective oppression and internal repression' (Ref. 17). But the most striking aspect of Hopple's study is the immense student enthusiasm that it uncovered. The response rate to the 1975 questionnaire was 67%. Of these, 87% evaluated the course as 'very good', or 'one of the best I have ever taken': 89% claimed to have 'enjoyed the course more than most courses'. Asked to compare the course with others taken at the University 45% rated the course as 'excellent' and 45% as 'very good'. Compared with other Government and Politics courses 81% claimed the film course to be 'better than most other courses' (Ref. 18).

There may be doubts about such a high evaluation, in terms of return bias, and the respondent answering in a manner he or she considers appropriate in terms of the researcher's expectations. The return rate of 67% is however a high one, and the guarantee of anonimity should prevent severe bias of the second kind. Furthermore, alternative techniques, as G. Hopple (Ref. 19) points out, are not perfect. The general conclusion offered by Hopple (Ref. 20), '...is that all types of students were affected by the course -- or at least attributed influence to the course. As a group, self-identified political liberals were somewhat more prone to evaluate the course positively and assert that the course affected them. But the strength of this tendency should not be exaggerated.' The response may also be exaggerated because of the novelty of using film, although 29% of the students had taken part in other film courses and their responses were not significantly different from the rest of the group. That any potential educational resource should elicit such overwhelming enthusiasm from students should persuade us of the potential success of that resource if a favourable context can be found. Nevertheless there is still room for the exercise of considerable care in using films.

A. Marwick (Ref. 21) expresses certain fears as to the woolliness of claims that film leads to new perceptions and intuitions which cannot be pinned down, and is especially worried about film work becoming 'smart cocktail chat or high flown woffle'. This clearly expresses the reluctance, to which I alluded earlier, of social scientists to accept the use of feature films in their field. The documentary is generally more used by political scientists, yet the danger of documentary is that it claims a relationship to the 'truth'. The feature film does not make such a claim; indeed, in *Buffalo Bill and the Indians* the feature film has even provided a document to encourage sceptical thought about the images we receive. Marwick's doubts lead him to propose (Ref. 23) three 'fundamental principles' to teachers wishing to use film.

1. ....before introducing a programme of film material, the organiser of the programme should clearly state his aims and objectives in so doing.

2. ....all film material should be integrated firmly into a specific teaching context: in other words the film should not merely be an optional extra, but, ... its relevance to the students' course of studies should be made abundantly plain. (e.g. film must be included in any assessment methods.)

3. ....every film, ...should be presented with the maximum of relevant information. (e.g. who made it, when, where, and why it is being shown).

These criteria are not too surprising. In fact they could be equally applied to any form of course material, which should surely be integrated into the course with particular aims in mind, and with as little mystification as possible. The second 'fundamental principle' is often not followed when films are part of a course. They seem to be generally considered as adjuncts to the 'real' course, not for serious consideration. In taking this attitude teachers are losing the potential of the resource which to a great extent relies on the active response of an audience to the film, not a passive viewing. In a course on American politics there would clearly have to be integration of relevant films with lectures and reading, but a course which did not attempt to integrate the unusual resource into the assessment would inevitably be a purely conventional course, with ineffective frills.

There will be a major difference between the use of film in political theory teaching and in any American Politics courses. In the former, both the course and the film are speaking to the same thing - the expression of concept(s) or idea(s) in some communicable form. Whether the film's symbolic content arouses archetypal reaction from the student, whether the ideas are in the film because the director put them there, or whether striking political concepts have appeared in the final copy of the film by an accident of its communal production matters little or nothing as long as there are significant problems of political thought expressed in the film. It is not so clear that the use of films relating to a nation's politics can be so abstract. I wish tentatively to suggest some uses of film which might contribute to a specifically American course.

Firstly there is the portrayal of political institutions and environments. The dramatic presentation of political institutions in action can add considerably to the observer's understanding of those institutions. Most educational and training films are notoriously bad: 'People are expected to ignore a film's badness for the sake of the allegedly more important purpose which it serves' (Ref. 24). The Open University in particular has been trying hard and with major successes to develop screen teaching methods, but, in my experience, even these very high quality educational films do not always maintain interest in a non-Open University class. On the other hand, when a commercial film producer bothers with political affairs the resulting film has the advantages of high budget, quality filming, often in colour, convincing acting, and so on. A film such as *The Best Man* can give an audience with some book knowledge of Convention practice a much more vivid comprehension of Convention politics and manoeuvring. *Advise and Consent*, though somewhat out of date, shows some of the forms of appointment and Senate committee workings in a clear and understandable manner. *Tora, Tora, Tora, Fail-Safe,* and *Dr Strangelove* each in their own individual way examine the process of decision making in government. Each of these films could be used to add depth to the students' knowledge of United

States politics. If well integrated into a course, with supportive reading and lectures I believe the understanding gained from the course would be increased; and if the political theory courses mentioned above are a fair indication, there should be a considerable amount of student participation encouraged by the addition of films.

Unfortunately for the most part Hollywood movies have avoided controversial topics, and political topics are almost inevitably controversial. Herbert Gans (Ref. 25) attributes this to the studio system's reluctance to narrow the audience for a film. In his estimation, Hollywood ignored the pluralist make up of society, and therefore did not make films to appeal to minorities - whether defined by tastes, demography, or political interest. He also suggests that the post war rise in the number of independent producers may rectify this imbalance. Certainly two recent films starring Robert Redford, *The Candidate* and *All The President's Men*, are hopeful signs.

By broadening this category to include 'political environments' however there are a number of other films that can prove valuable. For example the contemporary American fears of urban decay are expressed powerfully in *Midnight Cowboy, Taxi Driver* and a number of other films. Problems of the breakdown of urban services are central to *The Hospital* and *Serpico*. Intergenerational conflict forms the major theme of *Joe* and *Taking Off*. The themes of many such films are political sociology rather than the 'government' aspect of politics, but in choosing the relevant literature the teacher guides the course, and these films form a corpus of relevant literature.

My second category is of films valuable to a thematic approach. Since movies are complex and multifaceted forms they cannot be expected to fall exclusively into one category. For example the problem of racism may be examined in some courses as part of the contemporary political environment, in others as an historical theme of U.S. political life. Either way *Sounder, The Liberation of L.B. Jones, Nothing But a Man,* and *The Autobiography of Miss Jane Pittman* are films that could be useful in examining American racial conventions and tensions, and possible black responses. *They Shoot Horses, Don't They?* is an example of a film that may be read on quite different levels - either as an interpretation of the Depression years, or as a debate on the role of monopoly capital in American society. *Mickey One* might be a film about gangsterism, but is more likely to provide a response if one is examining alienation in American society.

The Western is a genre which produces quite a few sidelong glances at political and social themes. The use of genre can be quite significant for our purposes. To build an unfamiliar background, as for example in *Gone With the Wind* or *Streetcar Named Desire* takes a great deal of work, but to place a film in a Western genre (or Gangster genre, etc.) 'takes only a few suggestive strokes' (Ref. 26), freeing the writers and directors to explore diverse problems. Westerns have been examined for their relevance to chivalric codes and lawlessness (Ref. 27); as examples of the American attitude to culture and individual and national experience (Ref. 28); as individualism in action, the American closeness to nature, and the revolt against powerlessness in a world of machines (Ref. 29); as indicators of an American military tradition, and the democratic principle that the good hero wins if he holds out long engough (Ref. 30); and as vehicles of just, individualistic, anti-urban values (Ref. 31). An attempt has even been made to analyse Westerns in terms of the Presidential styles they are said to best reflect (Ref. 32). Conflicts over law, order, and justice form a distinctive part of this genre, and films such as *The Man Who Shot Liberty Vallance* explore that theme, using the debate at the same time to examine the conflict between Eastern 'urban' and Western 'farmer' values. The more recent 'cop' films also examine the potential conflicts between justice and 'law and order' in *Magnum Force, Dirty Harry*, and the like, where the individual good cop is seen as hamstrung by liberal Supreme Court decisions. Regional clashes of lifestyle and values are rarely presented with as much impact as in *Lonely Are The Brave*. A more ambiguous evaluation of traditional farming values is presented in *The Last Picture Show*'s vision of an agricultural community in decline.

One is tempted to use the Western as historical evidence, but this would clearly be a dangerous move. Historical fact is often sacrificed to dramatic content in a commercial film, and whereas the themes and debates within the work may still be immensely valuable, the 'story' must always be taken as a vehicle for the debate, not as fact (Ref. 33). Some films are praised for their verisimilitude; for example *Guns in the Afternoon*, of the Westerns, is reputed to portray a gold-rush town with surprising and stark reality. Furthermore, recent films such as *Tora, Tora, Tora,* and *All the President's Men* have been painstaking efforts to reconstruct particular events, what Swallow (Ref. 34) calls 'dramatised documentary'. But the existence of a few such excellent examples should not lead the teacher into treating other films with the same faith.

My third category concerns the use of films to examine the political ideas and conflicts of a chronological period. The approach would be to take a number of films made in a particular time span and examine them, comparing them with each other and relating the political ideas to the contemporary political scene. This may overlap to some extent with the currently expanding field of Cultural Studies, but it seems to me that a predominantly political analysis along such lines can be valuable, and that films may have particular significance for some such studies. For example, in the 1930s Hollywood appeared to discover sociology. Social problems, urban decay and gangsterism were sometimes allowed to have social roots. Warner Brothers, in particular, moved into the newspaper tradition of the exposé as, for example, in that studio's production of some of William Wellman movies, though in general targets were disguised (Ref. 35). W. Hughes, who is generally sceptical of the use of films, nevertheless sees value in the use of film 'for the history of opinions' (Ref. 36), giving as an example *The Grapes of Wrath* (1939) which, he says, 'provides us with a set of important contemporary opinions on (the) problems (of the American Depression and the plight of migrating workers)', while F. Isaksson and L. Furhammar (Ref. 37), in their book *Politics and Film*, claim that the films of the New Deal were typified by optimism, they also pick out *Grapes of Wrath* as an example of a hard hitting film. This film's impact is considered by the Editors of *Cahiers du Cinéma* (Ref. 38) to be the response of the Republican-controlled studio 20th Century Fox, and the studio's Republican Managing Director, Darryl F. Zanuck, to the faltering New Deal.

Another period about which film can provide a stimulating debate is the years of the House Un-American Activities Committee. The Committee, under the Chairmanship of J. Parnell Thomas, was quick to pinpoint the film industry for its investigations of Communist influence on American life. The subsequent investigations, and blacklisting of 'premature anti-Fascists' is a significant part of the Cold War hysteria. The film industry, being part of, not just a commentator upon, this era, produced movies which could be profitably shown on any course dealing with the period. An example of Hollywood's most extreme reaction is provided by *I Married a Communist (The Woman on Pier 13)*, a film produced at R.K.O. through the determination of Howard Hughes, who had to offer the film to fourteen directors to find one who would take it on. *Invasion of the Body Snatchers* is an allegorical story of a village gradually overtaken by beings characterised by their heartlessness, lack of warmth, callous murdering habits, sameness of opinion and sneaky, underhand methods. There may be some argument about whether the director was attacking Communists or McCarthyites, but that the film is a political document is not in doubt. *On the Waterfront*, quite apart from any potential it may have in connection with its picture of industrial relations, is also a statement on the morality of exposing corruption to government investigators. The director, Elia Kazan, had been one of the 'friendly witnesses' during the Thomas committee's investigations.

If one is going to use film in this way it is important to limit one's claims. To investigate the political ideas of the *films* of an era is not necessarily to examine the political ideas *of* that era. There is undoubtedly a connection, but to make the step from the former to the latter must necessitate some considerable knowledge of the sociology of the film industry. The films of an era may provide excellent stimuli to the study of the time, giving life to the problems and debates that were reflected on film, but they may not put all the sides, or even face all the major problems. Claims cannot be made that they represent solely the views of the directors, writers, Hollywood, or the public without more background work on the industry itself. This in no way undermines the value of films, it is just one of the pitfalls of the technique. Careful choice of films may rectify the major studios' imbalance of production; integration with other forms of literature and with lectures can fill any substantial gaps (though my guess is that there would not be many gaps to fill). Also, a course which included a discussion of the industry may be very valuable. The film industry was at one time the third largest in the country, and it has a history of connections with national and California politics. A course which looked at these factors, plus the problems of communications and the use of, and influences on, media, and which at the same time examined the products of those media, would cover a wide variety of important political and sociological themes.

The feature film cannot be used indiscriminately - it is all too easy to convince oneself that every film has *some* relevance to politics - but carefully chosen examples from this massive literature can be used with excellent results if integrated into relevant courses. The study of United States politics is particularly well served since that country has produced, and continues to produce, a large number of films from which to choose. It seems likely though that the studios and producers of other countries (Godard, Bertolucci, Sembene) have produced material which would fit into other courses. A well conceived use of such film may bring political institutions, themes, and conflicts into the experience of a student with a power that printed media can rarely achieve.

REFERENCES

1. The essay stems directly from my teaching on the workshop course at Maryland in 1974 and on a less ambitious 'Film and Political Ideas' course I was able to run at Lanchester Polytechnic, Coventry in 1975-6. Many of the details about the Maryland film course are taken from the following papers by members of the teaching team: Gertrude Steuernagel and James M. Glass (April 1976) *Films and Political Concepts: Psychoanalytic Theory and Its Relationship to the Study of Political Theory*, presented at the Midwest Political Science Meeting, Chicago; Gerald W. Hopple (April 1976) *The Use of Film in Teaching Political Theory: A Questionnaire Study*, presented at the Midwest Political Science Association meeting, Chicago. The first of these papers is written in sections, each author having written separate sections. When referring to this paper below I have mentioned the name of the individual responsible for the section to which I am referring. These papers have been very useful in the preparation of my own piece. If however I have at any point misrepresented their analysis the fault is entirely mine.

2. Glass, *op. cit.*, 2.

3. Hopple, *op. cit.*, 2.

4. Thomas S. Kuhn (1962) *The Structure of Scientific Revolutions*, University of Chicago Press, Chicago.

5. G. Steuernagel and J.M. Glass, *op. cit.*

6. Glass, *op. cit.*, 26.

7. *Ibid.*, 21

8. Quoted in I.C. Jarvie (1970) *Movies and Society* Basic Books, New York, 220. (This book contains a lengthy annotated bibliography on pp 229-366).

9. *Ibid.*

10. Ralph Stephenson and J.R. Debrix (1974) *The Cinema As Art*, Penguin Books, Harmondsworth, 28.

11. *Ibid.*, 101.

12. D.R. Young (1922) *Motion Pictures*, 6, Philadelphia. Quoted in I.C. Jarvie, *op. cit.*, 365.

13. U.E. Harding (1942) *Movie - Mad America*, Grand Rapids. Quoted in I.C. Jarvie, *op. cit.*, 284.

14. F. Fearing, Social Impact of the Mass Media of Communication, in N.B. Henry (1954) *Mass Media and Education*, Chicago. Quoted in I.C. Jarvie, *op. cit.*, 269.

15. Steuernagel, *op. cit.*, 14.

16. This course is not examined in detail since it was specifically aimed at *non* Social Scientists, in fact Modern Language students, to persuade them to discuss social and political theories. Though supposedly compulsory, the course was not assessed, and 'success' was measured in terms of managing to keep any of the class attending at all. The introduction of films into the second half of the course improved attendance and improved the amount and thoughtfulness of discussion contribution. The films shown were: *NADA; WR - Mysteries of the Organism; The Balcony; Family Life; Taking Off; Joe; Fahrenheit 451.*

17. Hopple, *op. cit.*, p. 12.

18. *Ibid.*, 23.

19. *Ibid.*, 37.

20. *Ibid.*, 40.

21. A. Marwick, Film in University Teaching, in P. Smith (ed. 1976) *The Historian and Film* Cambridge University Press, Cambridge.

22. *Ibid.*, 151.

23. *Ibid.*

24. Jarvie, *op. cit.*, 179.

25. *Ibid*, 36-7.

26. *Ibid.*, 144.

27. F. Woods, Hot Guns and Cold Women, *Films and Filming 5* (1959). Quoted in I.C. Jarvie *op. cit.*, 365.

28. J. Pratt, In Defense of the Western, *Films and Filming 1*, (1954). Quoted in I.C. Jarvie *op. cit.*, 329.

29. M. Nussbaum, Sociological Symbolism of the 'Adult Western' *Social Forces 39* (1960). Quoted in I.C. Jarvie, *op. cit.*, 323.

30. H.L. Jacobson, Cowboy, Pioneer and American Soldier, *Sight and Sound 22*, (1953). Quoted in I.C. Jarvie, *op. cit.*, 296.

31. F. Elkin, The Psychological Appeal of the Hollywood Western, *Journal of Educational Sociology 24*, (1950). Quoted in I.C. Jarvie, *op. cit.*, 263.

32. P. French, *Westerns*, Viking Press: reviewed by Tom Flinn in *The Velvet Light Trap* 12, 40 (Spring 1974).

33. W. Hughes, The Evaluation of Film as Evidence, in P. Smith (1976) *op. cit.*, 49-79.

34. N. Swallow, Television, the Integrity of Fact and Fiction, *Sight and Sound 45*, no. 3, 183-185 (Summer 1976).

35. R. Campbell, Wild Bill's Wild Boys, *The Velvet Light Trap 15*, 1 (Fall 1970) G. Klein, Wellman's 'Wild Boys of the Road', *The Velvet Light Trap 15*, 2-6 (Fall 1970).

36. Hughes: *op. cit.*

37. F. Isaksson and L. Furhammar (1971) *Politics and Film*, Studio Vista Publishers, London.

38. The Editors of Cahiers du Cinema, John Ford's 'Young Mr. Lincoln', printed in translation *Screen 13*, no. 3, 5-47 (Autumn 1972).

Film Analysis — the Structural Approach

Karsten Fledelius

INTRODUCTION

To the political and social historian as to the social scientist wanting to use film in research and teaching, film is not just 'film'. The scholar tends naturally to concentrate on the most factual material which in the case of film will mean newsreels, film reports, and the more factual of the films marked with the 'documentary' label. Unquestionably, factual film possesses a larger degree of credibility regarding the objects or persons referred to than any more or less fictional filmic treatment, but first of all it should be remembered that many films are a mixture of factual shots originating from real events, shots made of reenactments or reconstructions of real events, factual shots used to illustrate another event than the one they originated in, and shots of purely fictional events. To 'sift' a so-called documentary, for instance, in order to find out which shots can be considered authentic traces of the events referred to in the film and which not, is a laborious task. And for the scholar looking for authentic traces of real events the feature film normally falls completely out of consideration.

This sort of analysis, which in the expression of one of its foremost theorists, Niels Skyum-Nielsen (Ref. 1) from the University of Copenhagen, may be called the *documentality analysis*, is not, however, the only possible approach to the problem for film in historical and social science research and education. If films are treated as communicative sources conveying a message from a certain sender (or group of senders) to a more or less definite group of receivers, but at the same time containing a lot of more or less 'unwitting testimony', to use a phrase of Arthur Marwick's (Ref. 2), about their situation of origin, quite another strategy of analysis has to be used which puts its emphasis not so much on the relation between film and depicted reality as on the relation between the inherent possibilities of meaning in the film, with on one side its situation of origin, on the other side its situation of reception. In this case the significance of the documentality aspect is reduced; in fact it could be maintained that the less factual or 'documental' the film shots are, the better they illuminate, for example, the intentions of the film makers. It might be maintained that the more 'trivial' a feature film is, the more it reflects of the expected attitudes and tastes of the intended audience (Ref. 3).

Karsten Fledelius is Senior Lecturer in the Historical Institute of the University of Copenhagen.

The analysis of the inherent potential of meaning in a film (of what could be called the *spectrum of possible meanings* (Ref. 4)) demands two separate, but inevitably somewhat interconnected approaches, the 'structural analysis approach' and the 'sign analysis approach'. The former deals with what constitutes the 'macro-plane' of the film, the larger unities of meaning. The latter deals with the single units of meaning within visuals and sound track, the 'micro-plane' of the film. This contribution will concentrate on the former, the latter deserving a contribution of its own. It should not be forgotten, however, that a complete analysis of a film demands a combination of both approaches. The reason for starting with the structural analysis is that it is a comparatively simple form of analysis, governed by a limited number of principles and therefore easier to 'objectivise', whereas the sign analysis is often exceedingly complicated and strongly influenced by subjective interpretation; it therefore seems to be the safest and most profitable procedure to start with the film whole and analyse its composition, thus procuring the 'syntactical framework' for the analysis of the micro-level. A method to approach this 'syntax' of the film has been provided by Christian Metz (Ref. 5), whose system is based upon the *syntagma*, which for him denotes the smallest independent unity of the film's progress. To him a film can be described as a combination of syntagmas belonging to various categories; each such category can be characterized by some overruling structural principle. In the beginning we were rather sceptical with respect to the validity and usefulness of this system, but through the practical application of it in connection with the analysis of a Danish information film about modern Greenland (*Sisimiut*, Jørgen Roos, 1966) the original scepticism was gradually superseded by a growing conviction that, at least in connection with this film, the system made it possible to define the film's means of expression much more precisely and to get a better idea of its general structure (together with a better prospect for evaluating the 'spectrum of possible meaning', the values, and the attitudes) than any other analytical approach we know about. Naturally that does not mean that we believe that we have found *the* method for the historical or social science analysis of film - which ought, in my opinion, to be a combination of several methodical angles of approach - but I would not refrain from considering it one of the most promising forms of analysis concerning audio-visual media products which has thus far been developed.

THE BASIC CHARACTER OF METZ'S SYNTAGMATIC ANALYSIS

What is it that separates this form of analysis from others hitherto known and used? Let us first look at the similarities. Nearly all film analysis methods used up till now have, as Metz's, in one way or another originated in the basic idea of the film as a system of expression, a language, and attempted to approach that 'film language' with methods identical with (or at least analogous to) linguistic methods of analysis. The quantitative 'content analysis' is represented within film research by the German sociologist Gerd Albrecht, among others (Ref. 6); the qualitative analysis traditions on the other hand fall clearly into two groups which one could call the 'extroverted' and the 'introverted'. The former, which is rather widespread among younger analysts (at least in Denmark), determines dominating trends in the social background and attempts to find them in the films. The 'introverted' group of scholars, among whom the 'classical' film semiologists must be counted, puts the work itself, its inner logic and its message, in the centre. In its most absolute form this attitude leads to the conception of the work as something sovereign which has an existence independent of its originator(s) and consumer(s).

In semiotics it is, however, no precondition that a work be seen as something detached from originator and consumer - the basic problem of semiotics seems rather to be, to what extent the codes governing the work exist dependent or independent of the transmitter and the receiver.

One can imagine here two extremities in opinions: one which maintains that the individual artist creates his codes himself, and one which maintains that there are inherent in the human intellect some anthropologically- or sociologically-determined thought structures which constitute the unconscious but determinative structural basis for the expression. If the latter point of view is correct (at least to a certain degree), the consequence is that it will be possible to establish - for mankind as a whole, for specific cultures, or for particular classes or groups of society - certain inescapable (although as a rule not recognized) basic structures for thought and expression. Transferred to the analysis of the filmic expression: it would be possible to determine basic structures which are independent of the actual communication situation, but nevertheless control it.

If we accept the idea of these basic structures, independent of the communicating individual, we can go one step further and ask what their origin is. It would naturally be most 'radical' to assume that fundamentally they are biologically based. But one can also see them as the product of a given cultural community's natural, technical, and traditional conditions, possibly in combination with a common human, psychophysiological background pattern. (In both cases the problem remains, of course, to determine these conditions!) But one can go one step further and formulate the question as one of thought and expression as conditioned by the social context (the conditions of production in a given society and the role the communicator assumes within that community). Here we reach the point where structuralism could gradually merge into a marxistic model of interpretation. It is a fundamental point of view of Karl Marx that there are laws for the development of human society which are beyond the actions of individual people, and it is these laws which he has attempted to determine in his works and which he awards universal validity in the light of historical experience.

We have reached the duplicity which characterizes so much system theory and has characterized so much philosophy through the ages: on the one hand one refers to empirical evidence; on the other hand one requires of the world that it contain an inner logic - one assumes that experiences can fit into a logically coherent structure. Part of this structure is consequently not based directly on evidence, but rather on what one could call 'logical necessity'. Ultimately one requires of such a structure that it be confirmed by future experiences. If that does not happen there are two principal possibilities: revision or even rejection of the established structure, or re-interpretation of the experiences out of the structure's inner logic. It is the latter attitude which can make it necessary to operate with conceptions like 'false consciousness' and 'objective truth'.

Have we gone too far? Only apparently as far as I can tell. For what is a system such as the syntagmatics of Metz if not an attempt to fit empirical experiences into a logical structure which is supposed to be universally valid? The empirical evidence is here the forms of expression actually occurring in film - in this case, feature film (Ref. 7). The theoretical background stems (as mentioned above) from linguistics. The practical realisation consists of the clear arrangement of both the basic categories and the complex categories in a general table of dichotomic structure (Ref. 8).

One can regard the system as an attempt to determine a basic code for the 'syntax' of the 'film language'. The system is fundamentally descriptive and does not pretend to be a determination of the meaning of each individual syntagma type, only of the over-ruling structural principle that governs it. The ordinary filmic montage forms are not considered as elements of meaning in themselves, but as functional elements constituting the various syntagma types and thus determining the mutual relations between the individual elements of meaning. As a whole, one can regard Metz's system as an assertion that a distinction can be made with audio-visual communication between various ways of expression with specific characteristics and that these ways of expression manifest themselves in various types of structures which are objectively demonstrable and will always be present regardless of whether they are the product of the film's creator's consciousness or constitute an unconscious structure of expression, as they originate in man's use of the media.

Is Metz right? Only an extensive testing of the system can give some proof. And the system should be tested not only with feature film (for which it was originally developed) but also with factual film. *Sisimiut*, a complicated documentary dealing with ethnic and social development problems in modern Greenland, was chosen as the first test of the system's applicability to factual film.

THE SYNTAGMATIC CATEGORIES (ORIGINAL AND DEVELOPED VERSION)

Before we take a closer look at the composition of the syntagmatic system, we must emphasize that the system used is not a direct take-over of Metz's, but constitutes a developed version of it. The background of this version is in the first instance the experiences acquired in connection with the carrying-out of the structural analysis of *Sisimiut*, and secondly, the discussions about a paper describing it which has recently been presented at two conferences in West Germany and a seminar in Copenhagen (Ref. 9). The further development of the system is, by the way, quite in Metz's spirit: his model is in itself the product of a development and he has seen it as natural that it be further elaborated by others in the light of the experiences acquired through its use.

Table 1 shows, in English translation, the original syntagmatic categories according to Metz. The translation is taken from Fledelius (Ref. 10) but differs only slightly from Taylor's translation of Metz (Ref. 11).

TABLE 1 Original Syntagmatic Categories According to Metz

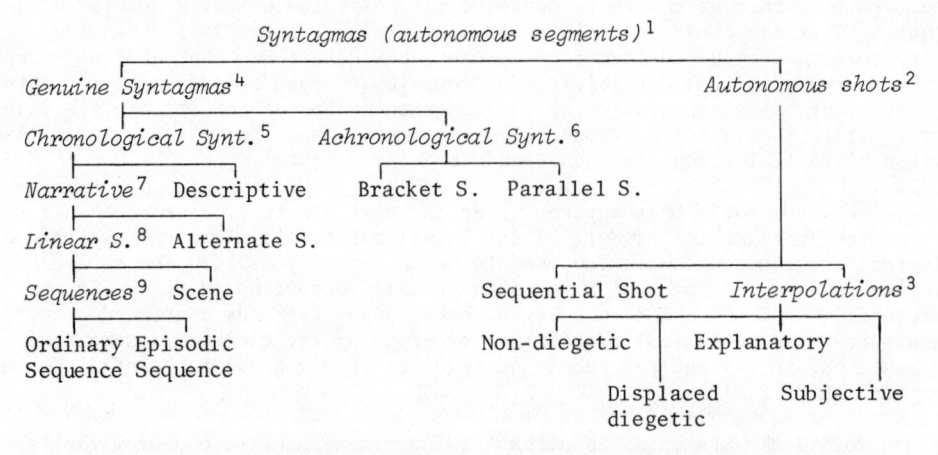

Syntagmas (autonomous segments)[1]

Genuine Syntagmas[4]   *Autonomous shots*[2]

Chronological Synt.[5]   *Achronological Synt.*[6]

Narrative[7] Descriptive   Bracket S. Parallel S.

Linear S.[8] Alternate S.

Sequences[9] Scene   Sequential Shot   *Interpolations*[3]

Ordinary Episodic   Non-diegetic   Explanatory
Sequence Sequence
             Displaced   Subjective
             diegetic

The words written in italics signify composite categories of syntagmas, the single categories being written in normal letters. The system is arranged in such a way that you have a choice between two alternatives at every level when you proceed from the top to the bottom (the only exception is the category *Interpolations*). The small numbers refer to the questions you ask in each case: they represent my own concise wording of Metz's definitions.

1. Does the syntagma contain one or more shots?

2. Can the shot be considered as an independent unit or does it have the character of an interpolation into another syntagma?

3. What is the relationship of the interpolation to the action of the syntagma it is inserted into? (Ref. 12)

4. Are the shots arranged according to some chronological principle or not?

5. Are the shots arranged according to a diachronic or a synchronic principle?

6. Does the syntagma consist of shots dealing with a single item, or does it contain a comparison between two (or more) items (e.g. contrasting rich people with poor people or to-day with yesterday)?

7. Does the syntagma contain only one sequence of events, or two or more alternating sequences of events?

8. Are only parts of the sequence of events represented, or is the sequence of events represented in continuity?

9. Has the selection of parts of the sequence of events been carried out according to simple considerations of relevance or according to some particular system (e.g. the condensation of a gradual development by means of shots showing the same object at long intervals)?

Tables 2 and 3 constitute the final stage of a gradual revision process. They are the consequence of a series of problems connected with the original outline of the system:

(1) The original outline ranges the governing principles of the syntagma categories in the following order: one shot/more shots - a chronological/achronological - diachronic/synchronic - linear/alternating - continuous/discontinuous. The question is, however, how theoretically satisfactory, and above all how practical, this order is. It seems to me much safer to arrange the principles in the following order: linear/alternating - chronological/achronological - diachronic/synchronic - continuous/discontinuous - one shot/more shots. In this way the very important (and most often uncomplicated) question of whether the syntagma contains one or two 'lines of action' (or 'lines of content') is put first, while the often tricky (and for the *meaning* mostly rather unsignificant) distinction between the 'unbroken' and the 'broken' cinematic record only appears in the conclusive phase of the categorization (Ref. 13).

(2) For Metz, the *Bracket Syntagma* is simply a syntagma kept together by a common item only, the item itself constituting the 'brackets'. Several examples can be found, however, of syntagmas delimited by real brackets: shots or sequences, either identical or similar, placed at each end of an achronological syntagma and constituting or underlining the item of the syntagma. This very distinctive type should constitute the real *Bracket Syntagma*, while the achronological syntagma only delimited by a common item or topic should be renamed *Topic-delimited Syntagma*.

(3) Of the Metz-category *Autonomous Shots*, only the *Sequential Shot* deserves the term *autonomous*. The Interpolations as such are not independent unities of meaning, and thus in fact not syntagmas at all! Moreover, it is characteristic that whereas the 'Genuine Syntagmas' are categorized according to differences in their internal structure, the Interpolations are categorized according to external criteria, i.e. their relationship to the action of the syntagma into which they are inserted. The

most radical (and my opinion the most satisfying) solution to this problem would be to let the Interpolations form a new sort of film unit: the *Hypotagma*, and to let this term cover not only interpolative shots, but also small sequences of an interpolative character (cf. the arguments put forward in paragraph (1) and Ref. 13 against laying too much emphasis on the distinction between shots and small sequences in the expression analysis). And why should it not be possible to arrange the hypotagma categories in a dichotomic way? In fact, a such arrangement would be an advantage in view of the fact that Metz's list of interpolations can hardly be considered as exhaustive, and a higher degree of systematizing would facilitate the elaboration of this somewhat neglected part of the system.

(4) A *Sequential Shot* is an independent unity of meaning constituted by an 'unbroken' cinematic recording. A distinction should be made, however, between a 'diachronic' and a 'synchronic' type. The former (and probably more frequent) can be named *Scene Shot*; here, some action is going on before the camera, with the camera either in a fixed position or following the movements of the acting persons or objects. The latter type can be named *Descriptive Shot*; here, there is no action before the camera, all movement being created by the camera itself. In other words: the Scene Shot is an uncut Scene, just as the Descriptive Shot is an uncut version of the Descriptive Syntagma. In order to avoid misunderstanding, the introduction of the category 'Descriptive Shot' should be followed by changing the name of the Descriptive Syntagma to *Descriptive Sequence*, as well as the introduction of the 'Scene Shot' should be followed by changing the term 'Scene' to *Scene Sequence*.

(5) Normally, no syntagma or hypotagma can be shorter than one shot. In some cases, however, a shot - a continuous filmic recording - can fall into smaller parts (which can be termed *positions* or *moves*) that constitute independent or semi-independent unities of meaning separated from each other by camera movements, not by cuts. As it is of minor importance for the expression analysis if a syntagma is delimited by a cut or, say, by panning, such segmented shots should be treated as if each segment were a separate shot.

TABLE 2   Revised System of Syntagmas

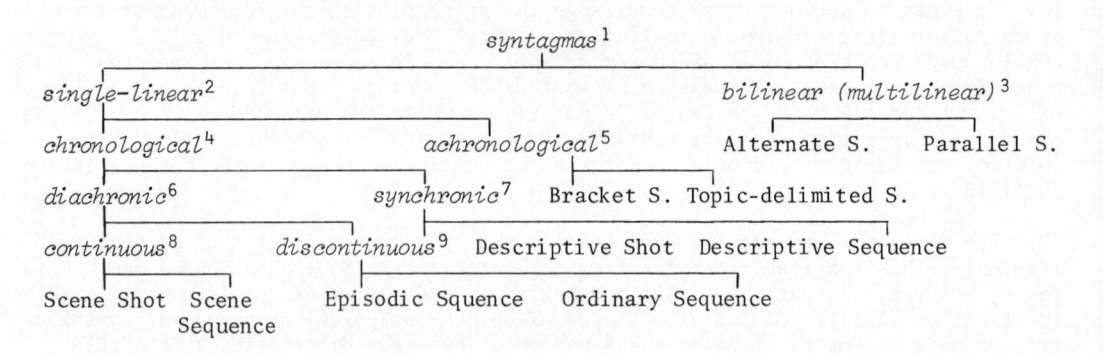

syntagmas[1]

single-linear[2]   *bilinear (multilinear)*[3]

chronological[4]   *achronological*[5]   Alternate S.   Parallel S.

diachronic[6]   *synchronic*[7]   Bracket S.   Topic-delimited S.

continuous[8]   *discontinuous*[9]   Descriptive Shot   Descriptive Sequence

Scene Shot   Scene   Episodic Squence   Ordinary Sequence
             Sequence

Words written in italics signify composite categories. In each case you have the choice between two alternatives. The criteria for the choice can be formulated as questions:

[1]   Is the syntagma built up on the basis of a single line of action or content, or does it contain two (or more) such lines?

[2-3] Is the syntagma constructed according to a chronological principle or not?

Film - Structural Analysis

4   Is the chronology of the syntagma of a diachronic or a synchronic nature?

5   Is the syntagma delimited by a 'frame' of identical or similar segments, or is it kept together by its topic only?

6   Is the sequence of events contained in the syntagma represented in continuity, or are only parts of the sequence of events represented, others omitted?

7-8 Does the syntagma consist of one or more shots?

9   Has the selection of parts of the sequence of events been carried out according to some particular system (e.g. the condensation of a gradual development by means of shots showing the same object at long intervals) or has the selection been carried out according to simple considerations of relevance?

TABLE 3 Proposed System of Hypotagmas

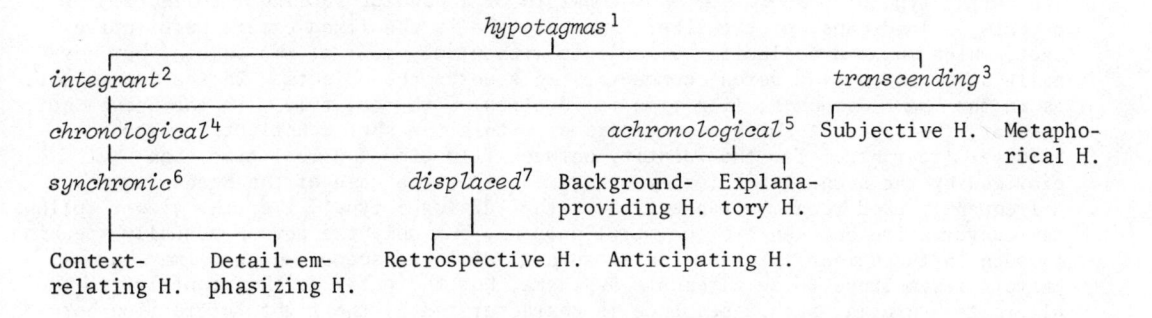

```
                              hypotagmas¹
                ┌──────────────────┴──────────────────┐
          integrant²                             transcending³
    ┌───────────┴───────────┐                   ┌──────┴──────┐
chronological⁴         achronological⁵    Subjective H.   Metapho-
    │                       │                              rical H.
synchronic⁶        displaced⁷  Background-  Explana-
    │                │         providing H.  tory H.
┌───┴────┐      ┌────┴─────┐
Context-  Detail-em-  Retrospective H.  Anticipating H.
relating H. phasizing H.
```

The criteria for classification can be formulated as questions:

1   Does the hypotagma show something which also forms part of the superordinate syntagma, or is its object external to the sequence of events or topic of the superordinate syntagma?

2   Does *time* constitute an important element of the relationship between the hypotagma and the superordinate syntagma, or is it of no importance for this relationship?

3   Does the hypotagma show something going on in the mind of one of the acting persons of the superordinate syntagma, or is it without any direct connection with the action shown in the superordinate syntagma?

4   Does the hypotagma refer to the action just going on in the superordinate syntagma, or does it refer to some earlier or later part of the film?

5   Does the hypotagma provide the superordinate syntagma with some sort of general background, or does it constitute an explanation to some specific part or aspect of it?

6   Does the hypotagma relate the action or object of the superordinate syntagma to its actual context, or does it draw the attention to some specific detail or aspect of the superordinate syntagma's content?

7   Does the hypotagma anticipate the content of a later syntagma, or does it refer to the content of an earlier syntagma?

Additional remarks may be made concerning some of the categories. The *Parallel Syntagma* contains a comparison between two (or more) items, most often in order to emphasize a contrast between, say, rich and poor, free and slave, good and evil; no wonder that it often occurs in propaganda films. The *Alternate Syntagma* shall demonstrate the synchronicity of two separate actions by cross-cutting between them. An often-seen variant is the 'bringing-together sequence': two actions (e.g. voyages) start from separate points, the persons move gradually towards each other, and eventually the two actions merge into one, the last shot(s) constituting the joint ending of the two lines of action. The distinction between the *Topic-delimited Syntagma* and the *Descriptive Sequence* is not always easy to make as it is often a matter of personal judgment whether or not time has had any real significance for the building-up of the syntagma. It is, however, no serious obstacle to the application of the system that some syntagmas are so vaguely constructed that it may be possible to attribute them to more than one category. Often, however, a closer analysis of the syntagma in question will reveal with certainty to which category the syntagma be assigned.

The normal type of *Descriptive Shot* consists of a panning showing a collection of objects, a landscape, or the like. Another type is the fixed-camera Descriptive Shot, which shows a collection of objects without movement of the camera, but normally accompanied by a verbal commentary related to the objects. In the *Scene Shot*, as in the *Scene Sequence*, film time is identical with real time. In the Scene Shot, however, the coherent succession of frames within the shot constitutes a much stronger 'guarantee' for the identity between film time and real time than that provided by the sound track (or by other means) in the case of the Scene Sequence. A frequently used Scene Sequence type is the 'dialogue type', i.e. the viewer follows the conversation between two (or more) persons, but only the person actually speaking is seen on the screen. In some cases such a 'dialogue scene sequence' may have a certain resemblance to an Alternate Syntagma, but the point is that contrary to the Alternate Syntagma, such a sequence is characterized by the tight interaction between the persons shown and the strict diachrony of the sound track. The *Episodic Sequence* is extremely rare. The example normally mentioned is a sequence from Orson Welles' *Citizen Kane* (1940) illustrating the gradual emotional disengagement of a married couple by showing it in the same situation (the breakfast table) with long intervals; in this way a long development is dramatically condensed. The same technique is used in natural science films in order to show processes too slow to be caught by the human eye under normal conditions (e.g. the growth of a mushroom or flower).

The *Metaphorical Hypotagma* is normally a suggestive kind of insert to evoke specific connotations to the phenomenon denoted in the super-ordinate syntagma. Erwin Leiser, for instance, used it several times in his film *Deutschland, erwache!* (1968) in order to counteract the tendency of the Nazi films quoted in his compilation (Ref. 14). The *Subjective Hypotagma* conveys the thoughts of one of the acting persons of the super-ordinate syntagma. Often it is used as some kind of 'personal memory insert'. The *Background-providing Hypotagma* is normally used at the beginning of a syntagma, often just in order to indicate the location of the action. But it may also contain more elaborate information about the background of the action. The *Explanatory Hypotagma* normally gives an explanation to some phenomenon shown in the super-ordinate syntagma; in some cases it may be difficult to distinguish it from the *Detail-emphasizing Hypotagma* when this is felt to have a more or less explanatory character, but the problem is normally solved by closer examination of the relationship between hypotagma and super-ordinate syntagma: if the hypotagma forms part of the chronological system of the syntagma, it should be considered as Detail-emphasizing. The same criterion distinguishes the *Context-relating Hypotagma* from the Background-providing Hypotagma.

THE SYNTAGMATIC HIERARCHY

A further development of Metz's system consists of the perception of the film in its entirety not as a single string of paratactic syntagmas, but as a pyramid-like hierarchy of superior and subordinate syntagmas. In fact, Metz himself has referred to the possibility of analysing a film on several levels and mentioned as example an analysis of a passage from Roberto Rossellini's *Viaggio in Italia* (1953) made by Adriano Apra and Luigi Martelli (Ref. 15). In this analysis Apra and Martelli, after having broken up the passage into syntagmas according to Metz, also identified units that were larger and smaller than these. Metz's conclusion is that a film can be viewed both as a series of sequences (as he has done himself), as a series of shots, and as a series of 'episodes', and that one must, at least theoretically, have analysed a film successively on all its levels in order to know its total structure. In practice, however, Metz has perceived the film as a single chain of consecutive, co-ordinated syntagmas (Ref. 16).

The analysis of *Sisimiut* led not only to the identification of units larger than the syntagmas, but also to the conclusion that these units can be classified according to the same categories as the syntagmas, only with the difference that they are syntagmas of syntagmas, not syntagmas of shots. In the case of *Sisimiut*, the 284 shots are grouped in 69 syntagmas (14 of which contain one, 2 of which contain two hypotagmas); the 69 syntagmas are grouped in 19 *super-syntagmas*, these again into 5 *mega-syntagmas*, and the whole film can be considered as one *giga-syntagma*. And this four-storied structure seems to be nothing exceptional, at least with factual films: the pattern recurs in other documentary films and newsreels we have tried to 'syntagmatize'. The film whole seems normally to be determinable as a mega-syntagma (films with a duration of 10-15 minutes) or a giga-syntagma (films with a duration of about 30 minutes), but probably long films of about one hour or longer may consist of more than one giga-syntagma, and in this case the film whole may be determinable as a *tera-syntagma* (syntagma of fifth order). We have not so far been able to ascertain if certain film series (as for instance the American war orientation series *Why We Fight*) are determinable as syntagmas of still higher order (*peta-syntagmas*) and the same applies to the question of whether feature films are normally less hierarchical in structure than documentary films. Even more than the 'basic' syntagmatic analysis, the hierarchical analysis is in its infancy, but it seems very promising because of its capacity for elucidating the composition of the film's larger structures (its 'parts' or 'chapters') and of the entirety of the film itself.

HOW ARE THE LIMITS OF THE SYNTAGMAS DETERMINED?

Christian Metz (Ref. 17) has dealt with what one could term 'the filmic punctuation', identifying three types of division between syntagmas: (1) 'hard' cut followed by a change in time, place or action, (2) 'hard' cut followed by a change in tempo, atmosphere or the like, (3) particular filmic effects as stopping down the lens, fading over, wipe or the like. This quite summary categorisation is influenced by the fact, already mentioned, that Metz systematically concentrates on the visuals. Meanwhile the 'auditives' lurk in the background of both category (1) and (2). How often is a change in time or place indicated through some vocal utterance, via particular 'natural' sounds or by means of characteristic musical stanzas? And how often does a change in atmosphere occur via the background music?

In my opinion the film must be considered as a range of parallel-running 'channels' of expression. The visuals can be divided into a *picture channel* (or several in the case of superimpositions, split images and the like) and a *text channel* (credits, translation via subtitles, inserted texts etc.). The 'auditives' can be divided into a *commentary channel*, a *synchronic-speech channel*, a *music channel*, and an *acoustic-effect channel*. (Of course, all of these channels do not have to be present all the time or in every film.) The distinction between the various components of the film's progress is created through the change in one or (often) several channels, and there seems to be a tendency towards the manifestation of the distinction between syntagmas of higher order by changes in more channels (or by more profound changes in one or two channels) than when distinguishing between syntagmas of lower order. Furthermore, it seems that the changes generally lie much closer in the visual channel(s) than in the auditive ones, so that it is often within the latter that one finds the decisive clues for the delimitation of the superior syntagmas.

But how are the limits determined in practice? The first and foremost remedy, if the analysis is to be carried out on a solid basis, is to make a shot-by-shot analysis of the film. It is possible to carry out a more summary syntagmatic analysis on the basis of a so-called 'sequency analysis' (a description sequence-by-sequence), but unless the film is very clearly structured on the basic level this is a risky procedure. Besides, if you want to penetrate beneath the syntagmatic level it is absolutely necessary to have the detailed shot-by-shot analysis as your starting point. Thus, as a principle, it is always advisable to enter upon the study of the film by making a detailed description shot-by-shot and channel-by-channel.

After the completion of the description, the minor and major changes are looked for. In the visuals there may be changes in person(s), place, time and object(s); in the speech channels the changes normally lie at the passing-over from one sentence to another (or from one period of sentences to another), and when another voice takes over. In the case of the music channel there may be changes from one motif or tune to another, or from one style of music to another. Finally, regarding the acoustic-effect channel, changes may occur by replacing one kind of accompanying sound by another, but quite often strong noises function directly as a kind of interpunctuation between syntagmas.

Then the segments between the changes are analysed more closely. In this connection it should be borne in mind that a syntagma is characterized by two more features than its delimitation: the existence of an overruling structural principle, and the independence of its content, i.e. its capability of being understood separately. The last problem can most easily be approached by asking if the syntagma can be given a simple title covering its content without referring to any other segment of the film; if this is not possible you most probably have a hypotagma, provided of course that it is possible to determine its relation to a super-ordinate syntagma. After having determined the (primary) syntagmas according to the syntagmatic categories, you turn to the segments between the major changes, trying to determine the larger segments according to the same rules - the existence of an overruling structural principle and the possibility of giving each syntagma a title covering its content. By making the analysis you move gradually upwards in the system, level by level, and it is very important to finish each level before you enter the next.

It may happen that it is difficult to attribute some segment to one single syntagmatic category; this may be due to two reasons: either the syntagma itself is ambiguous (e.g. because it can be understood both as an alternate and a parallel syntagma, in which case the ambiguity is real, perhaps even premeditated; the ruling principle is the alternation between two phenomena, but it is left to the viewer to perceive it in his own way), or the syntagma appears so heterogeneous that it is impossible to assign it to only one category without neglecting important features of its construction. In the latter case the syntagma should be broken up, the analyst looking upon it not as one single syntagma, but as a system, a hierarchy of syntagmas. By doing this you will find out which structural principle is in fact the overruling one and which principles are subordinate. Regarding *Sisimiut*, at any rate, it has been possible to break down every complex syntagma into syntagmas clearly ruled by one single principle, but placed on different levels (normally one belonging to the superior and the rest to the subordinate level).

Film - Structural Analysis

Another problem appears when you have identified between two changes, two unities which both from the criterion 'overruling structural principle' and the criterion 'separately understandable meaning' must be considered as syntagmas, between which, however, no clear 'demarcation line' can be drawn. In this case (which only occurs once in *Sisimiut*) we have the phenomenon of 'conjunct syntagmas', i.e. syntagmas which have one or more shots in common. Often the overlapping will consist of a hypotagma referring to both the preceding and the succeeding syntagma. In the same way, naturally, a syntagma of lower order can function as overlapping between two syntagmas of higher order; in this connection a very tricky phenomenon may appear which can be called a 'sliding syntagma': this is a syntagma with a built-in, gradual change of content which does not, however, interfere with the overruling structural principle of the syntagma. (This type does not appear in *Sisimiut*.) The final stage of the structural analysis consists in the summing-up of the hierarchy of the film in a general table.

SYNTAGMATIC ABBREVIATIONS AND SIGNATURES

In order to facilitate the analytical work it is recommendable to use some system of abbreviations and signatures. The following proposal for a syntagmatic 'notation' is based upon the experiences made up till now with different films. Every syntagma or hypotagma category is indicated by two letters, the latter of which has the following meanings: H = Hypotagma, S = Syntagma, § = Shot, $ = Sequence. The former letter always is the initial letter of the syntagmatic category in question. This gives the following list of abbreviations:

AH = Anticipating Hypotagma
AS = Alternate Syntagma
BH = Background-providing Hypotagma
BS = Bracket Syntagma
CH = Context-relating Hypotagma
DH = Detail-emphasizing Hypotagma
D§ = Descriptive Shot
D$ = Descriptive Sequence
EH = Explanatory Hypotagma

E$ = Episodic Sequence
MH = Metaphorical Hypotagma
O$ = Ordinary Sequence
PS = Parallel Syntagma
RH = Retrospective Hypotagma
SH = Subjective Hypotagma
S§ = Scene Shot
S$ = Scene Sequence
TS = Topic-delimited Syntagma

_ _ _ indicates boundary of hypotagma
_____ indicates boundary of syntagma
_____ indicates boundary of super-syntagma
========= indicates boundary of mega-syntagma
========= indicates boundary of giga-syntagma

Hypotagmas are not numbered. Shots are indicated with normal Arabic numerals, primary syntagmas with power numerals, super-syntagmas with Roman Numerals, mega-syntagmas with small Greek letters, and giga-syntagmas with capital Greek letters. In the shot-by-shot analysis, the numbers stand to the left, the corresponding syntagmatic categories to the right of the middle line. Numbers and categories of the superior syntagmas are placed at the beginning of that particular superior syntagma, numbers and categories of primary syntagmas at the end of the syntagma. Category abbreviations of hypotagmas are placed either at the beginning or at the end of the hypotagma, according to convenience.

A PRACTICAL EXAMPLE OF THE USE OF THE METHOD: EXCERPTS FROM THE
'SISIMIUT' ANALYSIS

Shot-by-shot Analysis of the Film 'Sisimiut' - English Version, 16 mm

VISUALS	AUDITIVES
shot no./meter no. at beginning of shot (small letters after shot no. indicate shot segments, cf. above, p.	
Text in the picture is written in capital letters, superimpositions are recorded in the right part of the column.	*Music and acoustic effects are recorded in the right part of the column.*
0/0.00 STATENS FILMCENTRAL (initial strip)	

                                      A/-/I   BS/-/PS

1/1.0 worker rolls out wire (evidently to detonator), Danish worker with yellow safety helmet, middle-aged, plump.

2/2.3 close shot of the preceding   DH

3/2.4 Grl. woman and 3 children look on (faces calm without smiles)

4/3.5 worker (with GTO-insignia) and another Danish worker, also with safety helmet

5/4.0 Grl. group of spectators (faces without smiles). In the background view over part of the city.   music begins (guitar)

6/4.7 worker gives signal with his hand (medium close)   'Hehp!!' - howling sound

7/5.2 Grl. leave

8a/5.8 long shot of hillside-explosion superimposition of   1   O$ howling sound becomes peal of explosion

        SISIMIUT   speaking choir shouts Grl.

8b   PRODUCTION
           THE DANISH GOVERNMENT FILM   aggressive music (drums and
               COMMITTEE   guitars among others) begins

8c/(7.6) C/O STATENS FILMCENTRAL COPENHAGEN 1966

8d/(8.6) PRODUCED BY MINERVA-FILM A/S AND JØRGEN ROOS

8e/(9.8) ASSOCIATE PRODUCER MORTEN SCHYBERG
           ASSISTANT DIRECTOR HANS ENGBERG

8f/(10.2) COMMENTATOR TOM BROWNE SOUND NIELS ISHØJ

8g(10.6) CAMERA ROLF RØNNE ASSISTANT CAMERAMAN MICHAEL SALOMON

8h(11.1) SCRIPT PALLE KOCH

8i(11.6) A FILM BY JØRGEN ROOS   2 TS

Film - Structural Analysis

α/II	PS/O$
9/12.1 harbour and fjord region with ships	sound of a cutter motor
10/13.0 harbour region - panning to the right (camera follows small boat) D$ ³	On the Western coast of Greenland lies the town of Sisimiut. The Danes call it Holsteinsborg.
11/15.8 hut with two openings, boy comes out of left opening, goes towards the right	
12/17.2 View down over mountain side with house. Fjord region in background. Two boys walking (under 12 years old)	one of the boys says something
13/18.3 The boys go and run down a stairway along the mountainside	
14/18.8 The boys are on the way down the lowest section of the stairs. They are followed by panning to the right.	
15/19.9 The boys run over a wooden bridge - sit down together and talk	laughter
16/21.2 Elderly Grl. woman walks along stone building with small windows, with sack on back.	BH
17/21.8 The two boys sit and look at something with a grave, intent expression	
18/22.7 Boy with satchel passes by building site - the boy is followed by panning to right	AH
19/23.7 The two boys seen earlier, seen from behind. Dogs run towards left. In background a little higher up, a wall. ⁴	O$
20/24.7 The boy with the satchel passes by over rocks past the house from left to right, the camera follows him, so there is a panning to the right	guitar and jew's harp
21/27.2 more school children with satchels cut terrain on their way towards the camera	The new Greenland is moving ahead
22/28.4 school children from behind on way into school ⁵	At school the children meet their first hurdle: the Danish language music fades out O$
23/29.2 girl with satchel bends over book	Kan I stave til 'Danmark', kom! (Can you spell 'Danmark', come! (not translated)
24/30.0 close shot of boy spelling ⁶	D - a - n; Dan, m - a - r - k - DANMARK S$
25/31.7 children in class room (medium shot)	(teacher's voice?): 7 minus 4?

26/32.4 Grl. teacher from the side, student from the front (medium close shot) The teacher nods.	............3!
27/33.6 three children in group in the class, one scratches his neck and gets ready to take notes, the second takes notes, the third stares with big eyes.	10 minus 7??
28/34.3 same as 26 - the boy looks at his fingers	3!

7 | S$

III | TS

29/36.6 well-dressed, well-fed Dane comes out from door in bay of 2-storey house, goes down the stairs, and diagonally towards the camera swinging a little from side to side. Church in background (red on hill). Clip ends in 'american shot', slightly worm's eye view between portals of whale's jaws which close the chain in the foreground.	The days of the king-like district commissioner are gone. To-day he is a trade commissioner. He is no longer all-powerful but still holds an important position in the town.

8 | S§

30/38.9 Dane in overalls gets out of red landrover with KGH's insignia and goes over to large store which sells various items (furniture, textiles etc.), black church gable in background. In background to the right commissioner's house from the gable. Danish workman on way out of store with bag in his hand.	The manager of the Royal Greenland Trade Department Store is also a Dane.

9 | S§

31/40.5 Dane on his way into the telegraph office (corner of red VW pick-up to right) He runs agilely up the stairs.	The Danish chief telegrapher provides contact with the outside world.
32/41.9 fat Greenlander typewrites (with two fingers), microphone in front	The station also employs Greenlanders.
33/42.8 close shot of chief telegrapher bent over microphone - speaks Greenlandic	The chief telegrapher has been here for many years, he is one of the few Danes in the town who speaks Greenlandic.

10 | O$

34/45.2 Dane in windbreaker goes towards the camera while putting on white safety helmet, climbs into black and white landrover marked G.T.O. 5906 with pipe in mouth, slams door.	Sisimiut has a Danish builder, who is the local head of Greenland's technical organisation

11 | S§

35/46.8 policeman in full uniform with cap with white cover gets out of green car marked POLICE 5810, he smokes cheroot and goes into police station, camera follows him, he meets Grl. police officer in just	The Danish police superintendent helped by a Greenlandic force is responsible for law and order. 'Godmorgen, har der været noget spændende i nat? Nej, det har der ikke været. Nåh.

Film - Structural Analysis

as full uniform going in opposite direction.		(Good morning, has anything exciting happened tonight? No, it hasn't. Oh. (not translated))
	12	S§
36/49.3 Dane in red-chequered heavy jacket gets out of land rover marked ELVÆRKET 5706 and is followed on his way into building.		Also a Dane is in charge of the town's electricity supply.
	13	S§
37/50.9 harbour scene, Citroen ID19 stops at quay, Greenlander in boiler suit gets out and camera follows him to right through door of a red house		But the chairman of the town council is one of Sisimiut's own people, elected by them. He is a foreman at the harbour.
	14	S§
38/52.8 Doctor goes through door to ward (Dane with glasses) followed by 4 Danish ladies in white smocks and one Grl. who functions as interpreter, they stop at a sick bed, Grl. girl with bandaged foot in the air.		The head of the hospital is a Danish doctor. The nurse acts as an interpreter between doctor and patient.
39/54.2 close shot (medium close) of Grl. interpreter with doll in the background, turns towards doctor and answers in Danish, panning to the patient, pretty, smiling Grl. girl.		'Hvordan går det med foden?' ('How's your foot?' (not translated)) Grl. translates Grl. answers - 'Det går bedre' ('Better' (n.tr.)) 'Og smerterne de er mindre?' ('There's less pain?' (n.tr.)) Grl. translates Grl. answers - 'Su' ('Yes' (n.tr.))
	15	S§
	β/IV	TS/BS
40.56.5 woman on her way up slope with two pails of water goes into red house with partially peeled off paint		music begins (same as before)
	16	S§
41/59.4 girl smoking cheroots (close shot)		Amos was once a hunter, but the days of the sledge journeys and the kayak trips are over. His everyday life is now void of drama.
42/61.3 old Grl. woman with kettle, bent over old-fashioned stove, pours water into coffee pot, messy interior with wash drying		Amos and his wife still keep the old Greenlandic family solidarity in the new era.
43/62.3 comparatively large room with young women and children, Amos is sitting in corner with one of the children on his lap.		
44/63.0 close shot: panning from child's head to profile, young girl with knitted light-coloured sweater and braid.		
		DH

45/64.1 medium shot: girl in profile with child on lap in foreground, behind them slightly older children on sofa woman with black knitted sweater breast-feeding child of about 1½ years.

(CENTRAL SECTION OF FILM IS OMITTED FROM THIS EXAMPLE OF ANALYSIS)

279/312.3 Close shot of smiling Sofie seen full face, she looks to the left, Thomas glances to the left, now he puts his arm on her shoulder, his face looks at her smilingly from the picture's uppermost left edge and disappears again out of the picture.

280/313.0 Close shot of the bonfire, some herbs are thrown on - dimming down   voices

67 | O$

(A) /-/XIX | (BS)/-/O$

281/314.2 dimming up to flat, open place, the weather is a bit misty, in the middle-ground children with bags come diagonally towards the camera, to their right truck seen from behind The truck drives diagonally back to the left, the camera follows the children in a long panning to the left, here a school-like building appears.   guitar with Bach-like music

282/317.9 Long shot: children seen from the front moving on towards the left side of the picture (mostly boys)

283/318.9 Long shot: children, mostly girls, taken from the side walking to the left, the camera follows them in a panning, which ends at the school gate, through which a mixed group of boys and girls go.   music stops on a single note.

68 | O$

284s/320.7 School room (medium shot), boy in the foreground, picking at his face with his left hand, behind him two girls, the one on the left singing energetically, the girl on the right lies down on the table first on the one, then on the other side, behind them the boys, of which the boy furthest to the right plays at holding a telescope to his right eye (Age of children about 9-10).
    'Min dukke er våd'.
    (My doll is wet.)
    'M-i-n min d-u-k duk k-é ké dukke er é-r er v-u-d våd'

284b While the boy in the foreground spells to himself we zoom in on his face, his hand is still fiddling with his face. He holds his nose with
    spelling
      in chorus: 'M-i-n min d-u-k duk...'

both hands from each side, his fingers move up to the corners of his eyes and from there out to his cheeks which he sort of grabs.		speaker: Min dukke er våd *(slightly broken* - Danish is a very difficult language)
284c The picture is frozen where he is looking diagonally to the right with a questioning, astonished or slightly suffering look and slightly open mouth.	EH	guitar music (simple melodic lines followed by chords, plaintive character)
329.0 Dimming down.	69 S§	

THE END

Comments on the Excerpt of the Shot-by-Shot Analysis

Super-syntagma I does not form part of a mega-syntagma, because it constitutes the first part of the brackets of the giga-syntagma which comprises the whole film. That is why the place designated for the number of the mega-syntagma is empty at the beginning. The first mega-syntagma starts with super-syntagma II. The same applies to the last of the film's super-syntagmas, N° XIX, which is not counted as another mega-syntagma because it constitutes the second part of the brackets of the giga-syntagma (cf. the general table below). Super-syntagma I constitutes the opening of the film. It is considered as a Parallel Syntagma (a rather unusual one, indeed) because it plays on a contrast between the silent preparations for the explosion and the effectful and noisy presentation of the credits. This contrast does not in itself convey any separate meaning, it is only a way of presenting the credits in an entertaining and surprising way.

The explosion sequence in itself can be perceived as more than a simple registration of an event: due to the shifts between shots of the acting Danes and shots of the on-looking Greenlanders, an impression emerges of the Greenlanders as people of secondary importance for the development of their own country, as people who are not planning and acting, but planned for and acted for. The same impression emerges from super-syntagma XIX, in particular the last primary syntagma of the film ([69]) which describes the difficulties of the Greenland children with the learning of the Danish language. The first and the last syntagma of the film even end in the same way: with a freezing of the last frame which in both cases shows the Greenland consequence of Danish (or Danish-influenced) action.

The five mega-syntagmas contained within the brackets of the film's giga-syntagma all deal with aspects of life in Sisimiut and surroundings with particular attention directed to the social stratification of the community and the life patterns of different groups of the population. Only mega-syntagma α, which demonstrates the dominant role of Danish language and administrators, is covered by the excerpt. The following mega-syntagmas are dealing with β, Greenlanders' homes; γ, Greenlanders at work; δ, The role of Danish workers in Sisimiut; ε, Greenlanders' and Danes' activities after hours. This sounds rather like a mainly descriptive film, but both the structure and the way some signs and sign combinations are used raise the film above a merely descriptive level. We already touched on this question with reference to the giga-brackets, but let us proceed further and have a look at the overall structure of the film, such as it appears in Table 4.

TABLE 4 General Table of the Syntagmatic Structure of *Sisimiut* (with Comments)

Syntagmas	Super-syntagmas	Mega-syntagmas	Giga-syntagma
1-2 (O$ TS)	I (PS)		
3-7 (D$ O$ O$ S$ S$)	II (O$)	α (PS)	
8-15 (S§ S§ O$ S§ S§ S§ S§ S$)	III (TS)		
16-19 (S§ S$ TS S§)	IV (BS)		
20-21 (S$ TS)	V (PS)		
22-23 (O$ TS)	VI (TS)	β (TS)	
24-26 (S$ AS S$)	VII (PS)		
27-30 (TS D§ O$ D$)	VIII (TS)		
31-33 (D$ BS O$)	IX (TS)		
34-37 (D$ D$ D$ D§)	X (BS)		A (BS)
38-41 (O$ O$ O$ O$)	XI (TS)	γ (PS)	
42-44 (D$ O$ D$)	XII (TS)		
45-46 (D$ S$)	XIII (O$)		
47-50 (AS O$ AS O$)	XIV (O$)		
51-52 (S§ S$)	XV (O$)	δ (TS)	
53-55 (O$ O$ O$)	XVI (PS)		
56-62 (AS O$ O$ AS PS O$ AS)	XVII (TS)	ε (TS)	
63-67 (S$ S$ O$ S$ O$)	XVIII (PS)		
68-69 (O$ S§)	XIX (O$)		

The most important observations to be made from this table are:

(1) the dominance (62 out of 69) of chronological syntagmas at the primary level; of the remaining seven syntagmas, only two belong to the categories most suitable for transmission of message or bias: PS and BS.

(2) the dominance (14 out of 19, 5 out of 5, 1 out of 1) of achronological syntagmas at the super-ordinate levels; furthermore, five of the super-syntagmas and two of the mega-syntagmas are PS, and two of the super-syntagmas, three of the mega-syntagmas, and the giga-syntagma, are BS.

(3) the consequent pattern which appears with respect to the use of the PS: if some of the super-syntagmas within a mega-syntagma are PS, the mega-syntagma will not be a PS and, on the contrary, if none of the super-syntagmas are PS, the mega-syntagma will be a such.

This leads to the following conclusion: The PS-category, which is employed in this film to compare Greenlanders and Danes in Sisimiut, is used with great subtlety - it is not overused, nor is it always used at the same level; but it appears as an important structural element within every mega-syntagma so that the contrast between the two ethnic groups and their roles in society is always present in one way or another. In this sophisticated way, the film becomes much more than a plain description of life in the town Sisimiut. But it is only through a structural analysis of the super-ordinate levels of the film that it is possible to get hold of how exactly it is done.

THE SUB-SYNTAGMATIC LEVEL

A description of the 'micro-analysis' of films will surpass the limits of this contribution. Only a few remarks of a principle nature should be made with respect to the *sign analysis*. A *sign* can be defined as 'a signal understood as an element of meaning by either sender or receiver or both'. In other words: the basic condition for being a sign is to be understood as a sign. This means again that it is only possible to talk of signs with reference to specific groups of producers, transmitters, or receivers: the same signals are not understood as signs by everybody, and even if a signal is universally perceived as a sign this does not necessarily mean that it has the same meaning to everyone. Thus, in carrying out a sign analysis a clear idea is needed of whom you are referring to when you make your analysis and which general frame of reference the person(s) in question possess(es).

Signals can achieve their meaning(s) in different ways. A picture e.g. can become a sign to somebody in five different ways: through its causal connection with its situation of origin (its indexicality); through its ability to reproduce the visual features of the objects it depicts (its iconicity); through the conventional meaning it has got in common use (its preexisting symbolic value); through its actual position in the context of the film (its combinatory value); through the inaccountable connotations it may evoke in some individual's mind (incidental meaning through individual experience). The intriguing fact about this is that the same signal can achieve meaning in different ways - in fact become different signs - to the same person, dependent upon a combination between the context in which it is presented and the immediate personal attitude of the person (which is, however, to a higher or lower degree conditioned by the context). This can be expressed in the way that each signal contains a certain potentiality of meaning which is delimited by the context in which it is used and further delimited by the way it is perceived by its sender or receiver. This is the reason why structural analysis is so important a framework for sign analysis.

CONCLUSION

One of the most important outcomes of the structural or 'syntagmatic' analysis is that it makes it possible to observe some overruling patterns or 'modes' of expression with considerable significance for the character and content of the film's message. Perhaps these patterns are not realized by the film maker himself, but nevertheless they are there and they exert their influence on the message of the film. Thus, the structural analysis becomes of fundamental value for the 'close reading' of the film - the sign analysis. Besides, it facilitates this rather complicated and troublesome analysis by indicating, in combination with the aims of the examination, which parts of the film especially deserve closer analysis. In this way, structural analysis really may save time, in excess of placing the detail analysis on a safer ground.

A further value of the structural analysis is that it makes it possible to look on structure as a reflection of the communication situation in society, or in other words: to use structure as source material in its 'own right' for the study of the cultural background and the preconditions for film production and, perhaps, of the underlying socio-psychological structures.

Thirdly, syntagmatic analysis makes it possible to get an idea of the *rhythm* of the film - rhythm understood as an important structural phenomenon which acts as guidance for the receiver both by emphasizing certain elements of expression and by anticipating such elements. *Sisimiut* makes for instance often use of Background-providing hypotagmas at the beginning of super- and mega-syntagmas, and the background music is used to underline the larger syntagmatic entities by giving them a certain unity of cadence and atmosphere. The rhythm may be considered as a way of 'programming' the perception pattern of the receiver, of creating certain expectations - and sometimes also breaking them! And this effect does not depend on any process on the conscious level, on the contrary it seems to be most effective when it is not (wholly) realized by the receiver. The structural analysis may serve as a means to emancipate the analyst from a strong emotional impact from this 'hidden source'.

In the end, it should always be borne in mind that the syntagmatic relations between the shots in a film is a question about relations within the framework of the film itself, but not necessarily between the objects, situations or events filmed by the camera. If there is such a thing as a 'syntagmatics of reality' this cannot *a priori* be identified with the syntagmatics of the film. The syntagmatic process is a creative one, through which reality is interpreted and encoded in order to communicate information and values - a process through which the fragmentary fixated reflections of reality, the shots, are grouped together in the way which, in the producer's opinion, best serves the transmission of his message. Of course this is most evident in the case of propaganda films. Here syntagmatics are often used to create more or less thoroughly faked events out of factual shots - Leni Riefenstahl has provided us with outstanding examples of how to use this technique in her *Triumph of the Will* (Ref. 18). But even in the case of scientific films trying to register reality as meticulously as possible, syntagmatic problems inevitably appear when the single visual (and auditive) recordings shall be combined to form a reliable reconstruction of the phenomena in question.

Therefore, if the historian or social scientist wishes to use film as an index of the depicted reality, he must penetrate the syntagmatic level and use the individual shot as the basic analytical unit.

NOTES AND REFERENCES

1. Niels Skyum-Nielsen (1974) TV-kommunikation set udefra (TV-communication from an outside view), in *Studier i Historisk Metode IX: Historikeren og Samfundet (Studies in Historical Methodology IX: The Historian and Society)*, Universitetsforlaget, Oslo-Bergen-Tromsø, 101-108.

2. Arthur Marwick used this phrase in connection with his presentation of the BBC Open University programme *Social Consequences of World War I* at the Imperial War Museum conference 'Archive Film in the study and teaching of Twentieth Century History', June 1972.

3. An interesting study of so-called Trivial Film by Waltraut Jirsa, *Verkürzte Perspektiven*, will appear 1978 at Fink Verlag, Munich.

4. Karsten Fledelius, Considerations about Content Analysis of Audio-visuals, in *History and the Audio-Visual Media I - Brandbjerg 1975. The Proceedings of the 6th International Conference on History and the Audio-Visual Media, 4-8 August 1975, Brandbjerg, Denmark*, Copenhagen, in press.

5. Christian Metz (1968) *Essais sur la Signification au Cinéma*, Paris. English translation by Michael Taylor (1974) *Film Language. A Semiotics of the Cinema*, New York and Oxford University Press.

6. Gerd Albrecht, Sozialwissenschaftliche Ziele and Methoden der systematischen Inhaltsanalyse von Filmen. Beispiel: UFA-Tonwoche 451/1939 - Hitlers 50. Geburtstag, in Moltmann and Reimers (1970) *Zeitgeschichte im Film und Tondokument*, Göttingen, 25-37.

7. The sound track is not considered in Metz's system. To him 'film language' indicates the visual, not the audio-visual, means of expression. This sharp distinction between visuals and 'auditives' I find rather unfortunate, but the system is sufficiently flexible to allow for the incorporation of the film's auditive elements into the analysis.

8. *Dichotomic* signifies the principle that there is constantly a choice between two alternatives; Metz's original table is not, however, entirely consequent in this respect, cf. Table 1.

9. Karsten Fledelius, *A Structural Analysis of the Film 'Sisimiut' with reference to an Assessment of the Applicability of Semiotics in Historical Film Research*, paper presented at the 7th International Conference on History and the Audio-Visual Media, Tutzing, September 1977 - and further at a working session of the Film Section of the German Society for Semiotics, Münster, November 1977, and at a seminar in the Department for Audio-Visual Media Research, Institute of History, University of Copenhagen.

10. Fledelius, *loc. cit.* (see Ref.4)

11. Metz, *loc. cit.*

12. The non-diegetic interpolation shows an object which is external to the sequence of events. The displaced diegetic interpolation shows a piece of the sequence of events removed from its 'normal' into a 'foreign' context. The explanatory interpolation explains or interprets something, for example through enlarging a detail of the image shown. The subjective interpolation conveys not the present instance, but an absent moment as experienced by one of the persons in the film (it is normally some kind of 'personal memory insert').

13. At the semiotical working session at Münster, November 1977, Karl-Dietmar Möller pointed out how Metz himself in his analysis of the film *Adieu Philippine* (cf. *Essais* p.160 or *Film Language* p.159) erroneously considered syntagma a sequential shot instead of a scene, because he had ignored several cuts. When such a thing can happen to a professional analyst, how often will not an average viewer do the same? It should also be remembered that a worn copy of a film often contains more cuts than a fresh copy because of the normal damage resulting from projection. Therefore, too much emphasis should not be laid on this distinction, however important it might be from other points of view. Also K.-D. Möller proposed at Münster to put the distinction between linear and alternating syntagmas in the first place, out of considerations similar to mine.

14. After having shown the triumphant ending of the film *Heimkehr* ('Return', i.e. the return of the 'Folk Germans' into the Reich; the film was made in 1941), Erwin Leiser thus inserts a scene showing a man walking slowly through a heavily bombed street and adds the following commentary, 'That was what became of the Reich into which they should return!'

15. Adriano Apra and Luigi Martelli, Premesse sintagmatiche ad un'analisi di 'Viaggio in Italia', *Cinema e film 2*, 198-207, 1967 (cf. Metz, *op.cit.*, note on page 122: age 120 in the English translation).

16. Metz, *op.cit.*, 151-181 (149-182 in the English translation). This comprises an analysis of Jacques Rozier's film *Adieu Philippine*.

17. Christian Metz, Ponctuations et démarcations dans le film de diégèse, *Cahiers du Cinéma 234-235*, 63-78 (décembre 1971 - février 1972).

18. cf. the analysis of the film in K. Fledelius, K. Rübner Jørgensen and P. Nørgart, *Der Film 'Triumph des Willens' als Geschichtsquelle* (in press, Verlag C.H. Beck, Munich).

19. I am grateful to Birgitte Bentzon of the Historical Institute, University of Copenhagen for her valuable help in making the analysis on pages 116 to 121.

SECTION IV
Sources

Having established the scope for using audio-visual media at a rigorous and constructive level in the fields of political science and history, it is necessary to ask how an increasing demand for access to relevant material might be met. It is clear that this involves not only technical problems of storage and viewing, but also more general matters concerning the partial nature of audio-visual coverage of politically-relevant subjects, and the equally partial retention of material for 'permanent storage'. At first sight, the picture that emerges is somewhat discouraging, but on closer examination it appears that there is room for hope if not outright optimism. Much material has survived, and a substantial portion of it is accessible to the serious researcher - albeit at considerable expense in some cases. Many problems remain, and demand most urgent attention given the increasingly audio-visual nature of both public and private communication. It is worth remembering, however, that many of the same problems apply to literary sources, particularly for early periods.

Alden Williams and Kathryn Rowan discuss the general issues involved in the retention and availability of film and television sources on both sides of the Atlantic, laying emphasis on areas of potential improvement. Although their viewpoints overlap in important respects, it is instructive to note the extent to which significant differences in national policy do emerge. Finally, James Ballantyne's annotated list of some European archives leaves us with an encouraging indication of what diverse sources are available even now. Clearly, an improved awareness of what sources are open to the academic user is almost as important as ensuring that future sources are even more complete and easily accessible - and this priority is a major concern of the British Universities Film Council's Information Service.

Seizing the Moving Image: Broadcast Television Archives

Alden Williams

Prodded by such bizarre defences of criminal behaviour as 'involuntary intoxication by television', British and American courts at last join the rest of society to ask precisely how television and human behaviour are related. Profound consequences for the medium, law, and public policy are at stake. Unfortunately, the answers must come from studies based on a tiny fraction of one per cent of all programmes broadcast during television's first three decades as an unprecedented mass medium of information and entertainment, persuasion and gratification.

The long road to broadcast television collections comparable to public archives of every other mass communication medium takes ironic twists. One occurred recently on American television at the end of a biting self-examination of how television reports the news. For an hour, former network reporter Daniel Schorr used television's unique combination of sound, motion, currency and propinquity to portray newsmen's courage and diversity, skill and irresponsibility. Some of the programme's more vivid images were worth at least a second look, in the lecture hall as well as the home. How might viewers take a second look? Apply for a printed transcript, they were told. For anyone who has wished that yesterday's television programmes were as routinely available as yesterday's newspapers, it was a familiar frustration. One might as well manage a football side by using radio broadcasts.

The problem of broadcast television as a rich source of social data and instruction begins with systematic, accessible storage of programmes as they appear on the home screen. In turn, preservation is justified by two very nearly undisputed observations. First, in cultures where there is television - already most of the world - large popular majorities consistently declare television their most influential mass medium. By strict behavioural tests they may not be entirely right, but whatever may be the extraordinarily complicated relationships between television and human behaviour, not to mention the complexities of television itself as institutional behaviour, effect itself is a fact. Secondly, if one properly defines television programmes as coherent, integrated audio-visual images which truly exist only as publics receive them, then more than 98 per cent of all the world's television programmes are

---

Professor Alden Williams is chairman of the Electronic Media Data Archives Committee of the International Studies Association and a member of the political science faculty of Kansas State University. During 1976-1977, he was senior visiting fellow in the Centre for Television Research, University of Leeds, continuing a study of worldwide broadcast television archives for teaching and research.

irretrievably lost or rendered effectively unavailable to scholars and the general public after they are first broadcast.

'Irretrievably lost' applies to easily two-thirds - probably more, although precise estimates elude us - of broadcast television. That total includes a small fraction of live broadcasts, and the much larger share which is recorded temporarily, usually on videotape, and then wiped. 'Effectively unavailable' describes the remaining third of the world's television product, materials reposing anywhere from Welsh caves to New Jersey vaults to odyssean syndication in search of new buyers and audiences. None meets the following standard of accessibility proposed by the television archive committee of the International Studies Association:

> Is the material available for public reference with effort similar to the effort required for access to published products of other mass communication media of comparable scope, audience, and putative effect?

For example, is last year's 10 o'clock news or domestic drama as easily available to scholars in serial, comprehensive, original form as last year's newspapers from world capitals? Television differs from newspapers and magazines in many significant ways, but the comparison here is valid because, for purposes of reference and scholarship, electronic and printed mass media records are equally invaluable in original forms as chronicles and stimuli of human and social behaviour.

ARCHIVAL NEGLECT AND ITS IMPLICATIONS

Yesterday's failures of preservation must be separated from the archival issues of today in order to keep tomorrow's obligations and opportunities in perspective. When television turned mass in the late 1940s, delayed by the Second World War after its debuts at Broadcasting House in 1932 and the New York World's Fair six years later, little thought went to preserving the product. The simplest reason was technical: most programmes were broadcast live, and until durable videotape appeared years later, programmes could be captured only on flimsy kinescopes or, extravagantly, on film. Early television fare consisted of live performances and old cinema films; the former could not be preserved, and no one thought of preserving films *as television programmes* simply because medium and audiences differed from cinema.

Scholars, the likeliest archive users, either did not recognize or, disdainful of the new medium would not admit television's monumental importance for history and social science. To be sure, there were scholarly doubts about television; would not the novelty eventually lose out to radio which could go anywhere and be enjoyed anywhere, neither of which television's unwieldly cameras and receivers could do? Pre-behavioural political science, not yet infatuated with survey aggregates and computer-assisted data manipulation, was not inclined toward associations between television and political behaviour and institutions. So-called 'communication science' was as much a preserve of hybrid natural scientists as of social scientists and had not begun the extreme fragmentation of today's communication studies.

Archivists and librarians were preoccupied with backlogs from the war. The natural almost symbiotic relationships between archivists and their principal social science clients, akin to those between government documentarians and diplomatic historians, never developed. The longer time passed without preserving programmes, the more scholars assumed, as they do today, that someone, somewhere, must be doing the job, much as academicians assume the preservation of printed materials which, realistically, they expect never to consult. It was inconceivable that it could be otherwise. Television implied that archives exist by regularly offering nostalgic, commemorative, and obituary programmes. The reality was, and is, that such programmes consist of materials saved often by chance for their exceptional content. They compare to a family photograph album of newborn children and holidays, but devoid of pictures of workaday ordinary family life. The totally false assumption that archives must exist somewhere is still a major obstacle to mobilizing academic and public support for preserving television.

The most serious implication of the failure to preserve early programmes and to impose social science criteria was the time lost in developing archival procedures and standards fully suited to television as chronicle and data source. Programmes tended to be regarded, where they were regarded at all, as not quite respectable, deviant forms of cinema film, rather than as contemporaneous and extemporaneous chronicles of events and culture as different from cinema art as the sitting room and pub are from the theatre and museum. In both Britain and America, there is a misinformed but widespread feeling that only the 'best', 'most significant', 'most memorable' or 'most representative' of television's many kinds of programming can or should be preserved. Such an argument is not only technically wrong, but also antithetical to the dependence of history and social science upon the ordinary as well as the exceptional, and to social science's pursuit of patterned, recurring behaviour and institutions among individuals and groups, most of which by definition is not 'exceptional'.

More recently, archival issues have become enmeshed with, and sometimes victim to, tensions among the industry, various publics, and government involving the operation, management, and regulation of the medium and its supposed audience effects. These tensions exist on both sides of the Atlantic, outweighing most of the structural differences between British and American television. With ample constitutional and professional justification, broadcasters in both countries jealously guard their artistic, journalistic, and economic interests against assault from all sides, most of whom a free and responsible mass medium must sooner or later antagonize. Many of these assaults are based on partial, reckless, irresponsible analyses of television, but they are no less effective with publics inclined to see television as scapegoat for assorted social ills. In defence, broadcasters would like to preserve only their finest products, but besides being historically awkward, that solution simply cannot work in a day of videotape recorders in private homes. Moreover, broadcasters have far more to fear from slipshod, biased scrutiny of parts of their product out of context than from responsible analyses based on access to the complete product.

Big broadcasting and big business, in some ways natural allies, have come at odds especially to the extent that broadcast journalism and drama question values cherished by established industrial and governmental interests. Governments, the most acquisitive and certainly the wealthiest archivists, play several roles: as sometime owner-manager, regulator, arbiter of rights and duties, and of course, legislator and guardian of the copyright.

Copyright protections are an exaggerated barrier to opening up old television to scholars. British and American efforts to adapt copyright laws to modern economics and technology show how complicated the issues are. By one reading, both British and American copyright law forbid almost any unauthorized duplication of television programmes, but most of the practical issues are unresolved. Even the industry contradicts itself. For example, on copyrighted programmes for the National Broadcasting Company (NBC), NBC's parent Radio Corporation of America (RCA) advertises home videotape recorders, albeit with muted warnings about copyright infringements. As private recording (not to mention such exotic possibilities as direct interception of satellite signals) becomes easier and cheaper and copyright less enforceable, it takes no prescience to see resolution through a return to the fundamental purpose of copyright. It is, simply, to protect the integrity and market value of a producer's work against piracy. Unfortunately, television archives became an issue at the same time that authors and publishers were losing sales to easy Xerography and shrinking academic book markets. Yet the issues are quite different. Copying books to avoid buying them is not the same as copying one-off television programmes which are otherwise unavailable for teaching and research. The great majority of television programmes have no commercial value after they are first aired, and those few which do - mostly dramatic programmes - can be adequately protected for marketing purposes. The crucial difference is between piracy of materials with intent to secure revenues rightfully belonging to the producer (or artist, creator, performer, investor), and the scholar's situation: non-commercial examination of the product for the purpose of combination with other data and the scholar's own creative faculties to produce an analysis essentially no different from studies of copyright printed materials. Most fears of copyright infringement should be allayed by actual scholarship in well organized public archives.

THE IDEAL TELEVISION ARCHIVE

The International Studies Association (ISA) archives committee defines a true public archive of broadcast television as comprehensive, systematic, and accessible. After a ten year study of feasibility, the ISA committee concluded, first, that compromises for the sake of economy or expediency shortsightedly aggravate the problem, and second, that none of the challenges is beyond existing technology or modest political, corporate and professional accommodation.

How much less than the total daily television output is a 'comprehensive' record of the medium? The question is easily begged. Some historians and social scientists can never have too much evidence. Others, for example public opinion analysts, do nicely with almost incredibly small fractions of the universes they study. The nature of the problem under study and canons of proof, including statistical norms, make all the difference. Television archives potentially offer data for studies as different as individual biography and macrocosmic social analysis. Norms of sample size and reliability do not apply equally. Therefore we cannot know what size or what kind of sample is needed until much more work shall have been done. Scholarly integrity demands that, initially, television archives err in the direction of saving more, rather than less. The risk of doing less is, as always, invalid and unreliable findings based on insufficient data. News and 'serious' programming may have less to do with behaviour than advertisements and so-called dross and pap. Television archives cannot be designed like a statesman's memoirs to preserve only one side of the medium and its culture, any more than hospitals record only the healthy patients they discharge.

To be sure, the problem of bulk with videotape and film is formidable. One day's programming from two BBC-TV channels and just one of the ITV channels, stored conventionally, would occupy about a meter of shelf space, or a kilometer in fewer than three years. Comparable storage of three American networks' national programming would consume nearly 500 meters of shelf space a year. Few depositories can afford to commit such space and support indefinitely. And yet, a century ago, one could have been equally pessimistic about preserving newspapers and other serial publications. The answers for the printed media lay in miniaturization and centralization with remote retrieval. The same technology promises to reduce storage space needs for television by orders of magnitude. Broom closets, not library wings, can house years of audio-visual images which can be retrieved for reference with no significant loss of fidelity. The technology which produced superminiaturization also developed search and display mechanisms, coupled with plain language indices which would allow split second retrieval of, for example, a single ministerial statement on devolution, a season of football riots, or all broadcast mentions of the North Atlantic Treaty Organisation during five years, if they were on file - which they are not.

Beyond comprehensiveness, systematic and accessible archives depend primarily on indices and abstracts linked to retrieval mechanisms, and on the ability to compile selections from programmes for study. Again by comparison with newspapers, one cannot imagine consulting *The Times* or Hansard without an index, and no less should be expected of television programmes. The Television News Archive at Vanderbilt University in Tennessee, described more fully below, is almost alone among world television collections in its straightforward, plain language cataloguing and compilation facilities for research. Using the VTVNA *Index and Abstracts* toward a study of Vietnam prisoner of war issues during fifty months between 1968 and 1973, for example, this author screened nearly 2,200 hours of television news, including POW mentions on 634 broadcasts, from which some thirty hours of POW coverage was compiled for detailed isolated and contextual examination. The study, designed to test conventional wisdom about television news and Vietnam diplomacy, could never have been done without the ability to select and compile.

THE STATE OF EXISTING COLLECTIONS

Nowhere in Britain or America, or for that matter in the world, is there a comprehensive, systematic, accessible broadcast television archive by general research standards. The closest approximation, but limited to early evening national news in the United States, is the Vanderbilt University Television News Archive. Other storehouses of past television range from holdings of dozens to hundreds of thousands of hours' material, covering a bewildering variety of subjects, cataloguing and use procedures, and most important from the academic researcher's standpoint, sponsorship and function. Collections maintained by broadcasters to serve broadcaster needs tend to be larger, potentially more comprehensive, adequately if not luxuriously financed, and largely out of bounds for, or unsuitably organized for, teaching and research. Non-broadcaster collections, principally those associated with universities and government archives but also including scores of uncatalogued private caches, tend to be smaller, marginally financed, non-standard and highly selective, but somewhat more accessible.

Among broadcaster archives, the BBC Television Film and Videotape Library is the world's most complete storehouse of one corporation's programming over the longest period. Whereas the BBC Television Library houses a range of BBC programming, British Independent Television programmes are divided between news collections at the ITN and UPITN Film and Videotape Library in London, and other programmes scattered among regional ITV companies with varied archival policies. Both the BBC and ITN and ITV companies donate, sell, and otherwise transfer materials to more accessible collections, notably those of the National Film Archive and the Imperial War Museum, but severe restrictions of cost mean that preservation criteria are largely artistic rather than historical or sociological. For their parts, understandably, broadcasters' basic decisions about what to preserve and how to preserve it are governed primarily by broadcaster needs: possible re-broadcast in whole or in part, or research by production staff.

Aside from problems of cost, maintenance, and copyright, broadcaster and archivist procedures are sometimes not only contradictory, but mutually exclusive. For example, a news programme which appears to the viewer as an integrated whole may actually be transmitted in discrete segments electronically blended at the studio. Broadcaster needs dictate storage by segments, not programmes, and excluding advertisements in the case of commercial networks. The scholar in search of whole news programmes, or measuring such variables as item placement and intensity in context, is at a loss unless the programme shall have been recorded off the air. Such problems are not insoluble, however. Just as folders of cuttings in some newspaper morgues have been replaced by high-speed retrieval and display of individual items electronically, so can parts and series of television programmes be searched, found, and displayed without destroying the integrity of the original broadcast. As prerequisite, however, broadcasters and academicians need to agree on mutually useful classifications for cataloguing and retrieval, agreement which need not wait for liberal funding and rules of access.

Government's role as central television archivist is an issue in both Britain and America, but movement has been slow, beset by red herrings, and complicated by provincialism, perceived costs, and frequently, academicians' failure to define their needs. In Britain, the National Film Archive offers one kind of structural nucleus for comprehensive archives, while the Social Science Research Council links government and academe and could promote standardized cataloguing and exchanges. In the United States, the National Archives (NARS) accepted uncatalogued news programmes from the Columbia Broadcasting System (CBS) and more recently from NBC while CBS sued the much older, but private, Vanderbilt news archive for alleged copyright infringement. The suit was dropped after Congress, in an omnibus copyright revision effective in 1978, took two actions effectively permitting recognized libraries to duplicate television programmes for reference, and authorizing an 'American Television and Radio Archives' in the Library of Congress, separate from the National Archives. However, the Library of Congress Archives in 1978 was still years away from full operation and has already been defined as a selective collection for a relatively few scholars rather than the broad academic community.

University-based collections are typically selective, under-financed, erratically housed within their institutions, and idiosyncratically catalogued to suit resident researchers. In their defence, collections such as those at Leeds (Centre for Television Research, specializing in election campaign and referendum coverage), Leicester (Centre for Mass Communication Research), and Glasgow (Media Study Group), represent pioneering, hard fought efforts by scholars eager to get on with television-related research without waiting for archival perfection. In America, some two dozen colleges and universities have television film and videotape collections of potential use beyond their campuses. Holdings at the University of California at Los Angeles are associated with the National Academy of Television Arts and Sciences, while such varied organizations as the Aspen Institute Program on Communications and Society, the RAND (Research and Development) Corporation, and news study groups at the Massachusetts Institute of Technology and Indiana and George Washington Universities sponsor programs leading to archival development.

Nonetheless, the Vanderbilt Television News Archive stands alone at the forefront of systematic, accessible broadcast television archives. The heart of the VTVNA's collection consists of virtually complete holdings of early evening news broadcasts by all three major American commercial networks -- ABC, CBS, and NBC -- dating from the tumults of August, 1968, when the Democratic Party nominated Hubert Humphrey for president and Vietnam dissent reached a peak. Inspired by a retired businessman and Vanderbilt alumnus, the VTVNA publishes a monthly *Index and Abstracts* (see Figure 1) and is open to responsible users on campus or elsewhere by loan of videotapes compiled from VTVNA master tapes. Duplicate and compiled tapes are never sold, and users sign an agreement neither to reproduce the materials nor to use them publically and commercially. Without the VTVNA's example of scrupulous television archiving, it is doubtful that Congress would have revised the copyright law to permit library holdings of broadcast television. Still other encouragement, visionary but practical and universal, has come from the International Institute of Communications and its wideranging publication, *Intermedia*.

SCHOLARLY ACCOMMODATION TO A NEW MEDIUM

For the student of government and politics, television is clearly a variable in political behaviour, as well as chronicle of and part of the environment of its

Broadcast Television Archives 135

Tuesday January 31, 1978 CBS

5:30:00 INTRODUCTION WALTER CRONKITE (NYC)

5:30:00 MIDEAST / MIL. TALKS / SADAT CARTER MTG. / ALGIERS MTG.

(S) Resumption of Mideast mil. talks in Cairo noted. Pres. Sadat's listing WC
of differences in basic principles of 2 sides rptd.

(Cairo, Egypt) Pres. Sadat's mtg. with group of Am. Christians & Jews who John
praise his peace initiative noted. Sadat's upcoming mtg. with Pres. Carter Sheahan
mentioned & details given re: topics to be discussed, incl. question of
self-determination for Palestinians. [SADAT - says way must be found to
incl. term "self-determination" in agreement, otherwise whole thing will
collapse.] Troubles in US mediation efforts between Israel & Egypt out-
lined. Israeli def. min. Ezer Weizman's return to Cairo for mil. talks,
while pol. talks remain halted, stated. Weizman's attitude upon arrival
contrasted to that of Egyptian def. min. Gen. Abdel Ghany Gamasy. [GAMASY -
has no statement to make.]

(S) Mtg. of for. mins. from hard-line Arab ntns. of Syria, Libya, S. Yemen & WC
Algeria & PLO rep. in Algiers rptd. Film shown. Length of Sadat's trip to
US noted, as well as Israeli for. min. Dayan's expected arrival in US for
speaking tour on day before Sadat's departure; no plans for them to meet
yet rptd.

5:33:30 (COMMERCIAL: Geritol; Mr. Coffee Water Filter.)

5:34:40 VN SPY CASE

(S) Alexandria, VA, ct.'s indictment of State Dept. employee & VN ntl. on WC
charges of spying for VN govt. rptd.

(DC) Details of charges given; arrested are USIA employee Ron. Louis Humphrey Barry
& Troung Dinh Hung, who is Stanford U. grad. [HUMPHREY - isn't spy, never Serafin
suspected Troung & is cooperating with authorities.] Ct. proceedings de- Artist:
scribed; will cont. on Wed. when pleas to be entered. Roxie Munroe

(S) Possible sentence for 2 men, if convicted, noted. WC

5:36:10 CANADA / USSR SATELLITE

(S) Rpts. of location of more pieces of crashed USSR satellite near Great WC
Slave Lake, in Canada's Northwest Territories noted. Details given; photos
shown. Other suspect areas cited.

5:36:30 RHODESIA / MALTA TALKS / SMITH TALKS

(S) Update on dvts. at Malta conf. on Rhodesia settlement re: maj. rule; WC
negotiators incl. UN amb. Andrew Young, British for. secy. David Owen &
guerrilla ldrs. Robt. Mugabe & Joshua Nkomo. Film shown. Bishop Abel
Muzorewa's return to talks with Prime Min. Ian Smith in Rhodesia rptd.

5:37:20 (COMMERCIAL: Lowenbrau; All-Bran.)

Fig. 1 In the abstracts portion of the monthly *Television News Index and Abstracts* guide to the Vanderbilt (University) Television News Archive, each of the three national networks' early evening news programmes is described by individual item duration (to the nearest ten seconds), item content, and news reader or correspondent. An index to names, places, and events accompanies each issue.

times. Somewhat less obviously, television in and of itself is an eminently political institution, a reflection of a culture's ways of establishing authority, allocating values, and making and adapting rules. In the end, television archives will develop according to the uses and demands which scholars put to them, and according to the knowledge derived from television data, together with other evidence, which could not have been acquired any other way.

In both teaching and research, broadcast television materials pose problems that stem both from their being beguilingly familiar, and uncomfortably revolutionary. Among academicians, some regard classroom television as merely another audio-visual crutch like transparencies and film. Even if not contemptuous, they are put off by the time and bother required to put Ivor Richard, Morarji Desai, or Andrew Young on a screen for a few minutes when it is so much easier to paraphrase them, or to show rioters in Buenos Aires actually doing that which textbooks call interest articulation. Other academicians, perhaps more sensitive to the fact that communication is not a separable craft or discipline but rather an element of all behaviour, are discovering broad epistemological implications of data from the youngest mass medium.

Mechanical problems of working with television archival materials in teaching and research are simpler than the theoretical and epistemological problems. Basic hardware consists of a television receiver, ranging from a household set to a monitor of studio quality, attached to a videotape recorder/player, to which may be added editing features for compilations and a timer for unattended recording. As of 1978, the initial equipment could be purchased for £1000-1500 ($2000-3000). Videorecording tapes are expensive, costing up to £12 ($24) for a 60-minute colour tape, but they can be wiped and re-used scores of times without losing fidelity and can be stored indefinitely in a wide temperature and humidity range. Tapes may be open reel-to-reel, permitting more precise editing, or cassette enclosed, with greater protection against damage. While assorted tape gauges on the market impede easy exchange among non-standardized collections, tapes in gauges to suit one's equipment are available from established lending collections such as the Vanderbilt Television News Archive. Finally, by adding a videocamera to the basic equipment, instructors may record and preserve non-broadcast events, such as local council meetings or seminars with visiting scholars.

Far and away the most formidable challenge for the scholar using television as variable or data source is understanding the subculture and production constraints of the medium itself. Both television and academe have roles to play as reporters, analysts, and interpreters of society, but their perspectives, restraints, and responsibilities are not identical. Not surprisingly, as scholarly attention has turned to television, broadcasters have been far less defensive about copyright and other proprietary issues than about reckless, uninformed, polemic attacks upon broadcasters' professional integrity. Television, no less than the family, church, bureaucracy or other established variables in social behaviour can be understood and evaluated only in terms of its own resources and responsibilities, not the resources and responsibilities of academe.

Beyond this fundamental obligation to understand the television medium in its own right stretch the many questions of method and theory which evermore are engaging social scientists. If television is to be 'content analysed', of what does its content consist, precisely, and what are its effective properties? How appropriate are the tools and techniques of printed mass media content analysis for examing television? Can researchers 'scan' television at high speed, and at what risks of distorting the original images? Now that television pervades society more thoroughly than any breakfast cereal, religious faith or political doctrine, where does the empirical scientist find unexposed control groups? What viewer and social needs does television serve, and how? In the case of no other social institution, perhaps, has so much been attributed with so little empirical support as has been attributed to television. Much of what is said and written about television is no less brilliant and persuasive for being impressionistic. However, the future of comprehensive, systematic, and accessible archives depends on whether scholars are content to let it rest at that.

Audio-visual Sources and Research into Modern British Politics

Kathryn Rowan

There are two distinct types of audio-visual material at the disposal of political scientists in Britain. First, material made for broadcasts or for distribution such as film, television and radio programmes; second, recorded interview material. For some time historians have referred to and utilized a wide variety of audio-visual materials. Why have political scientists neglected this potentially valuable source of evidence? The purpose of this paper is to examine this phenomenon.

A group at the Open University (Ref. 1) which is exploring the value of audio-visual materials for research to complement developments in the teaching field has raised the question of why this source has been neglected. The question arose out of a research review that the group conducted to document projects where audio-visual materials are used in the field of modern British history and politics. This review, which is described below, throws some doubt on a statement recently made by Annan (Ref. 2) that 'Academics have long been aware that radio and television programmes are an invaluable source for studying the political and social life of the nation'. However, the group has found only one or two cases where this awareness has been translated into action. It should be noted that Annan is referring to television and to radio and not to archive film of the pre-television era. Also he is talking about sources and not about the analysis or the study of the medium itself.

The reasons for this neglect are developed in the following discussion. The first and most fundamental concerns the problems (not necessarily technical) of preserving broadcast material and of lack of access to it. The other reasons appear to stem from a distrust of the non-printed form such as the belief that the printed word provides a harder form of evidence than oral or visual material. Visual evidence is often seen simply as an illustrative adjunct to teaching. Another relates to a suspicion of technology and its effects. A final doubt expressed is that film evidence (including television) and the recording of retrospective interviews are both appropriate to the study of social history, but not to politics.

The paper attempts to demonstrate the weakness of these arguments. It suggests that the reasons why political scientists refer to newspaper but not to television sources are pragmatic rather than intellectual, and that the reluctance to record interviews has become less defensible. The following section reviews the main areas of research

---

Kathryn Rowan is a member of the Group for Audio-Visual Research into British Politics at the Open University.

where audio-visual materials and methods are used and outlines the limitations and the possibilities associated with them. The major sources of audio-visual materials for political scientists are then described, together with the contents of the collections and their preservation and access policies. Finally, the assumptions underlying the reluctance to refer to audio-visual sources are challenged in light of various groups' research experience both at the Open University and elsewhere.

RESEARCH REVIEW

A review of audio-visual research projects was conducted because the group wanted to explore the feasibility of establishing an audio-visual archive for a recent period of British government (in this case the 1964-1970 Labour administrations). The idea was to build up a collection of contemporary film, television and sound records of the period as well as retrospective interviews (to be recorded with those associated with the events and policies of the period). Intrinsic to the proposal was an interest in evaluating this material in comparison with the more traditional sources such as diaries, memoirs, newspapers and official documents. This led the group to review the methods and problems involved in a range of related projects spanning the fields of social and political history and also studies of politics and the media. It included a number of recent television programmes involving the reconstruction or filming of political events.

Social historians have pioneered the use of film as a source of evidence in its own right. Archive film, especially newsreel, is an important source in the specialist study of propaganda (Ref. 3). Film is also used as a source of factual evidence about past situations unavailable from other sources (Ref. 4). Political historians have also begun to refer to and use film as evidence. Aldgate for example has shown, at a purely quantitative level, that the Spanish Civil War was quite well covered by British Paramount and Gaumont British newsreels (Ref. 5). Although historians have focussed their attention on archive film of the pre-television era, many of the problems raised are relevant to the collection and the evaluation of television material and include questions of access, cost, preservation and use.

Although the serious researcher has access to the major U.K. collections of archive film (these are at the Imperial War Museum, the National Film Archive and the commercial newsreel companies such as British Movietone and EMI Pathé), this access is not easy. Since there is no national register of holdings (Ref. 6) and the collections own catalogues are often incomplete it can be both difficult to find out what exists generally and to locate particular items. Large quantities of material remain unidentified. Charges are made for viewing film, and making copies is extremely expensive - running into several hundred pounds for one hour of film (though videotape is considerably cheaper). The ease with which archive film can be identified depends to a large extent on the associated written documentation which is, on the whole, most complete for the large newsreel collections. Permission to view film may also be contingent on the existence and the condition of viewing copies.

The historian needs to know as much contextual information as possible in order to interpret film as document. For example who made the film, where and when? This is true whichever aspect of the interpretation of film is being stressed; as a source for the study of propaganda or as a factual source of evidence. This is a conceptual distinction and in practice it may be difficult to disentangle the two.

The review indicated that the researcher will encounter these difficulties, and probably to a greater extent, when using television material (see the next Section). Historians and social scientists who have approached television material as a source of evidence have been daunted by the problems of access and the impossibility of retrieving the complete coverage of an event of issue. Blumler and Dilks (Ref. 7), for example, found that the retention of broadcast material was haphazard and unrelated to scholarly requirements. Their solution to this problem was to take off-air recordings of programmes as they are transmitted, using a number of video-recorders. This is how they have established an archive of all the nationally networked broadcasting coverage of the February and October 1974 General Election Campaigns and the 1975 EEC Referendum campaign. The establishment of such an archive also opens up the possibility of systematic analysis of the content of political coverage. It was specifically with this view in mind that another group at Glasgow University took off-air recordings of all networked news programmes for several months in 1975 (Ref. 8).

These collections are invaluable for historians and political scientists in the future. But they do not solve the problem of access to, and retrieval of, programmes transmitted in the 1950s and 1960s. In the early days of television, many programmes were transmitted live. It is difficult to establish whether any of them were also recorded. Today with the advent of video-tape, most programmes are pre-recorded, or recorded on to video-tape at the same time as they are being transmitted live from the studio. Clearly only a certain proportion of transmitted programmes have been preserved since television began. But this does not preclude the use of the material which has survived (after all the number of written documents that have survived must be small compared with the number originally produced).

Television material, if one considers news, current affairs and documentary programmes, is an important source of evidence because the sources of television news do not fully overlap with newspaper sources and they may, therefore, contain different or new information; because the comments and interpretations offered may be different; and because it provides a visual dimension to our perception of events (for example, a sense of the mood of a political party conference).

SOURCES OF AUDIO-VISUAL MATERIAL

Audio-visual material generated in the post-war period and of interest to political scientists can be broken down into four categories; television, radio, newsreel and film.

Television (Ref. 9)

The major producers of television material are the BBC and the Independent Television companies. All have their own libraries where material is stored with an eye to its future use in programmes. The Independent Television libraries also have a commercial function as they aim to sell their material to outside bodies. By contrast, the BBC Film and Video-tape Library exists to serve the need of the Corporation. It follows that whereas access to the ITV libraries is possible (for a fee), it is impossible for an outsider to get access to the BBC libraries. Similarly, one can find out what is in the ITV collections, but not in the BBC's archives.

However, the above is oversimplified as a description of television collections in Britain. There is also a national film archive, into which a considerable amount of both BBC and ITV material has found its way. Secondly, the provision and storage of news stories for both the BBC and the ITV companies is something of a separate enterprise. Independent Television News, provides the news bulletins for the independent network and the News Division at the BBC Television Centre has its own library. The BBC have their own correspondents but they also get news stories from a syndication service called VISNEWS. VISNEWS is owned by a group of national broadcasting corporations, (Britain, Canada, New Zealand and Australia) and Reuters. ITN material is stored in the ITN & UPITN news library and VISNEWS also has its own news libraries. In both cases it is possible for the various researchers to gain access.

There are several Independent Television companies based in London and the regions which tend to specialize in different types of programmes and each has its own library or collection. Some hold more material of national political significance than others. Granada, for example, has a complete set of its *State of the Nation* programmes, its *Decision* series and the *World in Action* programmes. The scripts of the programmes are also filed. For those interested in regional events, Yorkshire has preserved all the material from its news magazine *Calendar* from 1969 to the present. Current affairs programmes such as *Weekend World* produced by London Weekend Television go out live from the studio but a video-tape record is made at the same time. Programmes for the last two years have been stored. Unlike Granada which has its own film library, Thames Television and London Weekend Television have no such formal arrangements. Access to Granada and Yorkshire Television libraries is possible by appointment. But London Weekend and Thames Television film researchers will cooperate with outside enquiries.

On the whole, it is very difficult to find out what is in the BBC Film and Video-tape Library, because the outsider is not allowed access to the crucial catalogues. He does, however, have access to the BBC Reference and Registry Services for a basic charge of five pounds a day. The Programme Information Unit, which is a section of the Services, compiles an index of all the programmes transmitted on radio and television and collects and indexes radio scripts, excluding news bulletins. Television scripts, which are available for a fee, are held in the Registry section. But no effort is made by this section to keep track of the programmes or material actually retained by the BBC and this information is only available in the Film and Video-tape Library which is open neither to the public nor to the serious researcher. At the moment there is no way of knowing how much current affairs material generated in the 1960's has been preserved (programmes such as *Gallery*, *24 Hours* and *Panorama*). The author understands that the BBC Film and Video-tape Library has recently begun to take off-air recordings of current affairs programmes such as *Tonight* to speed up their cataloguing process. Previously they had had to wait for the filmed inserts to arrive from the department involved.

The problem of preservation and selection of material is more acute at the BBC than at the ITV companies because of the amount of material involved. The BBC state that all complete programmes and sequences are initially kept by the library and nothing is destroyed without first being offered to the National Film Archive. There is a non-stop review procedure with sequences reviewed after six months and programmes after five years. Critics of the BBC are concerned that the preservation policies are formed and applied by the heads of department who advise the Film and Video-tape Librarian, and that valuable material may be destroyed without anyone else knowing about it (Ref. 10).

Although there is no automatic or statutory archive storage of British television transmissions, the television companies share the archive function with the National Film Archive. The NFA is a major division of the British Film Institute and was set up in 1935 to maintain a national repository of films of permanent value. Television forms only a part of this collection and of this, news, current affairs and documentary material is an even smaller part. It relies on the voluntary co-operation of the BBC and the Independent Television companies for the material. The Independent Television Companies Association currently gives £30,000 per annum to the NFA to spend on ITV programmes. Apart from this it has at present a television acquisition budget of £21,800 which it spends on BBC material; clearly this is insufficient.

The NFA has a dual role: to ensure the preservation of all material acquired and to provide a centralised collection for the researcher. A shortage of funds means that preservation takes precedence. Apart from items in the VISNEWS library, the NFA provides the only access to BBC material. It holds a significant collection of news, documentary and current affairs material which can be viewed provided viewing copies are available. But the NFA has a backlog of material to deal with, so sometimes they are not available.

VISNEWS, ITN & UPITN libraries all hold complete collections of transmitted news stories as well as many unused stories. VISNEWS has stories dating from 1957 which are indexed chronologically (main entries are under location and date) and also by subject and personality. 'Shot lists' and 'dope sheets' (Ref. 11) are available for each news story on microfilm which give information about the sequence of film shots and the spoken commentary. The ITN library has film dating from 1955, when ITN began transmitting daily news bulletins on the newly formed Independent Television Network. It works on a similar principle to VISNEWS, but in addition to the shot lists and dope sheets, the library files list the contents of every programme produced.

For newsfilm, access to the catalogues is both possible and free of charge, but there is a fee for viewing. The material has been systematically preserved, not in the form of the news programmes as transmitted, but as individual news stories.

Newsreel

In the immediate post-war period, the BBC's news coverage took the form of filmed newsreels, with a format borrowed from newsreel companies such as Movietone and British Gaumont. It is somewhat anachronistic that some of these companies continued to produce weekly newsreels until 1970 and one, Movietone, is still doing so. There is no problem of access to this material, but its value to the political scientist has yet to be assessed.

Radio

Access to the transcripts of BBC radio programmes is possible through the Reference and Registry Services (see earlier), but, in addition, the researcher can listen to any sound material that has been preserved at the British Institute of Recorded Sound. The function of the BIRS is to keep a duplicate set of the material in the BBC Sound Archives and to make it available to the public. Much of the collection at the BIRS is of music and drama though they do have some 'political' material. This largely takes the form of extracts of speeches or interviews, which as they are out of context and their selection is somewhat arbitrary, is rather unsatisfactory for the researchers.

Film

A range of specialised film is also available. The Central Office of Information and the nationalised industries have their own film sections and produce propaganda and promotional film. Several large or international companies such as Shell also have film units for much the same purpose. The Index Film and Television Library holds film from several of these sources. Documentary film produced by radical or left wing producers can be found at a number of libraries. One of these is The Educational and Television Films Archive though most of its collection is pre-Second World War. Another is The Other Cinema which specializes in post-war 'political' documentaries made by independent British film makers.

Finally, there is the potentially important category of amateur film and 'home-movies', although the problems of locating this material are obvious.

ARE THE ASSUMPTIONS VALID?

Television and Film Evidence

Both the research review and the investigation of sources made it clear that part of the Open University's archive proposal (to collect existing film and television film material) was not feasible. As we have already seen, television companies do not give material away and the expense of duplication is hardly justifiable in the current economic climate. But two crucial problems had emerged. They were concerned with how to secure research access to existing sources, and how to develop procedures for handling television material as evidence, as a particular form of document.

It is difficult to assess the value of television material as evidence until these two problems have been solved but it would appear some of the basic doubts can be challenged on logical grounds. Firstly, the argument that the printed form is a 'harder' form of evidence (than the visual form) is not particularly useful. Visual evidence is different, but it is comparable with the printed form. Both are highly selective in what they portray or seek to represent. This is equally true whether one is referring to primary sources such as minutes, memoranda and letters, or to secondary accounts, such as biographies. One of the main differences is that visual material is nearly always produced or made by an observer whereas most primary written material is a product of participants.

The distinction between primary and secondary sources which has been made in relation to the printed form can be usefully applied to visual evidence. One procedure that the political scientist might adopt would be to compare certain categories of visual with certain categories of written material. For example newspaper news reports can be compared with television news stories. Television current affairs programmes and magazine programmes such as *Tonight* can be seen as a form of a political diary. In the same way that a historian should take account of possible personal and political bias when he uses a written diary as source of evidence, so should the political scientist with the television programme. And although several people are involved in the production of a television programme, an analysis of the values, if not the bias and the criteria involved in the making of the programme is not impossible (Ref. 12).

However, a degree of caution is necessary when referring to current affairs material. A standard format for a programme such as *Panorama* is the studio discussion when one or more politicians or trade unionists are brought into the studio to discuss, or to be questioned on, a recent political event or issue. The studio situation is itself in the nature of a 'pseudo-event' and should be recognised as such (Ref. 13). But pseudo-events often make news. Sunday's television discussion becomes Monday's newspaper headlines. Such material provides evidence, not of events, but of attitudes.

Documentary or actuality film can also be compared with printed material. Like a good historical account, it may be both interpretive and original. Documentaries are most comparable with secondary sources - analytical accounts or biographies. Like these, they may involve investigative research and bring to light new sources and evidence. The nature of the medium, the appearance of reality, suggests at a common sense level that the documentary provides a primary source of evidence. But the filmed sequences are carefully edited and put together to convey the image or impression that the producer wants to be communicated to the audience. Newsfilm should be treated with the same caution.

A further problem of interpreting film as evidence is raised when only parts of programmes are found to have been preserved. Newsfilm is preserved, not in the context of the news programme as transmitted, but as individual news stories. Similarly in the past the filmed inserts of current affairs programmes were preserved but not the interlinking studio presentation. The value of this material may depend on the availability of contextual information (scripts etc.).

In a strict historical sense none of the television material described counts as primary evidence, but it may provide a witting or unwitting testimony, the witting testimony being the message that the producer was intentionally conveying, and the unwitting testimony being the information not consciously included (Ref. 14). As Marwick has pointed out, the unwitting testimony provides information about patterns of behaviour and concrete situations. The political scientist who uses television material has the additional advantage of contemporary written accounts which refer to particular occasions when political programmes were being made. One such is Grace Wyndham-Goldie's recent study which details the wheeling and dealing that lay behind the making of several current affairs programmes (Ref. 15).

Finally, it has been argued that film as a source of evidence is of little use for 'political' history. However, it is difficult to argue this case for television which in the post-war period has both extended its political coverage and become inextricably intermeshed in the political process.

Recorded Interviews

The second part of the Open University's audio-visual archive proposal was to develop a collection of interviews to be conducted with those associated with the events and policies of the period. The group found few precedents in Britain for such an enterprise. The developments in the field of oral history seemed to be relevant, but a quick glance at the range of contributions to the journal *Oral History* showed that they concentrate primarily on socio-economic history.

In America, by contrast, oral history techniques have been developed in relation to political subjects. Two well-known oral history programmes in the States are the Dulles collection and the Kennedy collection (Ref. 16). Both centre on the life of the particular man and the politics of his period of office. The concept of oral history has now become an integral part of all the Presidential Archives. In Britain, this function has been fulfilled, to a certain extent, by television. Periodically, a television company seeks an interview with a retired prime minister or politician. Several such interviews have recently been broadcast (with Eden, Macmillan and Wilson). The group felt that these interviews however well researched, are bound to be of a superficial nature and geared towards a popular appeal.

The interviews that the group was interested in conducting were those sought by political scientists for the purpose of academic research, that is related to specific research questions arising from detailed research of other sources. Political scientists and political historians cite such interviews as an important source, but few attempt to record them. Several explicitly reject the idea of recording, arguing that it inhibits the discussion. Some even refuse to take notes for the fear that it may interrupt the flow of conversation.

The Open University group decided to put this to the test as four members of the group were engaged in a research project into aspects of policy making in recent government. The technique of recording interviews was to be tried and evaluated in this context. The group found that the problems of method and the problems of memory are at least as great as the effect of recording in the use of interviews as a source of evidence and that while there are clearly some disadvantages of recording, the advantages can outweigh them.

In the context of method, Harrison (Ref. 17) has pointed out that the interview is but one stage in a sequence of events, which should begin with documentary research.

This may inspire an interview, initiate a correspondence with the informant, lead to further documentary research and finally to another interview. If the interview is to be worthwhile, the researcher must have a clear idea of what he does not know and what he hopes to find out. The purpose of the interview should be two fold: to check the printed record against the interviewee's own experience, and to pursue areas where the written account is inadequate. It follows that it is both permissible and logical for the researcher to remind the informant of events and to discuss the other sources with him.

However well-briefed the researcher, one of the problems of handling an interview can be the relative disparity in status between the researcher and the informant, if the latter is a minister or a civil servant, and the researcher a junior member of academic staff. The Open University group had two widely different experiences in this context both of which were equally disarming. In one case, a senior Cabinet Minister produced a stop watch and a tape recorder at the outset of the interview. In the other an ex-minister arrived three quarters of an hour late for the interview, but promptly disarmed the researcher by saying that he had cancelled the rest of his meetings for that day and had all the time in the world.

Most politicians and senior civil servants are adept at handling the interview situation and the researcher may find it difficult to get them to answer questions. One ex-minister retorted 'Let me do it my way' when a member of the group pressed for answer during an interview. But most respect, and are interested in, serious research and will co-operate as fully as their time permits.

The problem of memory is critical in this type of interviewing, and it has two facets. One is the straightforward question of whether the informant remembers or not. The second is more complex. It is how to evaluate what the informant claims to remember. Paul Thompson (Ref. 18) has argued that we perceive the past in terms of two sets of norms - the norms that influenced our perception of events in the past and the norms that influence our perception in the present. It may be impossible for the researcher to disentangle the two from the interview alone, but reference to other sources, in particular contemporary television interviews, may help.

The political scientist faces a particular problem of memory. The informant is usually aware of at least some of the documentary evidence and it may be difficult to abstract his own memory of an event from other accounts he has come across. Members of the group experienced this difficulty when interpreting an interview given by an ex-General Secretary of the TUC. During his period of office relations between the TUC and the government were reported in detail by Peter Jenkins of *The Guardian*. The transcript of the interview reveals phrases and arguments, similar, and in one or two cases identical to those used by Jenkins in his earlier articles. There was a sense of '*déjà-vu*'.

The researcher should not be unduly dismayed by these problems. No source is perfect; the process of selection, perception and interpretation are always there whether the past or present is being discussed and whether the source is oral or written. Thompson (Ref. 19) has gone so far as to argue that one of the greatest advantages of using interviews is that 'they raise the basic problem of method and bias in information which is not generally recognised in other material'.

Recording interviews poses two additional problems. It may inhibit the informant as we have already mentioned. Also it may create a sense of 'audience' for both the researcher and the informant. This sense may encourage both researcher and participant to perform and may make the informant give a more coherent picture of the past than he would otherwise have done. On the other hand, both the inhibiting effect and the 'audience' element involved in interviewing may be imperceptible. Another example from the Open University group's experience illustrates this. The ex-General Secretary of the TUC was far from being inhibited by the recording equipment. He spoke freely and appeared totally unaware of the microphone, not noticing at one stage that he knocked it over when reaching for a book to illustrate the point he was making. Much depends on the individual personality.

The decision to record or not must be made in relation to each case. Clearly, the chief reason many political scientists do not consider recording is their fear of not getting 'non-attributable' information. Informants may be inhibited from speaking 'on the record' by the Official Secrets Act. One solution to this is to offer an embargo on sections of the tape. The researcher also has to consider whether note taking is more disturbing than recording when weighing up the pros and cons. The author noticed during an unrecorded interview with an ex-junior minister that her note-taking had an inhibiting effect. Nothing was said but only when pen and paper were put on one side did the informant begin to talk more freely.

The advantages of recording are mentioned less frequently and they should be stressed. Firstly the reader of a research paper or monograph no longer has to take on trust the author's interpretation of the 'hundreds of interviews on which this study is based'. The transcripts (the evidence), should be kept for as long as possible to allow for challenge or for reanalysis. (This is normal procedure for many of the social sciences.) The second advantage is to the researcher himself. However careful he may be, he cannot help listening selectively during the interview. Recording prevents the loss of information and gives the interview a wider value as it can be used by other people. Finally, it may encourage some politicians to give interviews and to record for posterity their views on controversial issues.

A general point is that political scientists can be very secretive about their sources of evidence in comparison with other social scientists. While the Official Secrets Act plays a part in this, much of interest can be uncovered publicly without impinging on it. This has been demonstrated by the interviews conducted for Granada Television's *Inside British Politics* series (Ref. 20). Interviewing for television provides the most public context possible, yet Keith Kyle managed to reveal some remarkable information about the conference at Sèvres (a secret meeting between the English, French and Israelis, preceding the Suez invasion) in interviews conducted for a series of programmes on the Suez crisis (Ref. 21). It was, of course, an explosive and controversial issue, and the most revealing interviews were with the French and Israeli participants. Where there is greater consensus, informants may be more reticent, but these examples suggest that some rethinking is in order.

CONCLUSION

It is clear from the preceding discussion that sources of television material need to be opened up further to the researcher, and that historians and political scientists should be able to advise on preservation policies. Further, any reluctance to record interviews as a matter of principle, needs to be reassessed in light of the new evidence. Audio-visual sources provide additional information for the political scientist, but more importantly they provide a different sort of evidence: the witting and unwitting testimony already referred to. At present though, it appears that one of the richest records of political life in Britain is being virtually ignored.

NAMES AND ADDRESSES OF BRITISH FILM AND TELEVISION ARCHIVES AND LIBRARIES

BBC Film and Video-tape Library,
(Reynard Mills Industrial Estate),
Windmill Road,
Brentford, Middx.

01-567 6655

BBC Reference and Registry Services,
BBC,
London, W.1.   01-580 4468 ext. 4647

British Movietone News,
North Orbital Road,
Denham,
Uxbridge, Middx.

Denham 2323

Educational and Television Films,
247a, Upper Street,
Highbury Corner,
London, N.1.

01-226 2298

EMI Pathé Film Library,
Film House,
142, Wardour Street,
London, W.1.

01-437 0444

Granada Television Film Library,
Manchester,
M60 9EA

061 832 7211

Imperial War Museum Film Archive,
Lambeth Road,
London S.E.1.   01-735 8922

ITN-UPITN Film Library,
48, Wells Street,
London, W.1.

01-637 2424

National Film Archive,
81, Dean Street,
London, W.1.   01-437 4355

Visnews and Video-tape Library,
Cumberland Avenue,
London, N.W.16

01-965 7733

Slade Film History Register,
c/o British Universities Film Council,
81, Dean Street,
London W1V 6AA

01-734 3687

The Other Cinema,
12/13, Newport Street,
London, WC2H 7JJ

01-734 8508/9

Yorkshire Television,
The Television Centre,
Leeds
LS3 1JS

0532 38183

NOTES AND REFERENCES

1. The Group for Audio-visual Research into British Politics.

2. *The Report of the Committee of Enquiry into the Future of Broadcasting*, Cmnd. 6753 (1977), 461, H.M.S.O., London.

3. N. Pronay, The Newsreels: the illusion of actuality, in P. Smith (ed) (1976) *The Historian and Film*, Cambridge.

4. P. Smith (ed) (1976) *The Historian and Film*, Cambridge.

5. A. Aldgate, 1930's Newsreels: Censorship and Controversy, *Sight and Sound 46*, 154 (summer 1977).

6. A selective register of holdings is provided by the Slade Film History Register which is in the care of the British Universities Film Council. Lack of funds has halted the progress on the Register but details of it are available through the BUFC.

7. David Dilks, School of History and J.G. Blumler, the Centre for Television Research, Leeds University - personal communication.

8. Glasgow University Media Group (1976) *Bad News*, Routledge and Kegan Paul, London.

9. I am grateful to James Ballantyne of the BUFC who provided me with much of the information referred to in this section of the paper.

10. The BBC has set up an Archives Advisory Committee under the chairmanship of Lord Asa Briggs. Its task is to advise on the ways in which the BBC archives might best be exploited in the BBC's and the national interest.

11. Shot lists and dope sheets are the film librarians' major written documentation of the film stored. Further information is provided in H.P. Harrison (1973) *Film Library Techniques*, Focal Press, London.

12. J.G. Blumler, Producers' Attitudes Towards Television Coverage of an Election Campaign, in R. Rose (ed) (3rd edition, 1976) *Studies in British Politics*, Macmillan Press, London.

13. This concept was developed by Daniel J. Boorstin in the context of the American media 'industry' where he argues newsmen create non existent news. D.J. Boorstin (1963) *The Image*, Pelican Books.

14. A. Marwick (1975) *War and Society*, Archive Film Compilation Booklet A301, The Open University.

15. G. Wyndham-Goldie (1977) *Facing the Nation: Television and Politics 1936-1976*, Bodley Head, London.

16. The Dulles Oral History Collection, The Princetown University Library; The Kennedy Collection, The John F. Kennedy Library, Federal Records Centre, 380 Trapelo Road, Waltham, MA 02154.

17. B. Harrison, Oral History and Recent Political History, *Oral History no 3*, 30-48 (1972).

18. P. Thompson, Problems of Method in Oral History, *Oral History no 4*, 1-48 (1972).

19. *Ibid*.

20. Granada Television *Inside British Politics*; a series of seven programmes produced by Brian Lapping and transmitted between June 12th and July 25th 1977.

21. BBC 1 *Tonight* programmes transmitted on 8th, 9th, 10th and 11th November, 1976.

Some European Film Collections: an Annotated List

James Ballantyne

The film archives and film libraries listed below are chosen for their relevance to the matter of this publication. The list is not exhaustive, for example British collections are not included as these are referred to in the paper by Kathryn Rowan. Entries are arranged alphabetically under country. Where a considerable amount of detail is given about a collection this was received in answer to a request for information that I sent out in November 1977. In the briefer entries the figures given for holdings of books and posters cannot always be strictly compared one with another as the number of duplicates within different collections can be as low as 3% or as high as 50% of the total. Readers wishing to know more about other collections in Europe and elsewhere in the world are advised to consult the publications listed at the end of this summary. The *FIAF Directory* in particular gives a wealth of detail about supplementary documentation such as scripts, newspaper clippings, scrapbooks, programmes, sound recordings, etc. It should be noted that many of the film archives and film libraries also collect television materials and/or television documentation. Lastly, readers should know that the major problem facing the film archivist today is the preservation of nitrate film, and the film researcher that of access to material. Consequently, the knowledge that an item exists in a collection carries with it no guarantee that the item may be borrowed, or even viewed.

AUSTRIA

Öesterreichisches Filmarchiv
Rauhensteingasse 5
A-1010 WIEN

Telephone: 529936/528172

Director: Dr Walter Fritz

Holdings: 20,000+ film titles, ca 3,500 books, 90+ current periodical titles, 200,000+ film stills, 26,000+ posters.

James Ballantyne is Information Officer, British Universities Film Council.

Öesterreichisches Filmmuseum
Augustinerstrasse 1
A-1010 WIEN

Telephone: 526206/523426

Directors: Peter Konlechner and Peter Kubelka

Brief history of collection: The museum was founded in 1964 by the directors. Since 1966 it organises the retrospective screenings at the Vienna Film Festival. More than 600 films a year are shown.

Holdings: ca 2,500 feature film titles, ca 2,600 newsreels, 4000+ books, 80+ current periodical titles, 128,000+ film stills, 2,000+ posters, 10,000+ souvenir film programmes. Press clippings, press books, etc., are also held.

Storage facilities: The nitrate film vaults are temperature and humidity controlled. Nitrate film constitutes about 14% of the total film holdings.

Catalogues and indexes: The film index is on microfilm: it contains information on about 200,000 titles. There are no published catalogues to the museum's own collection. Books are also catalogued.

Accessibility of materials and policy toward researchers: The library is open to all users without charge. Special arrangements must be made to view film material.

BELGIUM

Cinémathèque Royale de Belgique
Ravenstein 23
1000 BRUXELLES

Telephone: 5134155

Curator: Jacques Ledoux

Holdings: 5,000+ film titles, 8,000+ books, 200,000+ film stills. There is also a large collection of posters.

BULGARIA

Bulgarska Nacionalna Filmoteka
Ul. Gourko 36
1000 SOFIA

Telephone: 870296/899637

Director: Todor Andreykov

Holdings: ca 5,000 film titles, ca 2,000 books, 70+ current periodical titles, 7,000+ film stills, ca 5,000 posters.

CZECHOSLOVAKIA

Ceskoslovensky Filmowy Ustav-Filmoteka
Národní 40
11000 PRAHA i

Telephone: 260087

Director: Dr Slavoj Ondroušek

Brief history of collection: Founded in 1945 under the direction of the film historian Jindřich Brichta. It has four departments: film archive, cinematographic museum, film library, documentation department. By donation and purchase the archive acquired old films from small distribution companies and the positive and negative prints of the collections of the major Czech film production companies.

Holdings: ca 10,000 feature length films; the same number of short films, ca 5,000 negatives/features/and 6,000 short negatives; complete sets of newsreels since 1945 and large collection of early primitive films and silent comedies; 313,500 film stills, 87,150 press-sheets, personal documents on film-makers and actors.

Storage facilities: Two large vaults; new one being built.

Catalogues and indexes: All deposited films are indexed in the main working catalogue. Part catalogues on silent films and short films were issued recently. The catalogue on silent films was prepared in accordance with the FIAF guidelines.

Accessibility of materials and policy toward researchers: The archive provides viewing facilities for film-makers, authors, designers and actors, as well as for students of specialized film schools and all serious students of film history.

DENMARK

Det danske filmmuseum
Store Søndervoldstraede
DK 1419 KØBENHAVN K

Telephone: 576500

Director: Ib Monty

Brief history of collection: In November 1941 the institution known as Dansk Kulturfilm undertook to supply funds to set up a Danish film archive and the film museum was thus founded. In 1947 independent statutes for the film archive were drawn up and the official name, 'Det danske filmmuseum', was adopted. Until 1958 the museum was an independent institution financed by government grants: in that year it was placed under the administration of the Government Film Office. In 1964 it was given status as an independent state institution under the Ministry for Cultural Affairs. In June 1966 the museum moved to its present premises which it rents from the Danish Film Institute.

Holdings: 8,000 film titles + ca 150-200 a year; ca 26,000 books and pamphlets, ca 230 current periodical titles, 1,100,000+ film stills, ca 11,000 posters.

Film components stored: The museum has 8 mm, 16 mm, 35 mm and 70 mm films and the collection comprises both negatives and positive prints.

Storage facilities: The museum's 24 vaults at Bagsvaerd, outside Copenhagen cover an area of 600 square metres. Nine of the vaults can hold 1,500 reels of film each, the remainder 500 reels each. Air-conditioning ensures that temperature and humidity are kept constant.

Catalogues and indexes: Card catalogue of film titles and personalities. No printed catalogue.

Supplementary documentation: ca 3,000 unpublished film scripts, 1,500+ sheets of film music, 24,000+ files of newspaper clippings; programmes, pressbooks, scrapbooks, sound recordings etc.

Accessibility of materials and policy toward researchers: Films can be viewed at the museum's premises.

FINLAND

Suomen Elokuva-arkisto
Etaläranta 4B
00130 HELSINKI

Telephone: 659653/171010

Director: Seppo Huhtala

Brief history of collection: The Finnish Film Archive was established in 1957 as a private association. It has received a state subsidy since 1962. It has the same functions in Finland as the National Film Archive and the National Film Theatre in the UK.

Holdings: 2,500 feature film titles + ca 150 a year; 8,000 documentary, non-fiction and short fiction titles. Ratio of deposited/imported films is about 60%. 8,000 books + ca 300 a year; 160+ current periodical titles: 1,000 bound annual volumes; 1,000,000+ film stills, 10,000 posters, 15,000 folders of newspaper clippings and other documents about feature films; 2,000 scripts and dialogue lists.

Film components stored: Feature films are on 35 mm and are mostly black and white. Original negatives: 950,000 metres, 35 mm. Duplicate negatives: 10,000 metres, 35 mm. Master reversals: 10,000 metres, 16 mm. Preserved domestic nitrate film (to January 1st, 1977): 650,000 metres out of a total of some 2,000,000 metres to be preserved.

Storage facilities: Total area of premises - 1,200 square metres; safety film vaults - 450 square metres; nitrate film vaults (temperature and humidity controlled) - 60 square metres; paper material storage area - 250 square metres.

Catalogues and indexes: No published catalogues. Index of the 2,500 feature films. Index of all preserved domestic nitrate film items (1,000+).

Accessibility of materials and policy toward researchers: The archive arranges regular film screenings in Helsinki and four other Finnish cities. It also arranges Finnish Film Weeks abroad. There are private viewing facilities for film students and researchers. Copyright and film material ownership rest with the producer. The archive acquires screening rights for all of its non-theatrical showings.

FRANCE

Centre National de la Cinématographie
Service des Archives du Film
78390 Bois d'Arcy

Telephone: 4602050

Le Conservateur/Chef du Service: Frantz Schmitt

Brief history of collection: First vaults were ready to receive film from 30th October 1968. A government decree of 19th June 1969 charged the Centre National de la Cinématographie with the task of preserving cinematographic film. After the first seven years of operation the Service had received 300,000 reels of film (of which 70% were nitrate) from 600 depositors.

Holdings: 28,000+ film titles: 30,000 cans of newsfilm; 1,000+ books, 50+ current periodical titles, 28,500+ film stills, ca 5,700 posters.

Storage facilities: Two buildings with a total capacity of 300,000 cans of 35 mm safety film: a third building with a capacity of 180,000 cans of 35 mm film is under consideration. The nitrate vaults consist of 87 cells with 50 more cells under construction. All buildings are temperature and humidity controlled.

Catalogues and indexes: For internal use only.

Accessibility of materials and policy toward researchers: All collections are open to the public. Research is undertaken and charged for by special agreement.

Cinémathèque de Toulouse
3 rue Roquelaine
31000 TOULOUSE

Telephone: 489075

Curator: Raymond Borde

Holdings: ca 3,000 feature film titles, ca 4,500 short film titles; 3,000+ books; 60+ current periodical titles, 100,000+ film stills, 12,000+ posters.

l'Etablissement Cinématographique et Photographique des Armées (l'Ecpa)
Fort d'Ivry
Ivry sur Seine

Telephone: 6723777

Curator: Colonel Canniccioni

Holdings: 20,000,000 metres of film, or 90,000 cans or ca 14,000 titles. Almost 20,000 metres covering the period 1914-1918 have been preserved. In February 1976 a seven year programme, the aim of which is to preserve all nitrate film, was initiated. L'Ecpa produces about fifty documentaries a year.

Catalogues and indexes: Title and subject card indexes. It is hoped to produce a new catalogue using computer processing methods within four or five years.

Accessibility of materials and policy toward researchers: Permission to view material may be obtained from the Service d'Information et de Relations Publiques des Armées, 231 boulevard Saint-Germain, Paris (7e), which has also published a catalogue, 'Films de Cinémathèque, période 1919-1946'.

Gaumont Actualités et Société Nouvelle des Ets. Gaumont
1 Quai Gabriel Péri
Joinville-le-Pont

Telephone: 8864902

Director: Daisy de Galard

Holdings: 550,000 metres of edited material; 1,470,000 metres of unedited material; 203,000 metres of feature length and short fiction film. 1895 is the date of the oldest film preserved. The library also archives the Cinémathèque Eclair, the earliest documents of which date from 1933.

Catalogues and indexes: The original card indexes are on the premises. Where possible items are being reclassified to create a new index with separate subject, locations and personalities sections.

Société Nouvelle Pathé Cinéma
6 rue Francoeur
75018 PARIS

Telephone: 2571210

Chief Librarian: Mlle Jacqueline Charron

Holdings: Several million metres of newsfilm, documentary film, fiction film and television programmes on 35 mm and 16 mm. 1895 is the date of the oldest film preserved.

Film components stored: Nitrate and acetate film; negative and positive prints.

Catalogues and indexes: Card index for on-the-spot consultation but extracts from the index can be sent on request.

Accessibility of materials and policy toward researchers: On payment.

GERMAN DEMOCRATIC REPUBLIC

Staatliches Filmarchiv der Deutschen Demokratischen Republik
Hausvogteiplatz 3-4
108 BERLIN

Telephone: 2124324/2826404

Curator: Dr Wolfgang Klaue

Holdings: 40,000+ film titles, ca 3,000 books, 85+ current periodical titles, 112,000 film stills, 7,000+ posters.

Hochschule für Film und Fernsehen
Kronenstrasse 10
108 BERLIN

Telephone: 2292708/2292190

Head of Documentation: Prof. Dr Konrad Schwalbe.
Director: Dr Lutz Koehlert.

Holdings: The library of ca 80,000 books and 300+ current periodical titles covers cinema, theatre and the mass media. Note: This institution does not archive films.

GERMAN FEDERAL REPUBLIC

Bundesarchiv-Filmarchiv
Am Wöllershof 12
5400 KOBLENZ 1

Holdings: The Filmarchiv holds originals of many German films of the Third Reich including those which were captured by American forces and deposited with the Library of Congress after the Second World War.

Supplementary documentation: An extensive collection includes the records of Ufa and the Reichsfilmkammer.

Deutsche Wochenschau GmbH
Sieker Landstr. 39a
2000 HAMBURG 73

Telephone: 6771011

Director: Klaus Lensch

Archivleiterin: Mechthild Meyer-Rix

Brief history of collection: On behalf of the Press Office of the Federal Republic Deutsche Wochenschau looks after the issues of the weekly newsreel 'Welt im Film' which were produced by the allied occupation forces from 1945 to 1955. Deutsche Wochenschau and its subsidiary 'Cinecentrum GmbH' today produce newsreels, industrial films, documentaries and advertising films.

Holdings: Weekly newsreels in black and white, 35 mm, safety film, covering the years 1945-1977: 'Welt im Film' (369 issues), 'Welt im Bild' (213 issues), 'Neue Deutsche Wochenschau und Zeitlupe' (1022 issues), 'Ufa' (1092 issues), 'El Mundo al Instante (797 issues), 'O Mundo em Noticias' (658 issues): ca 6000 documentary and industrial films, 50% in colour, 50% in black and white, on 35 mm safety film; ca 300 issues of the monthly cinemagazine 'Deutschlandspiegel: Berichte aus Deutschland', 50% in colour, 50% in black and white, on 35 mm safety film. In all some 22 million metres of film are archived.

Catalogues and indexes: There is an alphabetical subject index and personalities index to the whole collection.

Supplementary documentation: The issue sheets of the newsreel material are filed.

Accessibility of material and policy toward researchers: All material is available for commercial and non-commercial use by, for example, domestic and foreign television companies, advertising companies, film producers and institutions of higher education.

Deutsches Institut für Filmkunde
Schloss
6202 WIESBADEN-BIEBRICH

Telephone: 69071-75

Directors: Dr Theo Fürstenau, Ulrich Pöschke

Holdings: 3,000+ film titles, ca 23,000 books, 270+ current periodical titles, ca 560,000 film stills, ca 23,000 posters.

Stiftung Deutsche Kinemathek
Pommernalle 1
1000 BERLIN 19

Telephone: 3036234

Director: Dr Heinz Rathsack

Brief history of collection: The Senate of West Berlin founded the Kinemathek on the 1st February 1963. The film director Gerhard Lamprecht's personal collection of films, scripts, film programmes and film apparatus, along with the Fidelius collection formed the basis of the Kinemathek's stock. In subsequent years further collections were purchased with the aid of funds received through the 'Deutsche Klassenlotterie Berlin'. In 1971 the Kinemathek was declared a foundation and from then on it has been funded directly by the Berlin Senate.

Holdings: 2,500+ feature film titles, 2,600+ short film titles, 20,000 books (administered, with the periodicals and scripts, by the Deutsche Film und Fernseh-Akademie in the same building); 180,000+ film stills, 8,000+ posters, 30,000+ film programmes.

Storage facilities: Capacity of vaults for nitrate and negative film - 6,000 reels: temperature +6-7°C; humidity 55-60%. Capacity of vaults for acetate material - 17,500 reels: temperature +9-10°C; humidity 55-60%.

Catalogues and indexes: Main record in vaults. The archive card catalogue lists films under title, and under country of production. There is also an index to directors.

Supplementary documentation: The Kinemathek publishes series of books and pamphlets. Much of its documentation is in the library of the Deutsche Film - und Fernsech-Akademie.

Accessibility of materials and policy toward researchers: Publishers, journalists, film writers and historians and television personnel may use the collection. Use of the three viewing tables (for 16 mm and 35 mm) is free for academic and scientific purposes. For the same purposes also there is no charge when material is viewed on the premises. There is a hire charge of 90 DM for each feature film screened off the premises. A film still costs 8 DM; 50 DM if used for commercial purposes.

GREECE

Tainiothiki tis Ellados
1 Kanari Street
ATHENS 138

Telephone: 612046

Curator: Aglaya Mitropoulos

Brief history of collection: The Greek Film Archive was founded in 1955 and reorganised in 1963 as a foundation. It is now partly subsidised by the State.

Holdings: 1,000+ film titles, 500+ books, 3,000+ film stills, 2,000+ posters.

HUNGARY

Magyar Filmtudományi Intézet és Filmarchívum
1143 Budapest XIV
Népstadion út 97

Telephone: 429599

Director: Dr Sándor Papp

Curator: Dr István Molnár

Holdings: ca 5,000 feature film titles, ca 7,000 documentary film titles, 5,300+ newsreels, ca 7,500 books, 100 current periodical titles, ca 47,000 film stills, ca 7,000 posters.

IRELAND (REPUBLIC)

Liam O'Leary Film Archives
Garden Flat
23 Wellington Place
Dublin 4

Telephone: 685875

Director: Liam O'Leary

Brief history of collection: Arising out of the 'Cinema Ireland' Exhibition held at Trinity College Dublin in March 1976 the archives were founded in July 1977 with the following aims:

1. To find a permanent home for Irish films worthy of preservation as artistic, historical or technically interesting records.

2. To collect posters, programmes, photos and other documents relating to the history of the cinema in Ireland.

3. To record the reminiscences of old-time film workers and the early recollections of film-going by prominent Irish personalities.

4. To research the newspapers and journals for information on the development of

the cinema in Ireland.

5. To publicise the need for an Irish independent National Film Archive.

6. Any other activities which will promote an awareness of the importance of the cinema in Irish life.

Holdings: Films so far acquired are deposited for preservation in a co-operating archive. 50 sound recordings. A collection of posters, programmes, photos, stills, negatives and slides is being built up. There is a large collection of books and periodicals. Special collections: drawings, letters etc. of Rex Ingram; rare photos and press books on classic films of the Twenties.

Catalogues and indexes: Irish Film Index: a card catalogue of 500+ cards carrying details of films made in Ireland between 1896 and 1976 as well as films of Irish interest; it is estimated that the Index will run to several thousand cards when completed. Index of Irish film personalities: several hundred cards cover directors, technicians and actors.

Supplementary documentation: Items such as photocopies of secret official documents concerning the cinema at the time of the Irish War of Independence are included in the collection. There is a list of films shown in all Dublin cinemas each week from 1896 to 1976.

Accessibility of materials and policy toward researchers: Accessibility is limited at the moment as Mr O'Leary and his colleague are operating on a spare time basis, implementing an initial five-year plan. Time allowing, all enquiries will be dealt with free of charge.

ITALY

<u>Cineteca Nazionale</u>
Centro Sperimentale di Cinematografia
via Tuscolana 1524
00173 ROMA

Telephone: 740046

Curator: Dr Lodoletta Lupo

Holdings: 15,000+ film titles, ca 7,000 books, ca 190 current periodical titles.

<u>Istituto Luce</u>
Piazza di Cinecittá 11
00174 ROMA

Telephone: 742641

President: Prof. Ernesto G. Laura

Director-General: Emilio Vesperini

Holdings: The Institute has a collection of newsfilm and news photographs dating from 1900 to date. It holds the copyright on pre World War Two and World War Two fascist material.

NETHERLANDS

NV Cinecentrum/BV Polygoon
's Gravelandseweg 80
HILVERSUM

Telephone: 03513851 ext. 340 to 345

Manager: Pieter M. Buis

Holdings: 35 mm black and white and colour newsreel material (partly colour since 1963) dating from 1921. Each newsreel issue has four stories per week on average.

Film components stored: Nitrate 35 mm negatives for the years 1921-52; acetate 35 mm negatives from 1952. From 1932 to date with sound on negative or separate optical soundtrack.

Storage facilities: All negative and positive prints, including soundtracks are stored in old army bunkers. Temperature and humidity are controlled.

Catalogues and indexes: Card index to the newsreel material. No printed catalogue.

Supplementary documentation: Press clippings, scene-lists, typed commentaries. Newsreel issue sheets for every week after 1946.

Accessibility of materials and policy toward researchers: On request items can be shown on editing table. From 1921 to 1945 only in negative, from 1945 until now also in positive. Search fee is Dfl. 30 per item. Film material regarding the Royal Family cannot be copied without governmental permission.

Stichting Nederlands Filmmuseum
Vondelpark 3
AMSTERDAM W

Telephone: 141646

Curator: Jan de Vaal

Holdings: 25,000+ film titles, ca 7,000 books, ca 180 current periodical titles, 255,000+ film stills, 15,000+ posters.

NORWAY

Norsk Filminstitutt
Aslakveien 14B/Postboks 5 Røa
OSLO 7

Telephone: 242994

Director: Jon Stenklev

Brief history of collection: Founded in 1955 with a budget of £500. 1978 budget is approximately £160,000. It is the State Film Museum and is funded by the Royal Norwegian Ministry of Ecclesiastical Affairs and Education.

Holdings: 2,100+ feature film titles and 3,800+ short film titles (ca 20% is nitrate, 15% colour); ca 6,500 books; 84 current periodical titles - 1,700 volumes of back issues; a large clippings and stills collection covering approximately 11,000 film titles; 1,500+ posters.

Film components stored: For Norwegian material, positive and negative prints, fine grain prints, effects track, etc. are held. Foreign films are usually positive prints.

Storage facilities: Nitrate vaults are built into a mountain. New vaults for acetate and colour film covering an area of 900 square metres and costing approximately £1,000,000 are under construction. The old vaults are temperature and humidity controlled as will be the new.

Catalogues and indexes: No printed catalogue. Film titles are listed on Kardex. About 70% of the collection has been fully indexed.

Supplementary documentation: Film programmes, scrapbooks, sound recordings, slides etc.

Accessibility of material and policy toward researchers: There is no charge for students and researchers who view film on the premises. There are regular screenings in the Institute's 48 seater study cinema.

POLAND

Filmoteka Polska
Ul. Pulawska 61
00975 WARSZAWA

Telephone: 455074

Director: Roman Witek

Holdings: 9,000+ film titles, 12,000+ books, ca 120 current periodical titles, ca 300,000 film stills, 30,000+ posters.

PORTUGAL

Cinemateca Nacional
Palacio Foz Restauradores
LISBOA 2

Telephone: 362531

Director: Manuel Felix Ribeiro

Holdings: 850+ film titles, ca 7,000 books, 17,000+ film stills, ca 70 current periodical titles, 400+ posters.

RUMANIA

Arhiva Naţională de Filme
Bd. Gh. Gheorghiu Dej 65
Casuta postala 126
BUCHAREST 1

Telephone: 133485

Director: Marin Pârâianu

Holdings: 5,000+ feature film titles, 10,000+ documentary non-fiction and short fiction titles, ca 4,000 books, ca 250,000 film stills, 19,000+ posters.

SOVIET UNION see USSR

SPAIN

Filmoteca Nacional de España
Ministerio de Información y Turismo
Avenida del Generalísimo 39, Planta 10
MADRID 16

Telephone: 4550442

Director: Florentino Soria Heredia

Holdings: 6,000+ film titles, ca 8,000 books, 30+ current periodical titles, 7,000+ film stills, 200+ posters.

Noticiarios y Documentales Cinematográficos: NO-DO
Joaquin Costa 43
MADRID 6

Telephone: 2617400

Jefe del Servicio Exterior: Carmen Diez de Rivera

Holdings: Newsreels and documentaries on Spain.

SWEDEN

Cinemateket/Svenska Filminstitutet
Filmhuset
Box 27 126
S-102 52 STOCKHOLM 27

Telephone: 630510

Director of Filminstitutet: Harry Schein
Cinemateket: Rolf Lindfors, Anna-Lena Wibom

Holdings: 7,000+ film titles, 21,000+ books, ca 240 current periodical titles, 1,250,000+ film stills, 30,000+ posters.

Föreningen Armé - Marin - och Flygfilm
Riddargatan 23B
11457 STOCKHOLM

Telephone: 670940 ext. 46

Managing Director: Captain J. Ellsén, RNR

Brief history of collection: Founded 1920. Most items in the collection have a military background but the scenes and people photographed also document Swedish life and culture from the end of the 19th Century. The oldest film dates from 1896 and shows the King and Queen opening the Stockholm Industrial Exhibition. There is also much foreign material covering the Balkan Wars and World Wars One and Two.

Holdings: 8,000 documentary film titles including 100 animated films and comedies totalling 200,000 feet of 35 mm nitrate film and 300,000 feet of acetate film (90% of which is on 16 mm). 75% of the collection is on black and white, 25% colour (including every film since 1960).

Film components stored: 6,000 negative films, 4,000 fine grain prints, 50,000 feet of effects tracks.

Storage facilities: All acetate films are stored at the head office with normal temperature and humidity control. Nitrate films are stored 20 miles outside Stockholm in special non-explosive culverts.

Catalogues and indexes: Main card catalogue - cataloguing methods are manual at the moment but data processing is planned. There is a published catalogue with twice yearly supplements: the new edition being produced at present will have an additional section on historical films.

Accessibility of materials and policy toward researchers: Viewing facilities are free. There is a small charge for the use of cutting tables, projectors and film room. If an operator is needed there is a further charge.

SWITZERLAND

Cinémathèque Suisse
12 Place de la Cathédrale
Case Ville 2512
1002 LAUSANNE

Note: The main sections of the Cinémathèque are in the process of moving to new premises at the Casino de Montbenon.

Telephone: 237406/7

Curator: Freddy Buache

Holdings: ca 4,500 feature film titles, ca 3,500 documentaries, non-fiction and short fiction titles, 7,000+ books, ca 190,000 film stills, 10,000+ posters.

USSR

Gosfilmofond
Stancia Bielye Stolby
MOSCOW

Telephone: 1361018

Director: Viktor Privato

Holdings: ca 40,000 film titles, 4,000+ books, 125 current periodical titles, ca 170,000 film stills, ca 30,000 posters.

European Film Collections 165

YUGOSLAVIA

Jugoslovenska Kinoteka
Knez Mihailova 19/1
11001 BELGRADE

Telephone: 622555

Director: Vladimir Pogačić

Holdings: ca 35,000 film titles, ca 11,000 books, ca 100 current periodical titles, 150,000+ film stills, ca 10,000 posters.

BIBLIOGRAPHY

Frances Thorpe (ed.) (1975) *Directory of British Film and Television Libraries*, Slade Film History Register, London.

An introduction to the resources of eight major British film and videotape collections which are described by their custodians. The history and organisation of each collection is detailed and information is given about the holdings of film and supplementary documentation, cataloguing practice, storage facilities, and availability of materials.

Brenda Davies and John Luijckx (eds.) (1976) *FIAF Directory of Film and Television Documentation Sources*, Netherlands Filmmuseum for Fédération Internationale des Archives du Film, Amsterdam.

As the title indicates this invaluable guide covers sources of documentation. Details are given about holdings of books, periodicals, scripts, newspaper clippings, stills, posters, programmes and pressbooks, scrapbooks, sound recordings, slides and special collections. Addresses, telephone and telex numbers and other useful practical information about staff, hours of service and photocopying charges are also given. A new edition is in preparation.

le Film Français, No. 22 nouvelle serie, No. 1726, 9 juin 1978

See special dossier 'Stock images (1)', pages 7-12, which features long articles about three major French archives, with briefer items on a further three.

le Film Français, No. 23 nouvelle serie, No. 1727, 16 juin 1978

Special dossier 'Stock images (2)', pages 9-14, features an article on the Services des Archives du Film at Bois d'Arcy and discusses the broader aspects and problems of French archives.

Richard A. Nelson, Germany and the German Film 1930-1945: an annotated research bibliography, Part III: Research Libraries, Archives and other sources, *J. University Film Association 30*, 53-72 (1978).

A valuable annotated survey containing a section on media archives in the Federal Republic of Germany and other European countries (p.61-66) and a section on American media archives (p.54-61).

Peter Cowie (ed.)(1978 or latest edition) *International Film Guide*, Tantivy Press, London.

An annual publication which always has a section listing film archives around the world. Gives the number of film titles, books, stills, posters etc. currently held. Also gives names of curators and directors.

World Directory of Stockshot & Film Production Libraries, (compiled by the Cinémathèque Royale de Belgique under the direction of its curator M. Jacques Ledoux). Oxford: Pergamon Press for the International Film and Television Council, 1969.

Lists 310 film production libraries and other bodies in 59 countries which can supply stockshot material. Organisations covered include film archives, television companies, newsreel companies, industrial companies, government agencies, film production companies and scientific and research film centres. Details given: date of constitution, date of oldest film document preserved, total footage held, film gauge and whether film is black and white or colour, rights of reproduction, restrictions on use of material, type of catalogue. Now somewhat out of date.

Ernest D. Rose (1974) *World Film & TV Study Resources: a reference guide to major training centres and archives*, Friedrich-Ebert-Stiftung, Bonn-Bad Godesburg.

An introduction to film and television schools and archives in 75 countries of the world. Entries dealing with archives give information about holdings, vault capacity, screenings, library stock, publications issued, names of curators and directors and telephone numbers.

Index

ABC 134
Advise and Consent 99
Aelita 37
Albrecht, Gerd 106, 124
Aldgate, Antony 140
Aldrich, Robert 25
All The President's Men 100-1
Analysis-film 66-8
Annan 139 *see also* Committee on the Future of Broadcasting
Apra, Adriano 113
Archives 4, 18, 129-166
Arhiva Nationala de Filme 162
Arsenal 36
Asians from Malawi 14, 22
Aspen Institute 134
Association of Revolutionary Cinematography 36
Audio-visual services *see* Television services in universities
Autobiography of Miss Jane Pittman, The 96, 100

BBC 3-8, 13, 20, 141-3, 148-9
  Archives Advisory Committee 149
  Film and Videotape Library 141-3, 148
  Reference and Registry Services 142-3, 148
Bad News 9, 12, 16
Balcony, The 96
Baldwin, Stanley 89-90
Ballantyne, James J. 127, 151
Battleship Potemkin 31, 34-37
Bay of Death 37
Bear's Wedding, The 35
Beaverbrook, 1st baron 89
Becker, L.B. 77-8, 81, 85
Bed and Sofa 38
Belsen 14
Bertolucci, Bernardo 102
Best Man, The 99
Bevan, Aneurin 3, 4
Bias against understanding 6, 9, 11, 20-1
Birt, John 6, 9, 20
Blacklisting 28
Blacks 11 *see also* Race relations
Blumler, Jay G. 70, 71, 73, 76, 79, 80, 84-5, 140, 149
Bolsheviks 31-33
Bond, R 74-5, 84
Boorstin, Daniel J. 150
Brandt, Willi 63, 69
Bridge, F.R. 54
Briggs, Lord Asa 149
British Film Institute 42, 142 *see also* National Film Archive

British Institute of Recorded Sound 143
British Movietone 91, 140, 143, 148
British Universities Film Council vii, viii, 1, 149, 151 *see also* Slade Film History Register
Broadcasters 7, 12, 19, 20
Broadcasting 3-8, 9-16, 17-24
Broadcasting House 130
Brynmor Jones Report 45
Buchenwald 14
Budget speech 3, 4
Buffalo Bill and the Indians 99
Bukharin, N.I. 34
Bulgarska Nacionalna Filmoteka 152
Bundesarchiv - Filmarchiv 157
Burn (Queimada) 96
Buscombe, Edward 2, 23, 25
Butler, David 74, 82, 84-5
Butler, R.A. 4

CDU 62-3, 65-6, 68-9
Calendar 142
California at Los Angeles, University of 134
Candidate, The 100
Capra, Frank 27
Carr, E.H. 17-18, 23
Carter, Jimmy 11
Cayrol, R. 76
Censorship *see* Hays Office, Official Secrets Act
Central Office of Information 143
Centre for Mass Communication Research 134
Centre for Television Research 71, 134
Centre National de la Cinématographie 155
Ceskoslovensky Filmowy Ustav-Filmoteka 153
Challis, C.E. 54
Chamberlain, Neville 4, 87, 89-93
Chancellor of the Exchequer 3, 4 *see also* Aneurin Bevan, R.A. Butler, Neville Chamberlain, Winston S. Churchill, Reginald Maudling
Chancellor of the Reich 60
Chaplin, Charlie 34
Characterising documentation 64
Cheka 35
Childs, W. 54
Chronological fact film 64
Churchill, Winston S. 3
Cine-Eye 38
Cinema
  as popular art 25
  as propaganda weapon 32
  box office as indicator 25, 26, 35

Cinema as Art, The 97
Cinema vans 90-91
Cineteca Nacional 162
Cinémathèque de Toulouse 155
Cinémathèque Royale de Belgique 152
Cinémathèque Suisse 164
Cineteca Nazionale 160
Citizen Kane 112
Clark, David R. 47-9, 56-7
Clark, William 4
Clarke, P. 73
Clockwork Orange 96
Collected Short Stories 96
Coltman, Peter 47-8, 57
Columbia Broadcasting System (CBS) 10, 134
Committee on the Future of Broadcasting 71
Communication 71-83, 87-9
Communication and Politics in the 20th Century 53
Communism 28, 62, 88, 95, 101
Conformist, The 96
Conservative Party 72, 77, 82, 89-91
Convention politics 99
Copenhagen University 105
Copyright 131-134
Cowan, J. 46
Cox, Sir Geoffrey 12, 15
Cranston, Maurice 87
Cries and Whispers 95
Crossman, Richard 6
Current affairs 6, 9-16, 145

DKP 62-3, 66, 68-9
Daily Mail 15
Danes in Greenland 116-122
Danske Filmmuseum 153
Davidson, J.C. 90
Davies, Philip J. 2, 95
Davis, D. 73, 78
Day, Robin 6, 20
De Bono, Edward 96
Debrix, J.R. 97
Decembrists 37
Decision series 143
Deliverance 96
Democratic Party 28, 134
Desai, Morarji 136
Deutsches Institut für Filmkunde 158
Deutsche Wochenschau GmbH 157
Deutschland, erwache! 112
Devils, The 96
Dilks, David N. 54, 140, 149
Dirty Harry 100
Discreet Charm of the Bourgeoisie, The 96

Disraeli, Benjamin 87
Directory of British Film and Television Libraries 165
Dr Strangelove 99
Documentality 61n, 105
Documentary 38, 61n, 105, 144
Dobson, D. 74
Dovzhenko, Alexandr 37-8
Dreyer, E.C. 74
Dulles Oral History Collection 145, 150
Dzerzhinsky, Feliks 35

Earth 37-8
East Bloc 63
Eden, Sir Anthony 145
Education and Science, Department of 9
Educational & Television Films 143, 148
Educational technology 47-8, 50
EEC Referendum 141
Effects of Mass Communication, The 84
Eisenstein, S.M. 31, 34, 37-9
Election campaigns 59-68, 71-83, 134, 141
Elliott, Philip 2, 17, 21, 23-24
EMI Pathe 140
Encyclopaedia Cinematographica 61
End of St Petersburg, The 34, 36, 37
Environment, Department of the 9
Ermler, Friedrich 38
Etablissement Cinématographique et Photographique des Armées 155
Eternal Jew, The 38
Ethnographic films 61
Eurovision 11
Evans, R.I. 46, 56
Exterminating Angel, The 96

FDP 62-3, 66, 68-9
Fail-Safe 99
Fairbanks, Douglas 34-5, 41
Fascism 87, 88
Fearing, F. 97
Federal Chancellor 63, 69
FIAF Directory of Film and Television Documentation Sources 151, 165
Film
  as observational medium 61
  feature films 95-102
  sound, advent of 90
  structural analysis 105-126
  see also Archives, Cinema, Documentary, Propaganda
Film and Television in the Study of Politics vii-viii, 1
Film Français 165
Filmoteca Nacional de Espana 163
Filmoteka Polska 162

Index

Fledelius, Karsten 61, 70, 105, 108
Fonda, Henry 28
Footlight Parade 25, 28
Föreningen Armé-Marin-och-Flygfilm 163
Forster, G.C.F. 54
Forty-First, The 37
Forward, Soviet! 35, 38
Fourteen-day rule 4
Fragment of Empire 38
Francis, Richard 20, 24
Franco, Francisco 91
Frank, Reuven 17, 23
Freedom of Information Act 6
Freud, Sigmund 96
Friendly, Fred 10
From Caligari to Hitler 25
Furhammar, L. 101
Future of Broadcasting, The 71

Gallery 142
Gamillscheg, Professor 65
Gans, Herbert 100
Gaumont Actualités et Société Nouvelle des Ets. Gaumont 156
Gaumont British 91, 140, 143
General Line, The 38
General Strike 15
Genet, Jean 96
German cinema 25, 33
Ghost That Never Returns, The 37
Gladstone, William Ewart 88
Glasgow University 47
Glasgow University Media Group 9, 12, 141
Glass, James M. 95, 97, 102-3
Godard, Jean Luc 102
Gone With The Wind 100
Gosfilmofond 164
Goskino 34, 35
Göttingen 59-60, 62, 65-69
Granada lecture 6
Granada Television 142, 147, 148
Grapes of Wrath, The 101
Great Way, The 38
Greene, Sir Hugh 13
Greenland 106, 117-122
Greenstein, F.I. 73
Guardian, The 22, 146
Guns in the Afternoon 101

HMSO viii, 71
Hansard 133
Hardiman Scott, Peter 2, 3, 19, 20
Harding, J.E. 97
Hargreaves, Robert 2, 9, 19, 20, 22
Harrison, B. 145, 150
Hays Office 27

Health and Social Security, Department of 9
Himmelweit, Hilde 74, 75
Historians
  relationships with producers 45-57
  use of documents 17-18
Historian and Film, The 47, 57, 93, 103, 149
Hitler, Adolf 14, 60, 63, 91
Hochschule für Film und Fernsehen 157
Hollywood 23, 26-29, 34, 37, 100-102
Hollywood Ten 28
Home Office 9
Hoover, Herbert 28
Hopple, Gerald 96, 98, 102
Hornshøj-Møller, Stig 43, 59
Hospital, The 100
Hughes, Howard 101
Hughes, William 101
Humphrey, Hubert 134
Hupka, Herbert 63, 68
Hypotagma 110-112, 115, 123

IRA 15
ITV 133
If 96
Images of Red Russia 38
I Married A Communist 28, 101
Imperial War Museum 133, 140
Independent Television Companies 141-143
Independent Television Companies Association 142
Independent Television News (ITN) 9, 12-15, 133, 141
Index and Abstracts 133-5
Index Film and Television Library 143
Inside British Politics series 147, 150
Institute for Scientific Film (IWF) 59-61
Intermedia 134
International Film Guide 165
International Institute of Communications 134
International Studies Association 129, 132
InterUniversity History Film Consortium 53, 89, 92
Interviews, recording of 139, 140, 145-147
Invasion of the Body Snatchers 101
Isaksson, F. 101
Istituto Luce 160

Jay, Peter 6, 8, 9, 16, 20, 24
Jarvie, I.C. 97
Jenkins, Peter 146
Joe 103
Jugoslovenska Kinoteka 165

Kafka, Franz   96
Katz, Elihu   76
Kazan, Elia   101
Keaton, Buster   34, 35
Kennedy, John F.   8, 145
  Kennedy collection   145, 150
Kerensky, Alexander F.   39, 95
King, Mrs Martin Luther   8
King of Hearts   96
Kinogazeta   35
Kiss of Mary Pickford, The   34
Kitching, John   45, 56
Klapper, Joseph   72
Kline, F.G.   73
Kozintsev, G.   37
Kracauer, Siegfried   25
Kraus, S.   73, 78
Kuhn, Thomas   96
Kyle, Keith   147

Labour Party   5, 77, 82, 140
Lace   38
Laing, R.D.   96
Lanchester Polytechnic   98, 102
Lansbury, George   89
Last Picture Show, The   101
Lazarsfeld, P.F.   72, 73
Leeds
  electoral research in   71, 74-6, 79
  University of   45-57
Leicester University   129
Leiser, Erwin   112
Lenin, V.I.   31, 33, 36
Leningrad   35
Leppmann, P.K.   46, 56
Liam O'Leary Film Archives   159
Liberal Party   14-15, 79
Liberation of L.B. Jones, The   96, 100
Library of Congress   134
Life of Emile Zola, The   96
Lippman, Walter   23
London Municipal Society   90
London University Audio-Visual Centre   47
London Weekend Television   142
Lonely Are The Brave   100
Lord of the Flies   96
Lorenz, Konrad   61, 69
Los Angeles   26
Love and Anarchy   96
Lunacharsky, Anatoly   34-37
Lyman, S.M.   87

M3 Motorway enquiry   12
McClure, R.D.   81
MacDonald, James Ramsay   89
McGovern, George   81

Mackelprang, A.J.   73
Mackenzie, Robert   4
MacLeod, Iain   5, 91
McLeod, J.M.   73, 79, 81
McLuhan, Marshall   97
Macmillan, Harold   5, 145
McQuail, D.   72, 76, 79
Magnum Force   100
Magyar Filmtudományi Intézet és
      Filmarchívum   159
Man Who Shot Liberty Vallance, The   100
Making of a Television Series, The   21, 24
Man With The Movie-Camera, The   34, 38
Marat/Sade   96
Margaret, Princess   14
Marktplatz-film   66, 69
Martelli, Luigi   113
Marwick, Arthur   98, 105, 145, 150
Marx, Groucho   92
Marx, Karl   107
Maryland, University of   95, 98, 102
Massachusetts Institute of Technology   134
Mattingly, H.B.   54-5
Maudling, Reginald   4
May Day holiday   22
Mayer, Louis B.   28
Mendelsohn, H.   81
Mérimée, Prosper   35
Metro Goldwyn Mayer   28
Metz, Christian   106-110, 113, 124-5
Mickey One   95, 100
Midnight Cowboy   96, 100
Mill, John Stuart   15
Miller A.H. and W.E.   75
Ministry of Information   49
Mr Deeds Goes To Town   27
Mr Smith Goes to Washington   27
Moss, J.R.   47, 49, 55, 56
Mother   36-7
Movies and Society   97
Murrow, Ed   10
Music Lovers, The   96
Mussolini, Benito   87, 91

NARS (National Archives)   134
NBC   17, 131, 134
NPD   62-63
Napoleon   39
Napoleon III   87
National Film Archive   133-134, 140, 142, 148
National Front   11
National Socialist State   60
Nationwide   7
New Babylon   36-37

Index

New Deal 101
New York Times 10
New York World's Fair 130
News At Ten 9, 10, 11
News on television
  criticised as shallow 9
  compared with other media 10, 17
  event-oriented 21
  verbal 19-20
Newspapers 19
Newsreels 140, 143
Nicholas II 32
Nixon, Richard M. 8, 81
Noelle-Neumann, E. 73, 76, 77, 80
Norsk Filminstitutt 161
North Atlantic Treaty Organisation 132
Northern Ireland 5, 11, 20-21
Nosferatu 37
Nossiter, T.J. 80
Nothing But A Man 96, 100
Novyi zritel' 38
Nuffield Foundation 54
NV Cinecentrum/BV Polygoon 161

ODSK 35
Observer, The 22
October 31, 34, 36-9
October Revolution 31
Oesterreichisches Filmarchiv 151
Oesterreichisches Filmmuseum 152
Official Secrets Act 6, 147
O'Keefe, G.J. 81, 82
Old and the New, The 38
On The Waterfront 101
Open University 99, 139, 144-6, 150
Oral History 145, 150
Our Hospitality 35

Page, C.F. 45, 47, 56
Panorama series 5, 7, 142, 144
Paramount newsreel 91, 140
Paris Commune 37
Parliament
  broadcasting of 3, 8
  State Opening 3
Past and Present in the Audiovisual
    Media conference 66
Patterson, T.E. 81
People's Commissariat for Internal
    Affairs 35
Petrov-Bytov, P. 36-37
Pickford, Mary 34, 41
Picture of Dorian Gray, The 96
Pilkington Committee 71, 83
Plekhanov, G.V. 32
Political broadcasting 71-83

Political education 63, 65
Politicians, attitude to broadcasting
    4, 5
Politics
  as theatre 87-8
  impact of broadcasting 71-86
  on television 3-24
  Soviet system in 1920s 31-42
  sources for 127-166
  teaching with feature film 95-104
Politics and Film 101
Postmaster General 3
Powell, Enoch 9
Pravda 34, 35
'Press as King-Maker, The' 79
Prime of Miss Jean Brodie, The 95-6
Privacy 14
Private Eye 15, 87
Production Code 28
Proletkino 34
Pronay, Nicholas 43, 45, 54
Propaganda 31-9, 60, 76, 89-90, 97
Protazanov, Y. 37
Proust, Marcel 16
Pudovkin, V.I. 34, 37

Queimada (Burn) 96

RAPP 36
RKO 28, 101
Race relations 9, 14, 78
Radio 3-4, 6, 10, 17, 19, 21, 139, 143
Radio Teleffs Eireann (RTE) 21
Radio Times 3
RAND Corporation 134
Reagan, Ronald 95
Reimers, Karl Friedrich 59, 60, 62
Reith, Sir John 3, 15
Report of the Committee on Broadcasting
    see Pilkington Committee
Republican Party 28-9, 101
Reuters 141
Richard, Ivor 136
Riefenstahl, Leni 124
Robin Hood 35
Robinson, John P. 79
Rock Around the Clock 96
Room, Abram 37-8
Roos, Jørgen 106, 116
Roosevelt, Franklin D. 25, 28
Rose, Richard 82
Ross, K.G.M. 54
Rossellini, Roberto 113
Rosten, Leo 28
Rowan, Kathryn 127, 139, 151

SPD 62, 63, 66, 68
SVD 37
Sade, Marquis de 96
Sanger, Gerald 91
Satire programmes 5-6
Sauerberg, S. 74
Schary, D. 28
Schlesier, E. 69
Schlesinger Jr., Arthur 25
Schleswig-Holstein 63, 68
Schonfield, Andrew 4
Schorr, Daniel 129
Scott, M.B. 87
Sembene, O. 102
Semiotics 106-108
Serpico 100
Seven-day rule 4
Shell International Petroleum 143
Shub, E. 38
Simon, Franz 69
Sinclair, Upton 28
Sisimiut 106, 108, 113-116, 121-123
Sixth Part of the World, A 38
Skyum-Nielsen, Niels 61, 105
Slade Film History Register 149, 165
Slevin, Carl 1
Social Morality Council 71
Social Science Research Council 134
Social Security system 14, 22
Socialist realism 39
Société Nouvelle Pathé Cinéma 156
Society for Research into Higher
   Education 45
Society of Friends of the Soviet Cinema
   see ODSK
Sodom and Gomorrah 34
Sounder 100
Soviet cinema 31-42
Sovkino 35, 36
Soyuzkino 36
Spanish Civil War 140
Spiral of silence hypothesis 80
Staatliches Filmarchiv der Deutschen
   Demokratischen Republik 156
St. Angelo, D. 74
Stalin, I.V. 31, 33
State of the Nation 142
Steele, E.D. 54
Steuernagel, G. 97-8, 102
Stephenson, R. 97
Stichting Nederlands Filmmuseum 161
Stiftung Deutsche Kinemathek 158
Stokes, D. 74, 82
Stoltenberg, Gerhard 63, 68
Stonehouse, John 14
Strauss, Franz Josef 66
Streetcar Named Desire, A 100
Strike 36-8

Structure of Scientific Revolutions, The 96
Studio confrontation 5, 144
Style 87-93
Suez 147
Suomen Elokuva-arkisto 154
Svenska Filminstitutet 163
Swallow, Norman 101
Swansea, University College 31
Syntagma 106-125

Tainiothiki tis Ellados 159
Taking Off 100
Taxi Driver 100
Taylor, Desmond 20
Taylor, Michael 108, 124
Taylor, Richard 2, 31
Television 3-8, 9-16, 17-24
   as source material 129-137, 140-143
   dependence on culture 21-22
   dependence on pictures 6
   effect on voters 71-85
   journalists 9, 10, 13
   value to historians 23
Television Services in universities 45-57
Thames Television 142
Thatcher, Margaret 11
The Other Cinema 143
They Shoot Horses, Don't They ? 96,100
Thomas, J. Parnell 101
Thompson, Paul 146, 150
Thomson, N. 74
Thorpe, Jeremy 14-15, 22
Times, The 8, 133
Times Educational Supplement, The 1
Tonight 142, 144
Tora, Tora, Tora 99, 101
Trades Union Congress (TUC) 15, 146-7
Trauberg, L. 37
Trenaman, J. 72
Trial 96
Triumph of the Will 124
Trotsky, L. 34
Truth About Communism, The 95
Turin, V. 38
Turksib 38
Twentieth Century Fox studio 101
24 Hours 142
Twilight's Last Gleaming 25

UPITN 133, 141, 143, 148
USA 27-8, 130-134 *see also* Hollywood
Ullswater, Lord 3
Un-American Activities Committee 101
University Vision 56

Vanderbilt University Television News
   Archive 133-6

Vertov, D. 34, 35, 38
Viaggio in Italia 113
Victoire de la télévision, La 76
Video cartridges and cassettes 51-56
Video tape recording 131, 136, 141
Vietnam 11, 25, 133
Vincent, John 87
Violence, reporting of 21
Visnews 141-3, 148
Voters 60-63, 71-83
  issue-voting 81

Wade, S. 78
Walker, Peter 11
War, First World 33, 90
Warner Brothers 25, 28, 101
Watergate 10, 81
Watt, Donald C. 47, 57
Wayne, John 28
Weekend 96
Weekend World 142
Weiss, Peter 96
Welfare State 14
Welles, Orson 112
Wellman, William 101

West Indian community 11
Westerns 100-1
White Eagle 37
Why We Fight series 113
Williams, Alden 127, 128
Wilson, Harold 5, 87, 145
Winter Palace 31, 39
World At One 6
World Directory of Stockshot & Film Production Libraries 166
World Film & TV Study Resources 166
World in Action series 7, 142
Wyndham-Goldie, Grace 145

Yorkshire Television 142
Young, Andrew 136
Young, Donald R. 97
Yutkevich, Sergei 38

Z 96
Zanuck, Darryl F. 101
Zhizn' iskusstva 36
Zvenigora 36